CALVIN'S DOCTRINE OF THE LAST THINGS

CALVIN'S DOCTRINE OF THE LAST THINGS

by
HEINRICH QUISTORP
Lic. theol.

Translated by
HAROLD KNIGHT

WIPF & STOCK · Eugene, Oregon

Wipf and Stock Publishers
199 W 8th Ave, Suite 3
Eugene, OR 97401

Calvin's Doctrine of the Last Things
By Quistorp, H.
Copyright©1955 James Clarke & Co
ISBN 13: 978-1-60608-762-6
Publication date 6/2/2009
Previously published by Lutterworth Press, 1955

Copyright©Lutterworth Press1955
First English edition 1955 by Lutterworth Press
This edition published by arrangement with James Clarke & Co

CONTENTS

	PAGE
Foreword by Professor T. F. Torrance	7
Preface	9
INTRODUCTION: THE ATTITUDE OF THE REFORMERS TOWARDS ESCHATOLOGY	11

1. HOPE — 15

1. HOPE AS THE WAY AND THE GOAL — 15
2. HOPE AND THE WORD — 16
3. FAITH AND HOPE — 16
4. HOPE AND FELLOWSHIP WITH CHRIST — 20
5. HOPE AS A PRESENT POSSESSION AND FUTURE INHERITANCE — 22
6. HOPE AND PATIENCE — 25
7. HOPE AND PILGRIMAGE — 27
   A. Combat and victory
      (a) *The combat as a soldier's service in the cause of Christ* — 29
      (b) *The struggle considered as progress in a race* — 31
   B. Cross and crown
      (a) *The cross as suffering* — 34
      (b) *The cross as mortification* — 37
      (c) *The aspiration towards eternal life* — 40
   Excursus: The meaning of *meditatio vitae futurae* — 51

2. THE IMMORTALITY OF THE SOUL — 55

1. DEATH AS SEPARATION OF THE SOUL AND BODY — 56
2. THE BEING OF THE IMMORTAL SOUL — 61
   (a) *The independence of the soul* — 61
   (b) *The two-fold basis of immortality* — 68

	PAGE
3. THE STATE OF THE SOUL AFTER DEATH	81
(a) *Provisional blessedness*	81
(i) *The rest of the soul*	82
(ii) *The waiting of the soul*	87
(b) *Provisional damnation*	92
4. THE QUESTION OF PURGATORY	102

3. THE GENERAL RESURRECTION — 108

1. THE VISIBLE PRESENCE OF CHRIST	109
(a) *The expectation of the second coming*	110
(b) *The signs of the second coming*	112
(c) *The event of the parousia*	122
2. THE RESURRECTION THROUGH CHRIST	126
(a) *The dual foundation of the resurrection*	128
(b) *The mode of the resurrection*	133
(i) *Bodily identity*	133
(ii) *The newness of the risen body*	137
(iii) *The transformation*	140
(c) *The universality of the resurrection*	143
3. THE JUDGMENT OF CHRIST	145
(a) *The judgment of grace*	146
(b) *The judgment of wrath*	153
(c) *The question of the millennium*	158
4. THE ETERNAL CONSUMMATION IN CHRIST	162
(a) *The deliverance of the kingdom*	162
(b) *Eternal blessedness*	171
(i) *The perfecting of believers*	171
(ii) *The perfecting of the church*	177
(iii) *The perfecting of the world*	181
(c) *Eternal damnation*	186
CONCLUSION: THE SIGNIFICANCE OF THE ESCHATOLOGY OF CALVIN	192
INDEX	197

FOREWORD TO THE ENGLISH EDITION

AMONG the great figures in the history of Christian theology Calvin stands out as above all a 'Biblical Theologian'. With the publication of his *Institutes* as a guide to the study of Holy Scripture, scientific theology was given a radically new turn in sharp contrast to the philosophical *Summae* and the *Common Places* of the Mediaeval Schoolmen. Instead of working out into a logical system our understanding of God and creation, grace and human nature, in terms of the divine Being and creaturely effect, theology came to be concerned above all with the Word made flesh. Its supreme task was to listen to God speaking in person in Christ and to give consistent expression to the response of the church in faith and understanding to His Word. Thus the basic discipline of theology was the exegetical study of the Bible through which it sought, in rational worship and obedience, to be renewed in the spirit of its mind in conformity to the mind of Christ. Then on that ground it sought to give articulation in the language of the day to the church's understanding of Revelation, in order to aid it in the preaching and teaching of the Gospel, and in building up its members in the Body of Christ.

That is the kind of theology to which the church everywhere is turning to-day, after the centuries of scholasticism, pietism, and humanism. Once again the theologian and the exegete are working together and *dogma* and *kerygma* are being knit together in the rise of a new 'Biblical Theology'. Our danger recently has been to allow exegetical work to replace the discipline of hard theological thinking altogether, with the result that exegetes too often work with an uncritical and sometimes with a very poor theology, much to the detriment of their Biblical research. In this situation it is to our great advantage to listen again to the voice of John Calvin, the father of modern theology —and how very modern it sounds to-day! His theology was grounded from beginning to end on the hard exegetical work revealed in his Commentaries, to which he gave consistent articulation in doctrine. It was that combination which endowed his theology with such great strength and made it so relevant to the life and work of the church that it is still widely used after hundreds of years.

Perhaps at no point do we need to listen to the teaching of Calvin to-day more than in our understanding of "the last things". We need Calvin's Biblical sanity and his doctrinal consistency to deliver us from the one-sidedness of so much modern literature. Calvin's main teaching about eschatology can be formulated by saying that eschatology is the application of Christology to the work of the church in history. It is the understanding of the church and all creation—in terms of the *Regnum Christi*. Calvin's teaching here pivots upon the doctrine of union with Christ. Because we are united to Christ and participate in His risen humanity, eschatology is essential to our faith.

This stress of Calvin upon the risen humanity of Christ has a double significance for eschatology. On the one hand, union with Christ means that we are already in the new creation, and are so joined to the new humanity that our whole life reaches upward and forward in eager hope and joy to the renewal of creation; but on the other hand, union with Christ and participation in His new humanity means that we must live out that humanity from day to day in the midst of history. "Thy kingdom come, *and* thy will be done on earth, as it is done in heaven." The church that engages in that prayer must continually meditate upon Christ and on its new life in Him which waits to be revealed, so that here and now the new life may be known and lived out among men. Through the church, in Word and Sacrament, the new humanity in Christ is already operative among men, and it is only through the operation of that new humanity that this wild and inhuman world of ours can be saved from its own savagery and be called into the Kingdom of Christ in peace and love.

Dr. Heinrich Quistorp has done us a great service in presenting us with this lucid and carefully documented account of Calvin's teaching in all its breadth and relevance. We hear the authentic voice of Calvin the Biblical theologian, who sends us back to our study of the Holy Scriptures with deepened insight and a firmer grasp of their teaching. This is altogether an admirable work, for the publication of which in a clear and fine translation we are indebted to Dr. Harold Knight. It is safe to say that all who read it will be immensely grateful.

T. F. TORRANCE

Edinburgh, 1955.

AUTHOR'S PREFACE

THE revival of evangelical theology in the last three decades has proceeded from the discovery of the fundamental eschatological character of the Gospel. This led to a new and serious acceptance of the eschatology of the Bible itself. It is not sufficient to entertain a general eschatological point of view and to place theology within the framework of " the last things ", but the latter must also be appreciated in their full and proper significance : not just as an appendix to Christian doctrine but as its crown and culmination, without which it remains a torso, or, as it were, a cathedral without its tower pointing towards heaven.

This new orientation of theology in the reformed churches implies at the same time a new consideration of its origin in the doctrine of the reformers themselves; above all in that of Luther and Calvin and in the church confessions which they shaped. The witness of the reformation, which is a witness to the truth of the Word of God in Holy Scripture, helped us and still helps us to hear afresh the message of the Bible in the obedience of faith. This applies also to the reconstruction of an evangelical eschatology which is above all necessary today. In the storms which have beaten upon the church and the world in the present era Christianity is summoned by its Lord to bear witness to the hope which He has given it in His word. Thus it is the task of an evangelical theology which truly understands its vocation—that of furthering the proclamation of the Gospel in the church of Jesus Christ—to sketch the outlines which this witness, if it is to be faithful to Holy Scripture, must follow. It is my hope that the present work may make a modest contribution to the fulfilment of this task, in that it gives a hearing to the eschatological witness of Calvin and attempts to show what we may learn from him both positively and negatively. My hope is too that it will at the same time fill a gap in our critical knowledge of Calvin.

This work was inspired by a lecture of Prof. D. Althaus at

Erlangen on the theme of the last things and by the meetings of a Society for Dogmatics held in the house of Prof. D. Karl Barth in Bonn during the winter term of 1934–5, which took as the subject for its consideration Calvin's eschatological writing *Psychopannychia*; unfortunately this theological seminary in the home of my revered teacher had to be broken up on account of the untimely suspension of his Bonn professorship by the National Socialist régime. It was just the immediate impact of the German church struggle at that time and in the following years when I worked illicitly as a curate of the Confessional Church, which brought home to me with particular force and clearness the full implications of the Biblical message concerning the last things for the life and preaching of the Christian Church in the urgencies of the present. The "stipendium Bernardinum" of Utrecht facilitated my execution of the task. I would also take this opportunity of thanking the theological faculty of Utrecht for their encouragement and request that this work may be considered as a token of abiding fellowship in the faith. I wish to express particular thanks to Prof. D. Ernst Wolf (then of Halle, now of Göttingen) who helped me in this undertaking and was always ready to give me advice in its performance.

Cleves, 1955   HEINRICH QUISTORP

Postscript

It is a source of great pleasure and gratitude to me that an English translation and edition of my book has been made available through the friendly sponsorship of Prof. Torrance of Edinburgh and the co-operation of the Lutterworth Press.

I hope that the widespread Anglo-Saxon peoples, in whose religious development Calvin and the reformation which he influenced have meant so much and still mean so much, will also pay renewed attention to his doctrine of the last things and will see it as a witness to the Biblical message concerning the future coming of our Lord Jesus Christ—a message calculated to inspire real hope and confidence especially in the apprehensive minds of men living in an apocalyptic era.

INTRODUCTION

The Attitude of the Reformers towards Eschatology

THE theology of the reformers is not primarily concerned with questions of eschatology (we are thinking especially of Luther and Calvin). Their chief concern is with the problem of justification and the matters immediately relevant to it. The reformers were somewhat afraid of the doctrine of the last things because they saw that in the hands of the Catholics it was misused in a speculative sense, while in the hands of the fanatics it was misused for apocalyptic purposes. They on the contrary showed a marked distrust with regard to eschatological questions. Yet their whole theology is eschatologically orientated in so far as it is, in the Biblical-Pauline sense, a *theologia crucis* demanding sheer faith in the hidden glory of Christ and His kingdom and also at the same time a lively hope of its future manifestation. Thus it stands in sharp contrast to the falsely anticipatory eschatology of the *theologiae gloriae* of Rome and of the fanatics which imperils both pure faith and pure hope. The eschatological orientation of reformed theology is especially clear from the conscious co-ordination of faith and hope which it discloses.

This fundamental attitude makes eschatology for the reformers as it were self-explanatory. But in consequence they neglect the special content of the Christian hope. Too preoccupied with their own peculiar theme and too much afraid of distortions, they never succeeded in attaining any conclusive and independent formulation of Christian eschatology. This had disastrous consequences for subsequent Protestant theology. It became more and more de-eschatologized, or rather subjected to a perverse spiritualization and individualization of eschatology—a process whose beginnings are to be found with the reformers themselves, who in this respect are not original but are following mediaeval Catholic and humanist prototypes.

It is characteristic of the eschatology of the reformers that they do not originate new doctrines but present and emphasize aspects of traditional doctrine, confining themselves to a partial purification and renewal. We do not find in Luther and Calvin any coherent system of eschatology, but rather they treat the last things from time to time at relevant points in their scriptural exegesis and preaching and in their exposition of the creed (apart from the special polemical work of Calvin, the *Psychopannychia*). In this connexion Luther and Calvin have in part different views. Their differences in the matter of eschatology which are also significant for the divergence in their theologies as a whole will be discussed at appropriate points.

Our chief concern at the moment is to expound what the reformers have in common in their testimony to the last things. Both have a strong though not identical expectation of the return of Christ. In regard to this central eschatological doctrine both emphasize their sharp opposition to the Romish falsification which sees in the coming Christ only the menacing Judge and not the Saviour of the elect. For the reformers the doctrine of the end is primarily a Gospel, a teaching about the joyful Day of Judgment (Luther) or about the day of our salvation and blessed resurrection (Calvin). For them too it is of course a day of judgment, but of the judgment of Jesus Christ and His grace. Both reject the Catholic doctrine of the fire of purgatory because it is unbiblical and derogates from the saving work of Christ. For this reason death as the eschatological boundary of our personal life gains enhanced significance. The hour of death becomes utterly decisive for our eternal future. Both reformers hold fast to a two-fold issue— either acceptance to an eternity of bliss or rejection to eternal damnation, and are opposed to any neutralizing tendency which would dissolve the decisive significance of the gospel and of faith.

But the eschatology of Luther and Calvin lacks very largely the cosmic breadth which is characteristic of the Biblical expectation of the end. They fail to do justice to the ideas of the perfection of the new humanity as a whole, of the church in the coming kingdom of God and of the new creation in a new

INTRODUCTION 13

heaven and earth. It was not without reason that both Luther and Calvin were unable to deal with the Revelation of John. Luther's mind could not, as he said, adapt itself to the book because he failed to find in it Christ—i.e. justification by grace through faith, even though in his later prefaces to Holy Scripture he appraised it more highly. Calvin did not indeed reject it, he frequently and respectfully quoted it even, but passed it over in silence in his otherwise complete exposition of the New Testament.

Thus the eschatology of the reformers offers us the occasion to sketch out and complete a scriptural doctrine of the last things. In the following pages we must base our investigations on Calvin as the reformer whose theology has a special eschatological orientation. In particular Calvin himself must be quoted.

Abbreviations Used in the Notes

C.R. = *Corpus Reformatorum* (Calvin's Works, ed. Baum and others, Brunswick, 1863–1900).

O.S. = *Opera Selecta* (ed. Barth and Niesel, Munich, 1928–1936).

W.A. = Weimar Edition (of Luther's Works).

I
HOPE

IT is of the essence of Calvin's whole theology that it is impossible to treat his eschatology as a separate part. For his whole dogmatic is more than that of Luther eschatologically coloured. If we call Luther the theologian of faith we may, even if with exaggeration, characterize Calvin as the theologian of hope. All his declarations are, so to speak, concerned with the future. This applies in particular to his ethics. Hope in the future determines the present life of the Christian and of the church. Hence it is advisable to begin a presentation of the eschatology of Calvin with his teaching about hope as the fundamental attitude determinative of the Christian life.

1. HOPE AS THE WAY AND THE GOAL

The idea of Christian hope according to the Scriptures has for Calvin a dual aspect: on the one hand it is the attitude of the Christian and of Christianity in man's path through this world to his eternal end, on the other it is the content and the object of this hope, the end itself. "We must never grow weary in our hope of eternal life . . . moreover hope in this connexion connotes equally the object for which we hope, in our case, our hope of heavenly glory. But if we understand that this is to be found in heaven we must be assured by faith of the promise of eternal joy."[1]

Attitude and object stand in indissoluble connexion. The attitude of hope stands or falls with the object of hope itself. Christian hope lives by virtue of its object. It is the orientation of the Christian life towards the coming of Jesus Christ and thus towards the future generally. When Calvin speaks of hope, he always implies this connexion, never an abstract hope without clear content nor a fanciful speculation about the after life which has no relevance to the Christian and his life

---

[1] On Col. 1:5; C.R. 80, 79.

here and now. For he witnesses to Christian hope, which according to the Scriptures summons us to have hope.

2. HOPE AND THE WORD

For Calvin the Christian hope is no indeterminate aspiration, but a firm and sure expectation based upon the unambiguous promise which God has given us in His word and by which He has bound Himself. God is faithful and will not deceive us. " Since it is certain that God does not deceive us in our hopes there cannot be any ambiguity about hope itself. What a wonderful word : ' According to my hope '. Hence it is certain that God cannot avoid meeting our hope which is grounded on His own word." [1] His word is the word of the Gospel. Hope flows from faith in this joyful message, for from it radiates the goal of our hope, which is eternal glory. But the sum and the heart of the gospel shines upon us in Christ. He Himself is our hope. It lives through Him, through the expectation of His future advent, and is therefore wholly related to the word which bears witness to Him. " Where the gospel is, there is the hope of eternal glory. Yet let us not forget that the sum of all things is contained in Christ." [2] Christian hope is therefore bound to the scriptural word of promise, and thus lives in virtue of its content for the sake of Jesus Christ, in whom all the promises of God are summed up. Hope no more than faith is conceivable apart from its constant relationship with the gospel.

3. FAITH AND HOPE

Faith and hope are therefore for Calvin closely related ideas. They are co-relative the one with the other. " Faith is the foundation on which hope rests, hope feeds and supports faith." [3] Faith is in fact a being convinced of the truth of the promises and as such necessarily merges in the expectation of their fulfilment. " Thus faith is certain that God is true; hope expects that at the seasonable moment He will manifest His

---
[1] On Phil. 1:20; *C.R.* 80, 17.
[2] " Nam ubi evangelium, illic spes est salutis aeternae. Sed meminerimus, summam omnium in Christo contineri." On Col. 1:23; *C.R.* 80, 91.
[3] *Inst.* III, 2, 42; *O.S.* 4, 53.

truth. . . . Faith believes that eternal life is given us. Hope expects that at some time eternity will be disclosed." [1] Faith is the mother of hope; it gives birth to it.[2] The latter cannot exist without faith. But on the other hand faith cannot live without hope. Hope is its inseparable companion which it needs for its own strengthening on the toilsome path to the eternal goal, so that it is not wearied and paralysed by the many trials and temptations. "No one can expect anything of God if he does not first believe the divine promises; but equally our weak faith, if it is not to sink under the load, must be supported and maintained by the fact that we hope and wait in patience." [3] Without the prospect afforded by hope, faith cannot persist in its course but collapses in weariness; it cannot carry on the struggle without hope. "Hope is nothing but steadfastness in the faith." [4] By the fact that hope directs the glance of faith towards eternity, faith learns to endure the oppressions of this life. In his exegesis of the Epistle to the Hebrews Calvin repeatedly points out that wherever it is a question of steadfastness in the faith the idea of hope emerges and even takes the place of faith. "Because the readers are to be exhorted to persistence hope here takes the place of faith. Hope is the fruit of faith but also its strength and stay." [5]

Hope is not only a spur but also a bridle of faith. It not only urges it on when it is inclined to slacken but holds it in check when it is too precipitate. "Since it waits quietly for the Lord it keeps faith within bounds so that it does not hasten forward unduly, and strengthens it so that it does not stumble in regard to the promises of God." [6] Thus hope both inspires and regulates faith.

Hope is in fact the touchstone of a true and living faith, for Calvin. However splendidly a man may be able to speak of his faith, if he cannot combine with it a true hope his faith is vain. By hope genuine faith is distinguished from mere

---

[1] *Loc. cit.*
[2] On 1 Cor. 13:13; *C.R.* 77, 515.
[3] *Inst., loc. cit.*
[4] On Heb. 3:6; *C.R.* 83, 38.
[5] On Heb. 10:23; *C.R.* 83, 136.
[6] *Loc. cit.*

assent. " Faith is far removed from a general assent to the proposition that God for example is righteous and true. So much may be conceded even by the impious. But because they do not grasp God's fatherly goodness in Christ no genuine hope dawns for them." [1]

Calvin consciously follows the Biblical position in that he often uses faith and hope interchangeably. " Because faith and hope are so closely bound together Scripture at times uses the words faith and hope interchangeably." [2] Yet faith for him is not merged in hope but both belong together as co-relative and complementary. Faith comes first, hope second in the life of the Christian. Faith makes the start by initiating us into the fellowship and service of God through our acceptance of the forgiveness of our sins and our trust in the mercy of the Lord; hope enables us to persevere by preserving us in faith until the time of our final deliverance. " Faith which brings us into a right relation with God without which we cannot obtain forgiveness, always precedes all else just as the foundation must be laid before the building can begin." [3] Faith and hope are related to each other as justification and sanctification. " Whosoever therefore wishes to persist in the course of a sanctified life must hold fast to hope in the return of Christ." [4] Faith and hope both look towards Christ. Therein lies their unity. But while faith looks back on the One who has come and His work of salvation, hope looks forward to the Coming One and to the consummation of His work which will then be manifested, the complete fulfilment of all the promises of God. " After we have accepted the testimony of the gospel to the transcendent love of God we wait until God fully reveals what is yet hidden in hope." [5]

But the relation of faith and hope is not consistently balanced in Calvin. As distinct from Luther, who emphasizes the present fact of salvation by faith, in him salvation is con-

---

[1] On Heb. 6:11; *C.R.* 83, 76.
[2] *Inst.* III, 2, 43; *O.S.* 4. 53. Cf. also: " Here I equate hope with faith." On Heb. 3:6; *C.R.* 83, 38.
[3] On 1 Thess. 3:13; *C.R.* 80, 159 f.
[4] *Inst., loc. cit.*
[5] *Loc. cit.; O.S.* 4, 54.

sidered predominantly under the aspect of hope.[1] Faith as the opposite of sight is itself hope.[2] " By faith we apprehend what is concealed from the senses of man. Faith yearns towards the future which is not yet. . . . So then we must hope against hope."[3] Calvin stresses particularly this characterization of faith in his exegesis of Heb. 11:1, remarking first of all that this word is not a complete expression of the idea of faith but " has reference only to the close connexion of faith and patience."[4] Faith is wholly directed towards the promise of God which will only be fulfilled in the future; it waits to appropriate the future inheritance which it possesses only in hope. Paradoxically its content consists of goods which it has only in expectation. " It is a taking possession of things . . . which at the present moment we can neither grasp nor even with the understanding have the remotest apprehension of."[5] It is a being convinced of the reality of what is invisible; hence the opposite of all other kinds of persuasion which result from demonstration. What is promised to faith is properly the contradiction of all that is visible; righteousness where there is sin; eternal life in place of death; resurrection in place of extinction; blessedness where pain; fullness where hunger and thirst; divine help where a helpless cry.[6] In face of these contradic-

---

[1] " It is therefore correct when Paul represents our salvation as a matter of hope." *Inst.* III, 2, 42; *O.S.* 4, 53.
[2] " In this waiting for the fulfilment of things faith is identifiable with hope." Peter Brunner, *Vom Glauben bei Calvin*, 1925, p. 150.
[3] On 2 Cor. 5:7; *C.R.* 78,.63.
[4] On Heb. 11:1; *C.R.* 83, 143.
[5] *Loc. cit.*
[6] "Sic apostolus noster admonet, non haberi Deo fidem de praesentibus, sed quorum expectatio adhuc suspensa est. Nec vero gratia caret antilogiae species. Fides, inquit, est hypostasis, hoc est fultura vel possessio, in qua pedem figimus. Sed quarum rerum? absentium, quae adeo pedibus nostris non subiacent, ut longe superent ingenii nostri captum. Eadem est ratio secundi membri, ubi elenchum, id est, demonstrationem vocat rerum non apparentium. Demonstratio enim facit, ut res appareant, nec vulgo pertinet nisi ad ea, quae sub sensus nostros cadunt. Itaque pugnant haec duo in speciem: et tamen optime conveniunt, ubi de fide agitur. Res enim absconditas nobis demonstrat spiritus Dei, quarum nulla ad sensus nostros pervenire potest cognitio. Nobis vita aeterna promittitur, sed mortuis: nobis sermo fit de beata resurrectione, interea putredine sumus obvoluti: iusti pronuntiamur, et habitat in nobis peccatum: audimus nos esse beatos, interea obruimur infinitis miseriis: promittitur bonorum omnium affluentia, prolixe vero esurimus et sitimus: clamat Deus, statim se nobis adfuturum, sed videtur surdus esse ad clamores nostros. Quid

tions between the divine word and reality, faith can only subsist through hope which trusts in the word of promise more than in the reality of the world and of ourselves. Therefore is faith " a sure expectation of what is hoped for . . ." (Heb. 11.)[1]

4. HOPE AND FELLOWSHIP WITH CHRIST

The hope of Christians is rooted in their fellowship with Christ. Through faith they are incorporated in His body. As members of His body they have an eternal destiny. " Believers should realize that their hope of the heavenly inheritance rests solely upon the fact that because of their implantation into Christ they are by grace viewed as righteous." [2] The head who has entered into glory will draw the members after Him : such is the hope of Christianity, of the body of Christ. Christ is the foundation of the Christian hope. Because He has risen from the dead and ascended into heaven we too look for resurrection to eternal life. That is the firm stay of our hope. " Hope is the anchor of the soul which presses on into the innermost sanctuary but only because Christ has gone before; . . . Since therefore our salvation rests upon the resurrection and reign of Christ in glory, faith and hope now find a solid basis . . ." [3] The exalted Christ has us in His keeping; to that fact our hope is pinned. Thus hope like faith turns primarily towards the Christ who has come and is risen from the dead.

In Him the eternal inheritance is already essentially given to us. The future good of perfect righteousness and blessedness already exists in Christ. We do not need to go outside Christ since we already possess everything in Him. For His priesthood

---

fieret, nisi spei inniteremur, ac mens nostra praelucente Dei verbo ac spiritu per medias tenebras supra mundum emergeret? " On Heb. 11:1; C.R. 83, 143 f.

[1] " Beyond all the possibilities of human insight, faith as it were with ' closed eyes ' grasps the paradox of an eschatological anticipation of salvation. For both Calvin and Luther in this paradox it is essentially a question of the *simul justus et peccator,* only formulated in different terms." W. A. Hauck, *Christusglaube und Gottesoffenbarung nach Calvin,* 1939, p. 142.

[2] *Inst.* III, 13, 5; O.S. 4, 220. Quoted W. Kolfhaus, *Christusgemeinschaft bei Johs. Calvin,* 1939, p. 83.

[3] On 1 Pet. 1:21; C.R. 83, 227.

effects our entrance into the Kingdom of God. " It is impossible for us to wish for ourselves anything better." [1] Outside the accomplished work of Christ and communion with Him there is no hope.

But because Christ has already performed everything for us, we wait in yearning and hope until the day of its full manifestation. Just as certainly as the future good expected by the church of the Old Testament was actualized in Christ, so we yet await its consummate fruition which will not be granted to us until the day of our resurrection at His future advent. " Of course since the foundation of the kingdom of Christ the disclosure of this future good has begun. But in this matter it is called future because we are still living on the plane of hope." [2] Christ is the foundation and the end of the hope of those who share communion with Him. His second coming is nothing other than the unfolding of the fruit of that atoning work which He accomplished at His first coming. His appearance is a unique event in that with His death all is decided for us; the complete removal of our sins and at the same time the conquest of death which became manifested at His resurrection. "We need not in any sense be anxious : the unique death of Christ suffices perfectly for us. Hence it is said : He appeared once in order to take away our sins by His sacrifice : when He comes the second time the effect of His death will be fully disclosed." [3] Our hope is truly pointed to that end. Hope in Christ is hope in His future coming. Thereby with His glory will our own, which as members of His body we already have in secret, become manifest. " The reason why God delays the manifestation of our glory is that Christ has not yet been revealed in the full power of His Kingdom." [4] Thus hope in the future advent of Christ is no mere appendix to our belief in Him, but its crown. We hope for the consummation of the work of Christ by which at the same time our fellowship with Him will be consummated through our complete union with and assimilation to our glorified Lord. " In

[1] On Heb. 9:11; C.R. 83, 109.
[2] On Heb. 10:1; C.R. 83, 121.
[3] On Heb. 9:27; C.R. 83, 120.
[4] On 1 John 3:2; C.R. 83, 330.

the head has begun what must necessarily be completed in all the members." [1]

But Christ is not only the foundation and the goal of the Christian hope, but is Himself the guide on the course it sets. He guides and sustains the life of the Christian in the path of hope. " But because on our earthly pilgrimage we are everywhere surrounded by darkness Christ furnishes His disciples with lamps. ... In fact Christ Himself is our sun and protects us against the risk of getting lost." [2] The Christ in whom we hope Himself keeps us in His fellowship until we have attained the end of our way. But we have and preserve such communion with Christ only through steadfast hope in His visible manifestation at the last day. " The only way to hold fast to the faith is patiently to wait for the life which has been promised to us. " As soon as anyone deviates only a little from Christ, he perforce collapses." [3]

It is not without reason that in the description of hope as relating to the communion of Christ, almost all the essential elements of Calvin's doctrine of the last things find an echo. Calvin's theology is Christology; this is equally true of his eschatology.

5. HOPE AS A PRESENT POSSESSION AND FUTURE INHERITANCE

Glorification in Christ is our hope. We have this only through faith, but nevertheless it is already present and actual for us. " Since in this way we already glimpse the inheritance of eternal life, there flows from our vision such an assurance of our glory that our hope may already be considered as a present possession." This present is real: before God. The contradictions of our actual situation cannot alter it at all. " If from the worldly point of view many a sorrow darkens the splendour of our glory—before God and His angels it glows bright and clear." [4] The present of our hope is a reality in Christ. In Him the translation of His own to the heavenly sphere of being has already taken place even though it is not

---

[1] *Inst.* III, 25, 3: *O.S.* 4, 435.
[2] On Matt. 24:43 and on Luke 12:26: *C.R.* 73, 678 f.
[3] On 1 John 3; *loc. cit.*
[4] On Rom. 8:30; *C.R.* 77, 161.

yet visible. If a glance at ourselves shows our salvation to be only hidden, yet already in Christ we possess blessed immortality and glory. Thus Scripture testifies. It shows us in the Head what is still concealed in the members. " But on account of the secret union between the Head and the members this glory is already in the members." [1] Christ Himself is the sure pledge of our hope which we now possess. In Him hope as object implies already an " is " though in us only an " as if ".

Calvin likes to describe the relation of present and future salvation by means of the Pauline image of childhood and inheritance. Through Christ the Son of God we are ourselves received into the status of sons and children of God. The inheritance which is thereby promised us will however only be revealed in the future. " Children must sometime enter into their inheritance and if God has accepted us as children then an inheritance is allotted to us by Him." It is " Heavenly, abiding, and eternal, and is imparted to us in Christ . . . for we are joint heirs with the only begotten Son of God." [2] The risen and ascended Lord has already entered into the divine inheritance on our behalf. His inheritance is also ours though it is not yet visible. " The fruit of our acceptance into the status of children is still hidden." There is yet a painful tension between our blessedness in heaven and our misery on earth. " Our happiness is already stored up in heaven . . . but we are at present imprisoned in the bondage of the flesh as slaves and thus far removed from free Lordship over heaven and earth." [3] So long as we live in this body we cannot enter into the full enjoyment of our inheritance.

But we already have a pledge of our inheritance (Eph. 1) and that is the Holy Ghost, who gives and maintains in us the hope of the complete fulfilment of the promise in Christ. The pledge of the Spirit is like the guarantee in a business matter, the specific assurance that the settlement cannot be

[1] " Et certe, quamvis salus noster in spe sit adhuc abscondita quantum ad nos spectat: in Christo nihilominus beatam immortalitatem et gloriam possidemus . . . nondum haec . . . in membris apparent, sed in solo capite: propter arcanam tamen unitatem ad membra certo pertinent." On Eph. 2:6; C.R. 79, 164.
[2] On Rom. 8:17; C.R. 77, 150.
[3] On 1 John 3:2 f.; C.R. 83, 330.

revoked. " Thus God has made His promises secure by imparting to us the Holy Spirit." The certainty of the hope arises from the fact that He gives us an intimate personal assurance of the promise of the Word. " Of course the promises of God are in no way insecure in themselves, but we cannot rest assured about them if the testimony of the Spirit does not support us." [1] The Holy Ghost is the link between the object of hope and the one who hopes, between Christ and ourselves. This significance of the Holy Ghost as *vinculum* between Christ and His own is important for Calvin's theology generally. " God raised up Christ by the Spirit and has given us also of this Spirit." [2] That is the secure ground of our hope in the resurrection. Hope in its fullness arises solely through the power of the Holy Ghost which is a gift of God already in the present.[3] Through the Holy Ghost the members of Christ bear the coming salvation already in their hearts. The eternal good stored up for us in heaven and awaiting us, from which in our pilgrimage upon the earth we seem so far removed, has become already our own (in the power of the Holy Ghost) through the hope which soars aloft to Christ. " If the faithful walk on earth as pilgrims yet their confidence soars far above all heavens so that they calmly hide their future inheritance in their hearts." [4]

The final ground of this certainty of the hope of the future inheritance which God gives us through His Spirit is our election in Christ. " This heritage does not depend on accidents but is prepared for us by God before our birth. It is promised to all the elect whom Christ here addresses as the blessed of His Father." [5] The doctrines of predestination and eschatology here meet as the two poles and guiding points of Calvin's whole theology: the heavenly inheritance flows from our eternal election and acceptance in Christ. " Just as the Christian life founded in faith in its retrospective view has its foundation

[1] On Eph. 1:14; C.R. 79, 154.
[2] On Rom. 8:11; C.R. 77, 146.
[3] Cf. on Rom. 15:13; C.R. 77, 275.
[4] " Quamvis nunc in terra peregrinentur fideles, fiducia tamen sua caelos transcendere, ut futuram haereditatem tranquilli in sinu foveant." On Rom. 5:2; C.R. 77, 89.
[5] On Matt. 25:34; C.R. 73, 687.

alone in God's eternal election so looking forward its goal is resurrection to eternal life as the equally incomprehensible crowning act of God." [1]

6. HOPE AND PATIENCE

While in what has preceded we have been concerned more with the objective side of hope, or with hope as object, we shall now turn rather to its subjective side or to hope as an attitude with significance for Christian ethics and for the life of the individual who stands by faith in Jesus Christ.

The first note of the Christian life which is shaped by hope in the future coming of Christ is, for Calvin, patience. Hope and patience are co-related to each other as are faith and hope. As faith has hope, so hope has patience as its necessary " constant concomitant ", indeed as " inseparable companion ".[2] But patience itself springs from hope. Because hope is the assured expectation of the return of Christ it generates patience. We wait patiently because we are certain of the goal promised to us. " Hope and patience belong together for we wait in patience for that which is the object of hope." [3] " Now hope keeps itself upright only through patience." [4]

But this patience of the Christian hope does not mean slackness or idleness, but for Calvin it is, in the sense of the New Testament, ὑπομονή, a waiting in controlled expectancy, in calm steadfastness, and alert readiness, shunning no trouble and zealously proving both faith and hope in the works of love. For this reason Calvin can envisage the Christian life as a whole from the standpoint of patience. " The essence of true Christianity is that faith should be decisive and effective . . . that all believers should show themselves honest in the fulfilment of the duties of love; that they should count other things as nothing in comparison with their keen waiting for Christ; that they should not allow themselves to be annoyed by the length of their wait but overcome all the temptations

---

[1] P. Barth, article " Calvin ", R.G.G. (2) 1, 1432.
[2] On Rom. 8:25; C.R. 77, 156.
[3] On 1 Thess. 1:3; C.R. 80, 141.
[4] On Rom. 8, loc. cit.

of the world."[1] Dissatisfaction with the things of this life arises from the hope in the new world of God. On the other hand patience flowing from hope enables us better to bear the miseries of this world. "But if you are going to despise the comfort of patience then you will sink wholly into despair."[2]

The hopeful patience of the Christian is—according to 2 Peter 3:12—a waiting and a hastening; a running in the direction of the heavenly glorious goal, an endurance in the distresses of this world. In the patient hopefulness of faith the tension of peace and dispeace is overcome. As opposed to unbelieving impatience hope warns us to wait; as opposed to disobedient hesitancy it urges us to press on, to run our course in love and to be zealous in good works. "What hitherto was separated is now joined together; we are to wait, eager and yet calm: as the proverb says: make haste slowly.[3] Through the patience of hope we are more conscious of our future of bliss than of our unhappy present. We consider not so much what we are as what we shall be."[4] There lies the comfort of patient expectancy in bearing our cross and in temptation. In that way patience truly proves its worth. For because it lives on the promise of hope it knows that what it awaits is still hidden and at present can only be manifest and grasped in its opposite. "If life is invisible, what we see must be death. If our honour is invisible we must in the present life quietly bear shame."[5] Because hope is directed towards future good therefore patience is necessary.

In order to test and practise us in patience God has not made known the day of the return of His Son. Otherwise we should lose faith and patience and lapse into a false sense of security or into a mistaken sense of haste. "God intentionally hides from us this day so that we should not feel secure but

---

[1] "Hinc colligenda est brevis christianismi veri definitio: ut seria sit ac vigoris plena fides . . . in officia caritatis strenue se occupent pii omnes . . . ut in spem manifestationis Christi intenti reliqua omnia despiciant et patientia armati tam longi temporis taedium, quam omnes mundi tentationes superent." On 1 Thess. 1, *loc. cit.*
[2] On Rom. 8, *loc. cit.*
[3] On 2 Pet. 3:12; *C.R.* 83, 476.
[4] On Rom. 8:25; *C.R.* 77, 156.
[5] *Loc. cit.*

constantly keep watch."¹ Otherwise we might suppose that we needed to prepare ourselves for the coming of the Lord only a short time beforehand. It is typical of Calvin's whole outlook that he here speaks of the possibility and indeed necessity of a long time of waiting. " It is far from the Lord to appoint a fixed day as though the Last Judgment were necessarily imminent. . . . He wills rather to educate His disciples in patient waiting : they must take heart and realize that still many a long stretch must be traversed before the day of complete salvation."² We must learn to be prepared for the final manifestation of Christ without knowing the time and hour. The patience of hope contents itself with what is already revealed to it in the Word of God and stands in constant readiness for the appearance of the Lord in judgment. That is the support furnished by patience. ." The Lord with His return will summon back the world to order. On this account souls may take heart and hope."³ The patience of the Christian must be as lasting as that of the sower who quietly waits for the time of harvest and does not become angry when the fruit fails to appear as quickly as he hoped. " We get all too hasty and impetuous if the day of our redemption is not awaited with a quiet disposition."⁴

Hope and patience are for Calvin almost synonymous. They are as it were two aspects of the same thing; both concepts can be employed equally for the one and the other. But patience denotes more the aspect of waiting, hope that of hastening in the orientation of the Christian life towards the second coming of Jesus Christ.

7. HOPE AND PILGRIMAGE

Calvin likes to represent the life of the Christian in its patient hope of future glory as the journey of a pilgrim through foreign lands into the country of promise. It is the toilsome and dangerous journey of a foreigner through enemy territory to his own true home. The life of the faithful is

[1] On Matt. 24:42; *C.R.* 73, 676.
[2] On Matt. 24:14; *C.R.* 73, 656.
[3] On Jas. 5:7; *C.R.* 83, 425 f.
[4] *Loc. cit.*

really a painful journeying through strange lands in bitter need, anxiety and humiliation. On earth the members of Christ are guests who are here only in transit to their abiding heavenly home. "Disciples must above all be equipped for the journey and pass through the world without thought of staying and seek their abiding home nowhere but in heaven. The children of God can only be such as know themselves to be tenants on earth."[1] The pilgrimage is painfully difficult, but a luminous goal gleams and beckons to the wanderer: the eternal fatherland. Thither our minds are turned as to the assuredly happy goal of our pilgrimage because there we are invited by the hope of eternal salvation, the return to the house of the heavenly Father.

Therefore we can and should be comforted, brave, and energetic, in this—moreover but brief—pilgrimage. "Thus two things are commended to the believer: to run with zest ... and to keep the end firmly in view."[2] They will do so gladly in the discipleship of Christ; not only journey with good heart but press on with perseverance to the attainment of eternal life. "Believers are willing to make their journey, for they are urged by a greater hope which is not of this world."[3] The pilgrimage certainly involves much toil and pain. But all that is not in vain because it takes place in the hope of the course which is resurrection and God's reward. This goal implies both comfort and stimulus, for the hope in the return of Christ to resurrection and judgment means both encouragement and warning. "Our work is not in vain because it finds its sure reward in God. That alone is the hope which gives the believer courage to dare to undertake his pilgrimage —and which again and again stirs us when we are inclined to faint."[4] Also the thought of judgment arouses our zeal that we might be pleasing to God when we appear before His Son. "Frivolity and forgetfulness of duty spring from the fact that we are so often unmindful of what should always be kept in

---

[1] " Deus autem filiorum honore non dignatur, nisi qui terrae inquilinos se agnoscunt ..." On Matt. 24:43; C.R. 73, 678.
[2] Loc. cit.
[3] On 2 Cor. 5:1; C.R. 78, 60.
[4] On 1 Cor. 15:58; C.R. 77, 58.

view, viz. that we are here only strangers for a short time and that after the completion of our course we shall return to Christ." [1] The last expression is especially characteristic: the way of the Christian pilgrim starts from Christ and proceeds to Christ, retrospectively determined by His epiphany and prospectively by His parousia.

The life of the Christian believer as a pilgrimage of hope, such as Calvin attests it, can be presented in detail from three points of view: as a life of combat with the prospect of final victory, as a life of cross-bearing in sight of the eternal crown, and as an endeavour to attain eternal life.

A. COMBAT AND VICTORY

(a) *The combat as a soldier's service in the cause of Christ*

Calvin often calls the Christian life the service of a warrior. In his journeying through this world the Christian has constantly to struggle with inner and outer temptations and trials which are the work of the devil. Here the reformer follows, as in his eschatology generally, the witness of Paul first and foremost. " The apostle compares the life of the Christian to a continuing warfare because Satan torments and attacks him tirelessly." [2] Therefore the Christian warrior must always be armed. His weapons are faith, love and especially hope. It is above all the certainty of the coming victory which gives to the Christian in his struggle the strength to persevere. " Whosoever stands in faith, love and hope will not be caught unprepared. . . . Thus Paul encourages believers to endure steadfastly in the fight by reminding them of the certainty of final victory." [3] It is of course the hope of our glory which beckons to the warrior of Christ; quite a different reward of victory from that which the commanders of this world can promise to their soldiers. " If the warriors of this world do not hesitate to fight in spite of the dubious outcome and the danger of death—with how much greater courage must we carry on the struggle under the leadership and banner of Christ when

---

[1] On 2 Cor. 5:9; *C.R.* 78, 60.
[2] On Thess. 5:8; *C.R.* 80, 170.
[3] On v. 2, *loc. cit.*

we are assured that victory is ours."[1] The Christian warrior receives strength and courage when he looks to the eternal reward and the garland of victory: eternal life, " glorious immortality and heavenly felicity."[2] It is the highest honour and joy of the *miles Christi* to be adorned by God with the crown of life in His coming kingdom.[3]

No doubt the fight is hard and we must pass through a long series, indeed an abundance, of evils.[4] We must not take the struggle too lightly. There are Christians who regard it only as a game and who are very slack in their service of Christ and who in consequence take the cares of this life far too seriously.[5] " Thus Christians are often so lax for many of them are willing to serve only as if it were a game whereas Christ calls His servants to fight seriously." We are indeed summoned to fight the good fight which means to struggle bravely in the discipleship of Him who has gone before us in the struggle and through whom we may be already certain of victory.

By means of such struggles God wills to test His own and to exercise them in faith and hope. Hence they can be a " furtherance of our salvation." Thereby " are believers truly prepared for the reception of the crown of life."[6] The end will not come until the community of Christians has undergone the trials of its Lord which come upon them in "severe temptations."[7] But in this struggle we cannot of ourselves merit eternal salvation. To suppose so would be foolish and a ruinous error. In the last resort it is God Himself who sends us such temptations in order to test us; and at the same time His love, just because of that, prevents us and helps us.[8] But only those will stand firm in the struggle against the tempter who love God more than the world.[9]

---

[1] " Si dubio eventu et cum mortis periculo pugnare non dubitant terreni milites, quanto meliore animo certare nos convenit sub Christi auspiciis et vexillo, postquam de victoria certi sumus! " On 1 Tim. 6:12; *C.R.* 80, 328.
[2] *Loc. cit.*
[3] On Jas. 1:12; *C.R.* 83, 89.
[4] *Loc. cit.*
[5] On 1 Tim., *loc. cit.*
[6] On Jas. 1, *loc. cit.*
[7] On Matt. 24:14; *C.R.* 73, 657.
[8] On Jas. 1, *loc. cit.*
[9] *Loc. cit.*

The end of the fight does not coincide with the end of our earthly life. For though death separates us from the scene of combat the victorious end of the struggle which Christian living involves can be expected only with the return of Christ to summon us to resurrection.[1] Here Calvin sees the completion of the individual life as an integral part of the universal consummation. At this point emerges the question of the intervening state after death, which will have to be treated later.

(b) *The struggle considered as progress in a race*

Like Paul, Calvin describes the struggle of the Christian life lived in hope as a race for the victor's palm. " Paul alludes to the runner or the wrestler to whom the palm of victory is appointed only on condition that they do not slacken in their course." False teachers and apostles therefore seek to deprive believers of the chance of winning by aiming to deflect them from the straight course. Hence all such must be avoided as a most pernicious plague. The right way consists in the simple obedience of faith and hope in Christ alone. " Anyone who turns us away from the simplicity of Christ ruins our chance of gaining the jewel of our heavenly vocation." [2]

It is especially characteristic of Calvin's ethic and its eschatological bearing that he views this struggle and race for sanctification as a progress of the new life towards perfection, involving both a gift and a task, an endowment and a summons by God. Perseverance in the hopefulness of faith and in the Christian life which it determines can only be achieved by daily progress. To stand still would be to go back. In our pilgrimage we must not linger in our course but struggle to go forward. "He alone is secure who daily strives to advance." [3] It is here a question of Christian living in daily penitence, according to Luther's first thesis, and which Calvin describes as a constant progress in the new birth and in conversion with the object of total perfection.

Yet we are still far removed from this latter and remain so

[1] Cf. on Phil. 1:6; *C.R.* 80, 9. Cf. p. 32, n. 3.
[2] On Col. 2:18; *C.R.* 80, 111.
[3] On 2 Pet. 3:18; *C.R.* 83, 479.

until the end, in spite of all our progress which of course is required of us. "Meantime I do not require that the Christian's course of life should breathe nothing but the perfection of the gospel—although that is desirable and we must needs strive to attain it." [1] Calvin is not so severe that he refuses to acknowledge as a Christian anyone who has not yet attained the perfection of the gospel. Otherwise one would have to exclude everyone from the church. But this consideration does not affect the demand for progress towards the goal. "We must keep that end in sight and direct our endeavours solely towards it. That goal must be fixed for us and all our exertions in running the race must be aimed at it." We owe our service with undivided heart to the offer and command of God, to His righteousness and holiness. "But in this earthly prison-house of the body no man is strong enough to run his onward course with whole-hearted joy." Most of us suffer from such weakness that we make but modest progress, swaying and limping, even creeping on the floor. "Yet every day according to the measure of our power given to every Christian we must register some small degree of progress." But we must not lose heart about the slenderness of our progress "if only to-day we show some gain over yesterday." Again, we must not fall into complacency if we are enabled to win a victory. These are but partial victories; the final victory is yet to come. "Therefore we must ceaselessly strive to become better than we were until finally we have won through to goodness itself . . . but we shall reach it only when we have put away from us the weakness of our flesh and are taken up into perfect communion with God." [2]

The consummation is already glimpsed with death when we lay aside the body with all its weaknesses. But there is further progress to be made beyond death "because the day has not yet dawned which will make manifest the hidden treasures of our hope." [3] Nevertheless, this progress after death does not

[1] *Inst.* III, 6, 5; *O.S.* 4, 150.
[2] *Loc. cit.*
[3] "Certamen vero morte finitur. Sed quia sic de ultimo Christi adventu spiritus in scripturis loqui solet, melius erit extendere progressum gratiae Dei usque ad carnis resurrectionem. Tametsi enim qui ex corpore mortali

represent any further development but only the passage from the provisional consummation implied in the immortality of the soul to the final consummation attained through the resurrection of the body. Only then will fulfilment be completed. " Then those who belong to Christ and have hoped in Him will be found worthy and pure in His presence when our life hidden in Him will be made manifest.[1] That is the goal of our calling." [2]

In the Biblical idea of growth which Calvin often uses,[3] progress is conceived as a unified imperative and indicative. We are bidden to grow in grace. But such growth must itself be the effect of grace. In the last resort our progress to perfection is not our doing but from beginning to end the result of the Spirit of God and of Christ. It is " a constant working of the Spirit which gradually mortifies the surviving traces of the flesh and implants heavenly life within us." [4] Through the Holy Ghost also sanctification in hope is the work of Him who is the Author and Finisher of our faith. Christ Himself completes the work begun in us until " the day when we must appear before His judgment seat." [5]

Calvin's teaching about sanctification in hope is a sort of ethic of progress, but not that of a false optimism; yet by its eschatological goal and direction it acquires an aspect of crisis and decision.[6] The progress of the Christian life, as certainly as it consists in individual acts of man, is nevertheless summed up in a single creative and renewing act of God—now hidden but at some time to be revealed. But it is a question whether for Calvin there is not at least a partial manifestation of this

---

sunt liberati, non amplius militent cum carnis concupiscentiis, sintque extra teli iactum, ut aiunt . . . nondum illuxit dies, qui revelat absconditos in spe thesauros. Atque adeo quum de spe agitur, semper ad beatam resurrectionem, tanquam ad scopum referendi sunt oculi." On Phil. 1:6; C.R. 80, 9.

[1] Cf. on Col. 3:3; C.R. 80, 118.
[2] On 1 Cor. 1:7 f.; C.R. 77, 312.
[3] For example on 2 Pet. 3:18; C.R. 83, 479.
[4] On Rom. 8:11; C.R. 77, 146.
[5] On 1 Cor. 1:7; loc. cit.
[6] " This progress is a secret process essentially hidden from human eyes; in this lies the difference between the Calvinistic faith in progress and that of rationalism and modern culture." Karlfried Fröhlich, *Gottesreich Weltreich und Kirche bei Calvin*, 1930, pp. 90 ff.

C

new life flowing from God. In the following theme we come once more upon the same problem. (See pp. 39f.)

B. CROSS AND CROWN
(a) *The cross as suffering*

The life of Christians in hope has not only the active character of combat but also the passive one of cross-bearing and suffering. The fight is truly fought to a finish in suffering. In fact it is essentially a matter of endurance in temptation. By their loyalty to their Head, Jesus Christ, in their trials His members attract to themselves the hostility of the tempter and of the world which belongs to him. In this oppression they must prove themselves through struggle. "Believers must their lives long pass through a veritable sea of sorrows ... they must ever strive passionately even though there is no danger of real lapse." For true believers the cross means severe assaults of temptation, but they cannot perish or fall therein, because their Lord sustains them to the end in obedience and in the hopefulness of faith as those who from eternity have been chosen by Him. "They are still tormented by much disquiet though leaning on Christ they persevere unmoved up to the end." [1]

Calvin sees the suffering and the cross of the Christian in closest union with his coming glory. The reason for this lies in his fellowship with Christ. Through our suffering we are made participators in His suffering, through our cross we are drawn into the communion of His cross, and hence we must be partakers in the glory of His resurrection. "Christ has exalted us to fellowship with Himself on condition that we should be sharers of His life and be content in this world to die with Him." [2] In this matter Calvin understands suffering for Christ's sake in a narrower and a broader sense. "For Jesus' sake" means primarily: for the sake of bearing witness to Christ. This direct suffering for His name is the real cross of the Christian. But because in faith we die daily and are tried by much misfortune and sorrow and have death ever before

[1] On Matt. 24:4; *C.R.* 73, 651.
[2] On 2 Cor. 4:10; *C.R.* 78, 55.

our eyes, all suffering becomes for us the cross that we bear " because we are His members—members of the crucified Christ." [1] The whole life of the Christian stands under the sign of the cross, under the shadow of suffering and death; it is a foreshadowing of death like the life of Christ. " Thus we must all be prepared for the fact that our whole life should be a dying until finally it brings forth death itself. " [2]

It is " a glorious comfort for us that in all suffering we participate in the cross of Christ " and that therefore " the end will be eternal bliss ". Just as the death and resurrection of our Lord are closely bound together, so our death is linked with our resurrection. And when we are promised that we shall rise again, " in that is implied that we must die before we can live." [3]

But the suffering and dying of men does not, as such, come within the scope of this promise. It is rather a question of curse and judgment and that not merely for the godless but also and precisely for the community of the Lord. For, as Scripture teaches, judgment must begin at the house of God. The suffering of the children of God is to be interpreted as a punitive discipline for their sin but also as a salutary training meted out to them by their loving Father. " God punishes unbelievers too and causes them to feel His judgments, yet He also specially visits His own with manifold chastisements, for whom the Lord loveth He chasteneth and through the cross of suffering He trains His children in patience." [4] The suffering of Christians is a testing of their obedience and a preparation for " their complete restoration ".[5] In this hard but wholesome school God teaches His children to free themselves from bondage to this world and to turn their thoughts to eternity. " Heaven is our home and in the school of suffering we must prepare ourselves for our final departure. Temptations serve

---

[1] *Loc. cit.*
[2] " Tota vita nostra . . . sicuti vita Christi nihil aliud fuit quam mortis praeludium . . . " On Phil. 3:11; *C.R.* 80, 50.
[3] " Haec vero eximia consolatio, quod in omnibus miseriis sumus socii crucis, si sumus eius membra, ut per afflictiones via nobis pateat ad aeternam beatitudinem. . . . Ideoque mortuorum resurrectio diserte exprimitur, ut sciamus moriendum esse antequam vivamus." *Loc. cit.*
[4] On 1 Cor. 15:19; *C.R.* 77, 544.
[5] *Loc. cit.*

to disclose to us our future redemption, they point us to the glory of the resurrection life of Christ in which we too are called to share—we who now are crucified with Him." [1]

Suffering serves to further our bliss but it is not the means by which we are to attain it. We cannot merit salvation by seeking suffering but it is God who sends us our temptations; [2] they are His means by which He raises to His own glory those who through faith are called into the communion of the life and suffering of Christ. "The saints must view the persecutions which they endure from the godless not as the ground of their salvation (which Scripture nowhere teaches) but rather as a very comforting sign that God is leading them heavenwards." [3] Thus in suffering itself we already enter into glory even though only in hope. Through faith suffering becomes for us the seal of our redemption—the seal of that love of God who is designing great things for us.[4]

On the other hand, in pain itself we are strengthened by the hope of glory. The hope and promise of the crown works in us patience and endurance in our crucifixion so that joy in our coming salvation effaces and conquers our present sorrows and distresses. "The hope of blessed resurrection . . . is our strength in all adversity." [5] When we compare the sorrows of the pious with the infinite good of eternal glory, they lose all bitterness.[6] The afflictions of this time become slight and inconsiderable to us, for they soon pass away. The cross is only temporal but the crown is eternal. Hence as Christians we must not allow ourselves to be overcome by sorrow. But Calvin requires no stoical calm from us. For if believers were not tormented by pain and made anxious by their distress they would not be able to suffer the cross patiently. Christians, like all other men, experience grief and sadness, but they are not overcome by their feelings. In that consists their inner conflict.[7]

---

[1] On Rom. 8:30; C.R. 77, 161.
[2] Cf. on 2 Cor. 4:17; C.R. 78, 54.
[3] On Phil. 1:28; C.R. 80, 21.
[4] "Sunt enim persecutiones filiis Dei quaedam adoptionis sigilla, si fortiter et aequis animis sustineant." Loc. cit.
[5] On Heb. 11:30; C.R. 83, 168.
[6] On 2 Cor. 4:17; C.R. 78, 58.
[7] Inst. III, 8, 8; O.S. 4, 167.

But they are victorious therein because they are above all strengthened by the hope of their future happiness. "How effectively can all the bitterness of the cross be alleviated for us, in that the more we are assailed by misfortune the more certainly we are strengthened in our fellowship with Christ."[1] This applies especially to suffering for the sake of the gospel and of righteousness and not least to the martyrs' death. "The more we are tormented and despised the more firmly we strike roots in Christ. When we are covered with shame and disgrace then we have all the more glorious a place in the kingdom of God. If we are slain there opens to us the gate of blessed eternal life."[2] Of course the suffering of Christians varies according to the measure in which the disciplining and helping hand of the heavenly Father is extended to them. Paul for example suffers more than the church in Corinth. Yet he knows that he is bound to them by the same faith and thus by the same hope of bliss promised to them all alike. "For where there is unity of faith there is also a common participation in the same inheritance."[3] Thus there is a correspondence between cross and crown. The cross discloses to us the crown, but in bearing the cross the crown strengthens us.

(b) *The cross as mortification*

Suffering in hope is part of the process of sanctification and penitence. Calvin distinguishes two aspects of this: mortification and revivification (*mortificatio* and *vivificatio*). In this connexion he does not merely mean a single turning from sin to grace but as we have already indicated the integral renewal of the man by God who justifies and sanctifies him in Christ: complete new birth. Both things come to us through our participation in Christ (dying and rising again). For if we truly share in the death of Christ then by His power our old man is crucified, then the body of sin dies so that the corruption of our old nature loses its power (Rom. 6:6). When we participate in the resurrection, then we rise to a new life in harmony with the righteousness of God. "Thus penitence in a word

[1] *Inst.* III, 8, 1; *O.S.* 4, 162.
[2] *Inst.* III, 8, 7; *O.S.* 4, 166 f.
[3] On 2 Cor. 4:13; *C.R.* 78, 56.

can be described as the new birth; and the end of it is to be sought solely in the restoration of the image of God in us ... that is the way in which it pleases the Lord to restore perfectly all those who are accepted as heirs of eternal life." [1]

Regeneration takes place, according to Calvin, in a gradual process of growth, as was pointed out above when we were considering perseverance in struggle. The renewal does not happen all at once. " God effaces in His elect the corruptions of the flesh by a continuing and slow process. ... He restores all their powers to true purity so that in the whole of their life they may exercise penitence : they must know that this warrior's service is ended only with death." [2] In so far as it is a question of the fight against sin it is a matter of mortifying the flesh. " For the sake of clarity we may distinguish an inner and outer dying." [3] While this conflict is more a matter of inner mortification and self-denial, suffering, especially when seen in the light of the promise of future glory, represents outward mortification which comes through the visitations of God. " The inwardness and the outwardness of mortification refer to different sides of man who is undergoing regeneration " (Alfred Göhler).[4] Following 2 Cor. 4 : 16 Calvin makes a distinction between the old and the outer man. The old man is he who is under the dominance of the flesh and sin (in the Pauline sense). By inner mortification he must more and more make way for the spirit, for the new man. The outer man is the man who is governed by the realities of the present. He must aim at eternal life through the outer process of mortification by the cross as a result of which the inner man grows

[1] " Utrunque ex Christi participatione contingit. Nam si vere morti eius communicamus, eius virtute crucifigitur vetus noster homo, et peccati corpus emoritur, ne amplius vigeat primae naturae corruptio (Rom. 6:6). Si resurrectionis sumus participes per eam suscitamur in vitae novitatem, quae Dei iustitiae respondeat. Uno ergo verbo poenitentiam interpretor regenerationem, cuius non alius est scopus nisi ut imago Dei quae per Adae transgressionem foedata, et tantum non obliterata fuerat, in nobis reformetur . . . Proinde ista regeneratione in Dei iustitiam, Christi beneficio instauramur, a qua per Adam excideramus : quo modo in integrum restituere placet Domino quoscunque in vitae haereditatem cooptat." *Inst.* III, 3, 9; *O.S.* 4, 63.
[2] *Inst., loc. cit.,* pp. 64 f.
[3] On 2 Cor. 4:10; *C.R.* 78, 55.
[4] *Calvins Lehre von der Heiligung,* 1934, p. 35.

in us. " There is a dual man as there is a dual life, an earthly and a heavenly. . . . The outer man must decline so that the inner man may wax strong."¹ There is also no doubt in the case of unbelievers a decaying of the outer man through suffering; but only with Christians who progress by daily regeneration towards their eternal end does there arise in consequence the life of the inner man. " We need not concern ourselves about the corruption of the outer man since it serves for the growth of the inner man."²

Mortification and rising again are implied in each other. And in fact mortification flows from the new life. Christ slays what is mortal in us by endowing us with a truly new life.³ The dying of believers is so to speak the shadow by which their new being is disclosed. The new life is in the strict sense invisible. That means a constant temptation for us. " Corruption is usually very visible, renewal happens invisibly. Hence our fleshly nature craves in spite of everything for the realities of the present."⁴ We are in danger of taking too seriously our sufferings in the present and of collapsing under their burden. Hence future glory which so much outweighs them must be thrown into the balance.

Once again we are up against the question of the manifestation of the new life in Calvin's thought. Whereas from the point of view of the active side of the Christian life in hope, of active struggle, we heard of a manifestation—even though only initial—of the new life, we noted in connexion with the passive side, that of bearing the cross, a greater emphasis on the hiddenness of the new man. A. Göhler has rightly pointed out that *mortificatio* is more prominent in Calvin than *vivificatio* and that Calvin can represent progress in regeneration as a humiliation, an increasingly humble awareness of our imperfection.⁵ But W. Kolfhaus on the other hand can point out

[1] On 2 Cor. 4: 16; *C.R.* 8, 56.
[2] On 2 Cor. 4: 17; *C.R.* 8, 58.
[3] Cf. on Rom. 6: 4; *C.R.* 77, 105.
[4] On 2 Cor. 4, *loc. cit.*
[5] A. Göhler, *op. cit.*, p. 44; cf. also p. 52: "The more a person is distinguished by holiness, the more must he realize how far removed he is from perfect righteousness, with the result that he trusts solely in the rich mercy of God ". *C.R.* 59, 317.

that Calvin speaks in many places of a visible renewal which does not appear only at the last day but is perfected then.[1] In this regard Calvin's exegesis of Romans 6 is typical where he says: " It is said however (v. 8) we shall live with Christ, but this *futurum* is not meant merely to comfort us by the thought of our ultimate resurrection but to impress upon us the constant progress of our new life for all the future." [2]

Thus Calvin is aware of both a hiddenness and a manifestation of the new life. In the proper sense our new life as life in and with Christ is hidden in God and that not only from the point of view of the world but also for ourselves. " Paul says not only that our life is hidden in the view of the world but also in our own perception : for our hope must prove itself in the fact that we, surrounded by death, seek our life elsewhere than in the world." [3] But we can and must show signs of this life in the activity and suffering of obedience, hoping for the final manifestation of our true life with Christ in our resurrection. Only then does the symbol become a reality. The new life on earth is doubtless only a figure of the life of eternity, but as such a real *signum* of our fellowship in the death and resurrection of Christ, a reflection of eternity in time.[4]

(c) *The aspiration towards eternal life*

The Christian life of pilgrimage, according to Calvin, may finally be presented and summed up by his characteristic idea of aspiration towards heavenly or eternal life, to which he devotes a whole chapter of his *Institutio* (III, 9 : *De Meditatione vitae futurae*). It is closely related to the preceding one which treats of the cross of the Christian disciple (*De crucis tolerantia. . . .*). This connexion was already clear in the correlation of cross and crown.

Meditatio vitae futurae is for Calvin more than mere reflection, meditation, or contemplation of eternity and the beyond; it is the orientation of the whole man and his whole temporal

[1] W. Kolfhaus, *op. cit.*, pp. 75 f.
[2] On Rom. 6:10; *C.R.* 77, 110.
[3] On Col. 3:3; *C.R.* 80, 119.
[4] E. Ellwein on Calvin's exegesis of Rom. 6–8 in *De novitate vitae. Vom neuen Leben*, 1932, p. 122.

life towards the future goal which can best be represented by the Biblical idea of endeavour. The classical text for this view of Calvin is Col. 3 : 1 ff. On this he says : " Here Paul exhorts the Colossians to aim at the life of heaven . . . the word consider (*cogitare* = φρονεῖν) expresses rather the perseverance and energy of zeal, as though he would say : let that be your whole aim (*meditatio*) let your mind and spirit be thus directed." [1] Here we find also the Christological basis of this Calvinistic doctrine. The aim of the Christian towards future or heavenly life is grounded in the ascension of Christ. Because the Risen One has glorified our flesh and has ascended in it to heaven where He sits at the right hand of God and makes intercession for us, therefore we must turn our minds thither and according to our spiritual resurrection ascend as it were ourselves in heart to heaven where our Head is and our true life is, which on His return will become manifest to us. " The ascension follows the resurrection. If therefore we are members of Christ we too must ascend to heaven, because He was raised from the dead, received into heaven, that He might draw us unto Himself." [2] It is Christ Himself who raises us aloft to Himself in that He directs our gaze to His heavenly glory and so turns our aspiration and endeavour towards the eternal life which is already secure in Him. " Why must we seek what is above ? Because there is the life of believers " hidden with Christ in God. Hence we can no longer lose our hearts to this world and this life, hence we are here in truth but pilgrims. " In order that you men whom Christ has raised to Himself in heaven may aspire only towards what is above, leave aside earthly things." [3] This total orientation towards the life of eternity necessarily produces a contempt for the things of this life.

In his exposition of the *meditatio vitae futurae* in the *Institutio*[4] Calvin starts rather from this negative angle because he is here linking it up with the *tolerantia crucis*. But it must not therefore be misunderstood in a pessimistic sense. Here

[1] On Col. 3: 1; C.R. 80, 117 f.
[2] *Loc. cit.*
[3] On Col. 3: 2; C.R. 80, 118.
[4] *Inst.* III, 9; O.S. 4, 170–177.

too Calvin proclaims the law of the gospel. But in so doing he brings experience and philosophy into the service of the Word of God.

In the light of this word the miseries of this life receive a positive meaning. The weight of present distress impels us to look forward to the future salvation promised to us. It teaches us to think little of earthly things. " Whatever troubles oppress us we must always keep well in view their end: we must accustom ourselves to hold in contempt this earthly life and so be spurred on to aspire to that of eternity." [1] But by nature we are all inclined to cherish this earthly life with a quite foolish fondness. We lust after it like animals. Yet we would like to be more than they and to appear as though our minds were fixed on eternity. But in reality we are chained to the things of earth; "our whole soul is entangled in the snares of the flesh and thus seeks its happiness on earth." By the sorrows which He sends us God wishes to release us from this bondage, for as a result of them the values of this present life become questionable for us, in fact contemptible. We come to recognize the fragility and transiency of earthly joys and the nothingness of this earthly life generally. Thereby God destroys all human self-security and self-complacency. By the fact that we recognize the shadows of all present happiness, it becomes clear to us that earthly life is in no sense really happy. Thus we are brought to turn aside from the things of earth and to direct our hearts towards eternity. " Our hearts will never seriously rise to a desire and a longing for eternity unless first of all they are filled with a contempt for the present world." [2]

Of course the miseries of this world do not suffice to fix us firmly in this new direction. We cling so much to the world that we only too quickly forget the dubiousness of it which we have now and then caught a glimpse of, or we only speak of it on serious occasions when we pathetically philosophize about the tragedy of all things human while failing to think

[1] " Quocunque autem tribulationis genere premamur, respiciendus semper est hic finis, ut assuescamus ad praesentis vitae contemptum, indeque ad futurae meditationem excitemur." *Inst.* III, 9, 1; *O.S.* 4, 170.
[2] *Inst., loc. cit.*

and act consistently thus. This life has so many charms which again and again seduce us to seek our happiness therein that not even the constant sting of evil can really shake us up to think seriously of the wretchedness of earth.¹ " Hence we must be led to a deeper recognition, to an insight into the root of evil itself. That is sin, to the bondage of which our whole present life is subjected." The bondage of sin alone makes death an end.² " Because of sin we learn properly to despise earthly life and on account of it we must learn to hate the world with all our hearts." ³

Yet we must not fall into a pessimistic hatred of the life which God has bestowed upon us. That would be ingratitude to the Creator. For as such it is one of the blessings of God and we must thereby receive divine benefits. For the godly the latter acquire a special meaning in that they become signs and tokens of future good, a foretaste of heavenly felicity, thus " furthering our redemption ".⁴ This life which sin has robbed of its values for us gains a new and higher meaning by the fact that both in joy and sorrow it is for us a passage into eternal life—and of that we are assured by the Word of God. " Scripture gives us many and quite plain testimonies to the fact." ⁵

It is finally the comparison with eternal life itself which leads us to a true valuation of the present both positively and negatively. Because our home is with Christ in heaven this life becomes alien to us; but we are here as it were stationed by our heavenly Father to watch as in enemy territory and must endure and prove our loyalty bravely until He calls us home. " Life is just like a sentry post at which the Lord has stationed us." ⁶ The aspiration towards heavenly life cannot therefore imply any flight from the world but rather impels us already in this world to live another kind of life. " Believers must in this world live the life of heaven." ⁷ The vision of the

---

¹ *Inst.* III, 9, 2; *O.S.* 4, 172. ⁴ *Inst.* III, 9, 3; *O.S. loc. cit.*
² On 2 Cor. 5:4; *C.R.* 78, 62. ⁵ *Loc. cit.*
³ *Inst.* III, 9, 4; *O.S.* 4, 173 f. ⁶ *Inst.* III, 9, 4: *loc. cit.*

⁷ " Docet enim, nihili aestimanda omnia praeter spirituale Dei regnum: quia coelestem vitam in hoc mundo vivere debeant fideles." On Phil. 3:20; *C.R.* 80, 55.

ascended Saviour whose body is transfigured means a promise for our whole life; even for our life in the flesh. "If Christ has been raised to heaven, then how far removed from a Christian must be all lust. For what has Christ after His ascension into heaven in common with the filth of this world?"[1] Through our implantation into Christ by faith, each of us is an integral part of the body of the Risen Lord, and in the resurrection, which He will effect, is destined to share in His heavenly splendour. "Since our soul and our body are appointed to heavenly life and immortality and to a crown that fadeth not away, we must therefore exert ourselves to see that they are kept pure and blameless unto the day of His appearing."[2] This eschatological basis and direction of our life essentially distinguishes the Christian ethic for Calvin from the philosophical. "Here are truly excellent foundations for the shaping of our lives and never will the like be found among the philosophers."[3] Our whole life in this world is disciplined by our orientation towards eternity. We must use all the gifts which God gives us for earthly life with a heart that is exalted heavenwards towards the contemplation of eternity.[4] "All the gifts of God are in fact only pounds which God has entrusted to us to use for a short time that we might prove ourselves and we must be able to take leave of them any moment, for nothing must prevent us from being able to depart from this life at any time." "A truly sober use of the world is that alone which does not deflect or check our course towards the goal."[5]

This goal, towards which we must constantly strive, is for Calvin two-fold. Longing for heaven means for him principally longing for death as the end of this our present sinful mortal life, which is thus nothing and contemptible. This means a real yearning for death. When by a comparison with the future life we have learnt to despise the present one then as a matter of course we look towards the termination of this life. "For if heaven is our fatherland what is the earth but a place of

---

[1] On 1 Cor. 6:14; C.R. 77, 397.
[2] Inst. III, 6, 3; O.S. 4, 149.
[3] Loc. cit.
[4] On 1 Cor. 7:29; C.R. 77, 420.
[5] On 1 Cor. 7:31; C.R. 77, 421.

exile? If the departure from this world is entrance into true life what is the world then but a tomb?"[1] Since as a result of sin the present life has become death, we long for its end, which Calvin thinks brings us the redemption from sin and death.

Of course there is also a false longing for death which arises from natural despair. There is a satiety of life springing from sheer discontent, knowing no higher aim and thus ever falling back into a blind love of the world. "The godless too long often for death because they are discontented with their present state; but after, the opposite inclination predominates, the love of life."[2] Once more they flee from the thought of death and would like to live eternally on this earth. Yet there are serious-minded heathen for whom the meaning and value of this life have become altogether problematical, so much so that they wish they had never been born or would like to die as soon as possible. Calvin justifies them in so far that when they are overcome by the miseries of life they, without genuine hope, can think no other; "for they lack divine light and the true fear of God and what should they see in life but what is unhappy and hateful?"[3] Understandable as is the life-denying attitude of such stoic philosophers, Calvin as a Christian philosopher must yet recognize it to be worthless, for his own criticism of life has quite other foundations and from the vision of eternity arrives at a right and relative valuation of this life. Hence he says with regard to them: "... they did not see that what is in itself neither happy nor desirable can yet serve the best interests of the godly; thus in their interpretation they failed to get beyond despair".[4]

But because we have a true hope we must overcome the fear of death more joyfully than unbelievers, for such fear is disgraceful to Christians. "It is quite monstrous that many men who profess to be Christians do not know this desire for

[1] "Nam si caelum patria est, quid aliud terra quam exilium? Si migratio e mundo est in vitam ingressus, quid alius mundus quam sepulchrum? ... Si liberari corpore est asseri in solidam libertatem, quid aliud est corpus quam carcer?" *Inst.* III, 9, 4; *O.S.* 4, 174.
[2] On 2 Cor. 5:4; *C.R.* 70, 61.
[3] *Inst.* III, 9, 4; *O.S.* 4, 173.
[4] *Loc. cit.*

death and instead are afraid of it so that they tremble whenever they hear it mentioned...."[1] Certainly Calvin does not deny that the fear of death is natural to us as men. "All men by nature are afraid of death." This applies also to believers. They too naturally flee from the dissolution of earthly life. "No man is glad to have his clothes taken from him." For Christians the loss of life is in itself no gain. "Believers do not wish for death in order to lose something but in order to gain a better life." Hence in their case the natural fear of death is overcome by the confidence of faith.[2] "Fear of death can and must be overcome by the overriding comfort of the Christian hope. It is only this changing, fragile, transient, jerry-built, decaying, rotten dwelling of our body which is shattered in order that it may be transfigured into the abiding perfect heavenly glory."[3] Death is thus for Calvin to be awaited with longing, because by the separation of the soul from the mortal and corrupt body it already effects our entry into eternal felicity. As long as we are compelled to wander through the world in the present life we are, according to the testimony of the apostle, "far from the Lord" until we depart hence. "Thus if we compare earthly with heavenly life we shall doubtless readily despise it and trample it underfoot."[4]

Yet our contempt of life and our desire for death are disciplined by the will and command of the Lord who has placed us in this life and who alone can call us away from it. Hence as a result the meaning of death is again made relative for Calvin. This is especially clear from his exegesis of Phil. 1 : 21 ff.[5] On this text he says: "The translation: Christ is my life, therefore to die is gain, is hardly correct." Instead of which Calvin understands the passage thus: Christ is gain to me in life and death. Paul declares in this connexion that the

---

[1] *Inst* III, 9, 5; *O.S.* 4, 175.
[2] "... quum (apostolus) dicit: fideles mortem non ideo appetere, ut sibi aliquid decedat, sed melioris vitae respectu: ... concedit enim, nos praesentis vitae solutionem per se naturaliter fugere: quemadmodum nemo se libenter patitur exui suis vestibus. Sed postea subiungit, naturalem mortis horrorem superari a fiducia." On 2 Cor. 5:4; *C.R.* 78, 62.
[3] *Inst., loc. cit.*
[4] *Inst.* III, 9, 4; *O.S.* 4, 174.
[5] *C.R.* 80, 17 ff.

difference between living and dying—which last he would prefer in order to be with Christ—is cancelled through Christ Himself. " And certainly it is Christ alone who makes us happy in life and death. Without Him death is sad and life is no better than death.... But if Christ is with us He blesses equally our life and our death so that both become for us happy and desirable." For Paul the question of life and death has become indifferent—or rather they are equally valuable through his fellowship with the Lord who here and now has called him to be His servant. This applies at bottom to all Christians. " For believers both living and dying hide equal good fortune." [1] " The God who is gracious to us in Christ is Lord of our life and death. He is the Disposer supreme and alone knows what most serves for His glory." [2] To recognize this helps us in all the situations of life. The certainty of the salutary lordship and guidance of God makes every situation bearable to us. " For God has laid upon us the yoke; it is His business to command to each when he is to rest and when he is to continue the race." [3] Here rest means for Calvin earthly happiness out-running earthly misery. The faith that we are constantly in the hands of God the Father of Jesus Christ gives us especially the answer to the question of death. " If God wills to lengthen our life amid trouble and sorrow we must not desire to depart before the time. If He wills to call us away suddenly in the blossoming time of our life, we must always be ready for our departure." [4]

It is the Christological foundation of his eschatology and whole theology which prevented Calvin from lapsing into a certain philosophy of death to which he perhaps was inclined. " It is rooted in the death and resurrection of Christ that in living and dying we should serve the glory of His name." [5]

The aspiration towards eternity is thus for Calvin not merely an aspiration towards death but also at the same time towards resurrection. The hour of death and the last judgment are

[1] *Loc. cit.*
[2] *Inst., loc. cit.*
[3] On Rom. 14.7; *C.R.* 77, 261.
[4] *Loc cit.*, p. 262.
[5] *Loc. cit.*

for him two aspects of one end. "No one has made true progress in the school of Christ who does not await with joy the day of his death and resurrection."[1] When Calvin speaks of the end of the Christian pilgrimage it may mean two things: the end of our bodily life, and the final consummation. We must with our whole being strive towards this dual, and yet one, end. "Because on the return of Christ our body which is doomed to die shall be awakened and glorified, therefore there is no part of us which with our whole desire should not aspire towards heaven."[2] Again we are here confronted by the ascension and parousia of Christ as the two poles towards which the life of the Christian must be directed. In the exalted Christ there is our not only hidden but secured new life which in His second coming only needs to be revealed, and it is the one thing for which in this life we must strive; fundamentally the one Christ Himself. "Our life lies under the infamy of the cross; ... it is buried and in nothing distinguished from death," but we must wait in patience for the day when it will be manifest. With Christ our life, in spite of all present appearances, is safe from all danger in God. "What a fine comfort is the thought that the return of Christ will be the disclosure of our true life."[3] Because there lies our true life we must not be seduced by any deceptive appearance on earth. "Visible life is not the ultimate reality, the latter is to be found only when we have renounced the world."[4] We must await with joy the manifestation of that life on the day of our resurrection. It is characteristic that Calvin in quoting Luke 21:28, which he is fond of alluding to in this connexion, adds in the *Institutio* the word: "Rejoice (and lift up your heads for your redemption draws nigh)."

The day of judgment of the Lord ought to arouse, in His own, not terror but rejoicing as it is the day of our final salvation and glorification. Hence we must aspire towards it in

---

[1] "Hoc tamen habeamus constitutum, neminem bene in Christi schola profecisse, nisi qui et mortis et ultimae resurrectionis diem cum gaudio expectet." *Inst.* III, 9, 5; *O.S.* 4, 175.
[2] On Phil. 3:21; *C.R.* 80, 56.
[3] "Pulchra consolatio, quod adventus Christi vitae nostrae erit manifestatio." On Col. 3:3 f.; *C.R.* 80, 118 f.
[4] On Matt. 24:40; *C.R.* 73, 675.

such wise that we not only desire it but with sighs and longing await it " as the most blessed of all events ".[1] Calvin sees in what the day of the resurrection brings us—and not in death —our " only hope and comfort ". Thus in our pilgrim's course we must in a very real sense hasten to meet it. Only when we have in view this final end can we with the singer of Psalm 73 overcome the trials which the present good fortune of the impious causes us—good fortune which at the last judgment will be turned into terror. " Only when their eyes are turned to the power of the resurrection does the Cross of Christ triumph over the devil and the flesh, over sin and impiety in the hearts of believers." [2] In these last words of his chapter *De meditatione futurae vitae* Calvin once more describes the circle from the Christ who has come to the Christ who will come and as the sign under which the Christian life of hope aspires to eternity.

Finally, *meditatio vitae futurae* is for Calvin nothing other than hopeful faith itself, which directs its confidence to the Christ of God who has brought us eternal life and will at some future date disclose its full glory. The man who stands firm in the *meditatio futurae vitae* lives here in this world already the life of eternity in proportion as he dies to the life of earth. In other words : " The faith by which man is united with Christ means that he is translated from this world into the life of heaven " (A. Göhler).[3] Inasmuch as faith is directed to the future, the invisible, the heavenly, the eternal, as became clear from Calvin's exegesis of Heb. 11 : 1, it has the same nature as this *meditatio* : It is " the contemplation of things incomprehensible to our intelligence, the abandonment of the world and the seeking of the kingdom of God ".[4] The aspiration to eternity and the contempt of the present life which that implies is no more than faith a part of human nature. In spite of all our temperamental or essential pessimism, we men are not inclined to desire eternal life; that desire must be implanted in us by God. " Our natural senses do not incline us to seek

[1] *Inst.* III, 9, 5; *O.S.* 4, 176.
[2] *Inst.* III, 9, 6; *loc. cit.*
[3] *Loc cit.*, p. 40.
[4] *C.R.* 78, 444 (quoted according to A. Göhler, *op. cit.*)

the eternal. . . . God must therefore make us prepared." [1] He teaches us in His word that we receive a hundredfold more than what we lose when we die to this world. And with the word He gives us the Holy Ghost as a pledge which shall arouse in us a right desire for the new world of God by the fact that it gives us an inner assurance of the divine promises. "The Holy Ghost has a two-fold task: first He shows believers what should be their aim, then gives them a powerful impulse to follow it and overcomes their doubts so that they persist in their choice of the good." Despite all their assurance unbelievers do not attain real peace because they set their confidence and hope utterly upon this life and yet fear its end. "But we live in peace and die in comfort because we have a better hope." [2]

But faith which aspires to eternity and turns to the word of promise receives, however, a certain visible support in the sacrament because it is still on its journey. The Christian on his pilgrimage through this world, living by the hope of the gospel, is strengthened through the Lord's own sacrament in which Christ with His crucified and glorified body and blood gives him the spiritual food and drink of eternal life. "Since our faith as long as we live in this world cannot dispense with props, we are reminded by Paul that the celebration of this memorial meal is bidden us until Christ appears at the last judgment. Because He does not now commune with us in visible form we need a sign of His spiritual presence by which our faith can be trained." [3] The Lord's Supper strengthens us in the fight against all the temptations which threaten us and increases our faith. "The sacrament which He gives us is intended to make us grow and confirm us in the faith until, on His second coming, He makes us sensible of the fruit of His death and passion, inasmuch as He calls us to the full possession and enjoyment of it." [4] As a gift and help from our exalted Lord the sacrament specially summons us to aspire towards Him and His heavenly life. "If therefore our Lord

[1] On 1 Cor. 5:5; C.R. 78, 62.
[2] Loc. cit.
[3] On 1 Cor. 11:26; C.R. 77, 490.
[4] Sermon on 1 Cor. 10:14 ff.; C.R. 49, 802 ff.

Jesus Christ continues . . . to care for our salvation by every means, we must exert every effort to ascend to heaven whither we are called and invited." In our temporal pilgrimage to our eternal goal we need the sacrament as a visible pledge and seal for the confirmation of our hope rooted in the Word, until that hope itself shall be manifestly fulfilled. " Thus it is necessary that the Holy Eucharist should remain until Jesus Christ reveals Himself to us and consummates our redemption in very truth." [1] Hence Calvin precisely in the Lord's Supper turns our gaze to things above. We must not cling to the earthly elements of the Sacrament but in faith look upwards to the Lord and the essential content of the meal, for He has ascended into heaven and will return from thence in order to share with us His eternal feast in the Father's Kingdom. " This has nothing at all to do with a mystical soaring of the soul into heaven but is rather a strict warning as to the necessity of an eschatological outlook " (Wilhelm Niesel).[2] Calvin saw more plainly than Luther that aspect of the Eucharist which is concerned with the parousia; thus he forestalls any prejudice with regard to the notion of eternal salvation being inherent in the sacrament; and at the same time his interpretation encourages life in the *meditatio vitae futurae*—life lived under the category, so important for his teaching about the Eucharist: *Sursum corda*, " Lift up your hearts that you may ascend with the Lord ".[3]

THE MEANING OF *MEDITATIO VITAE FUTURAE*
(In debate with M. Schultze)

Calvin's idea of the *meditatio vitae futurae* has become the object of discussion as a result of the works of Martin Schultze: *Meditatio vitae futurae, Ihr Begriff und ihre herrschende Stellung im System Calvin's*, Leipzig, 1901; and *Calvin's Jenseits-Christentum in seinem Verhältnis zu den religiösen Schriften des Erasmus*, Gorlitz, 1902.

As is already indicated in the title of his first study, M.

[1] *Loc. cit.*
[2] *Calvins Lehre vom Abendmahl*, pp. 80 ff.
[3] On Phil. 3:20; *C.R.* 80, 56. *Cf.* also the Lutheran Eucharistic liturgy: " Lift up your hearts ". " Praised be He who is to come ".

Schultze, following in the footsteps of Ritschl, expounds the thesis that this idea is fundamental to Calvin's thought and determines his whole conception of Christianity[1] to such an extent that his whole theology is properly speaking an eschatology and culminates in a quite negative world-denying ethical system; this latter seems to him especially sinister. It results from a monastic outlook[2]—what Troeltsch describes as an asceticism within the world.[3] Schultze tries to explain this by non-evangelical and non-Biblical influences in Calvin and in fact traces it directly to Erasmus and indirectly to Plato.

It is no part of our task to examine in detail the arguments of M. Schultze but only to appraise them as a whole. It is his indisputable merit, at a time when the meaning of eschatology for theology was not adequately recognized, to have discovered it afresh in Calvin even though with other intentions.[4] But he

---

[1] *Meditatio vitae futurae*, p. 1.
[2] *Calvin's Jenseits—Christentum*, p. 30.
[3] *Die Soziallehren der christlichen Kirchen*, 1919, p. 653.
[4] It is not fortuitous that subsequently nearly all Calvin researchers have discussed the thesis of Schultze; mostly indeed to reject it. We will mention a few here: The most penetrating study of it is that of E. Doumergue in his extensive work on Calvin, *Jean Calvin* etc. Vol. IV, p. 305. He points out in the main that the thesis of Schultze goes back to A. Ritschl's views on Calvin which can be summed up as follows: in so far as Calvin is anti-Catholic he is inspired by Luther but in so far as he deviates from Luther he returns to the ascetic ideal of the Franciscans and the Anabaptists. (Cf. Ritschl: *Geschichte des Pietismus*, I, 76f.). In contrast with this Doumergue endeavours to demonstrate the Biblical reformed character of the theology of Calvin. In opposition to Schultze he insists on three typical thoughts of Calvin which Schultze himself cannot deny and which are irreconcilable with heathen or monkish pessimism: 1. Life as vocation (the reformers' idea of vocation); 2. Life as preparation for eternal salvation; 3. The resurrection of the flesh. In Doumergue's opinion Calvinistic spiritualism has in common with Platonist asceticism only externals. A. Lang in his biography of Calvin (*Johs. Calvin*, pp. 75 ff.) grants that "the relations of Calvin to Erasmus are to be considered as more important than has been the case hitherto." But he emphasizes that as a result of Calvin's hope in the beyond, and the ethic which it determines, the evangelical idea of faith is not imperilled. Calvin's insistence on self-denial together with his eschatological emphasis is rather "a not inconsiderable reflection of his moral earnestness and sense of decision". Lang stresses as against Schultze that not Erasmus but Martin Butzer is the real father of these Calvinistic ideas and that his influence on Calvin is in general far-reaching (the most important after that of Luther and Melanchthon). In his article "Protestantism" (*RE*. No. 16, p. 170) F. Kattenbusch brings out the fact that Schultze has for the first time brought to light an essential trait in the personal piety of Calvin. The special significance for Calvin of the *meditatio vitae futurae* is recognized, but in

overshot the mark in his critical analyses when he declared outright that the *meditatio vitae futurae* was the principal idea in Calvin's system. In the meantime research has come to the conclusion that there is in fact no common denominator in the theology of Calvin.¹

The theological reason for this is that Calvin does not—as still seems to be the general opinion—build up a speculative system from some central principle but as a Christian theologian wishes to be nothing more than a pupil and teacher of Holy Scripture, which as the word of the God revealed in Jesus Christ he aims to hear, to teach, and to proclaim. " Calvin is concerned about this living Lord and not about any doctrines drawn from Scripture." He is the theme of the whole theology of Calvin (W. Niesel).² At the same time of course the question remains as to how far he has been faithful to his intention. As a humanist Calvin was certainly influenced by Erasmus and Plato even in his eschatology; Schultze was up to a point correct in this. But Calvin's humanism is of formal rather than material significance for his theology; it is pressed into the service of the Word of God in that it affords

---

this matter the reformer did not want to restore monasticism but rather to require that the Christian within the world must be dead to the things of this life. The *abnegatio sui* is, Calvin thinks, the supreme guiding star of the Christian life in the world. P. Wernle in his summing up *Der evangelische Glaube nach den Hauptschriften der Reformatoren* (III, p. 348) describes the interpretation of Schultze as at least one-sided and exaggerated. Although he too is averse to Calvin's eschatological orientation of ethics, especially to his strict view of a dual issue, eternal blessedness or eternal damnation—yet he has to agree that the reformer is in this a true witness to the Biblical message: " Early Christian thought with its strong impulse to perfection . . . proved to be powerful and persistent with the reformers ". A. Göhler (*op. cit.* p. 60) admits that Schultze has rightly referred to the *meditatio vitae futurae* as " an essential aspect of Calvinistic theology ". But unlike Schultze he understands it in a positive sense: " World-affirming activity is in Calvin rooted in his world-denying attitude ".

¹ Cf. Herm. Bauke, *Die Probleme der Theologie Calvins*, p. 3. Bauke characterizes the essays of Schultze as typical of the attempt of so many researchers to sum up the theology of Calvin from one single point of view and to bring it under a single formula. He considers this attempt to be intrinsically impossible, but also confirms that Schultze " has performed a valuable service for the historical knowledge of the theology of Calvin and has drawn attention to an important aspect of the dogmatics and piety of the reformer ".

² *Die Theologie Calvins*, pp. 26 and 233. (See translator's note, p. 54.)

a certain scheme of thought for the interpretation of Holy Scripture, but a scheme which Calvin allows from time to time to be shattered by the Biblical testimony. The question is to what extent he does so; and if we would understand him rightly we must not be afraid constantly to test his teaching by the norm of all Christian teaching which he restored to a place of honour—the Bible itself. We shall have to examine critically his special eschatology by its degree of correspondence with Scripture. In regard to his general eschatology as set forth under the idea of the *meditatio vitae futurae* we could do no more than indicate the questions involved, but had to note that—viewed as a whole—the emphasis on hope as the decisive feature of the Christian faith and life corresponds to the Biblical message, especially to that of the apostle Paul, the chief witness of Luther's and Calvin's reformation. It is just that, however, that Martin Schultze with his neo-Protestant presuppositions wishes to dispute because with this doctrine of Calvin no positivist ethic can be constructed; for that reason he emphasizes so strongly—too strongly—the influence of Plato and Erasmus. He would like to classify Calvin as a stoic-humanist pessimist (with a Christian outlook). But as a preacher of the Gospel the reformer stands in the last resort beyond the philosophical opposition of optimism and pessimism. " Calvin preaches neither pessimism nor optimism, but summons us to the discipleship of Jesus Christ." [1] His entire theology stands under this sign, as also do his ethics and his eschatology. They must be measured by this criterion.

---

[1] Niesel, *op. cit.*, p. 144. Niesel characterizes the orientation of the ethics of Calvin towards eschatology as intrinsically necessary: it is a question of discipleship to the returning Lord. Hence he calls Schultze's methods of procedure widely mistaken, for " all other considerations as to the origin of the idea of the *meditatio vitae futurae* are to be strictly subordinated to this insight " (p. 142).

[*Translator's Note*. An English translation of Niesel's book, *The Theology of Calvin*, is published by Lutterworth Press.]

2
THE IMMORTALITY OF THE SOUL

IN the treatment of eschatological doctrines proper Calvin expressed himself somewhat sketchily; only in one instance does he make an exception—in regard to the doctrine of the immortality of the discarnate soul in the interval between death and the Last Judgment.

This doctrine, generally accepted in the ancient and mediaeval church but only officially recognized at the Fourth Lateran Council of 1215, became the subject of debate in the reformation period. Calvin finds himself in opposition to Baptist opponents. In his writing against the Libertines of 1545 he names as such a certain Quintin (Quintinius Piccardus) whom he knew personally.[1] The latter sect seemed to him extraordinarily dangerous, and that not least because of its denial of the immortality of the soul, which was for Calvin of such decisive importance.

It is not without reason that Calvin devoted to this debate his first theological writing—the *Psychopannychia*, which he outlined even before the *Institutio* (1534), but published only later after formal alterations[2] (1542). This essay is distinguished by the special acrimony of his polemic against the Anabaptists.[3] It becomes clear from this how important for Calvin is the problem here posed. Later he scarcely changed the thoughts contained in it; we find them recurring in the relevant sections of the *Institutio* and indeed just in the final

---

[1] Cf. *Contre la secte des Libertins*, C.R. 35, 152.
[2] Cf. the letters of Calvin to Christophe Faber and Antoine du Pinet, C.R. 38, II, no. 29, 144; R. Schwarz, *Calvins Lebenswerk in seinen Briefen*, no. 10 and 28. Further, the introduction by Walther Zimmerli to his new edition of this work, Leipzig, 1932.
[3] Calvin included the Libertines in the Anabaptist movement, though as a special group whose pantheism he thought to be very dangerous. But whether the reproach of ethical libertinism is exact remains questionable, as direct sources are wanting. (Cf. W. Niesel, *Calvin und die Libertiner*, 1929, 1; pp. 58 ff.)

edition of 1559 in which the eschatological chapter, *De resurrectione ultima*, appears in quite new form; likewise in the appropriate sections of his scriptural exegesis. Sometimes we find formulations which are identical with those in the *Psychopannychia*. Wherever the question of the immortality of the soul emerges Calvin becomes animated and in fact impassioned, speaking with special emphasis. One notices that he finds himself here in a vital conflict with contemporary opponents and that for him much is at stake. In this connexion they disputed not so much the continued existence of the soul after death (this they did only partially) but asserted rather the sleep of the soul in the intervening state, i.e. between death and final resurrection. In this view they are up to a point in the good company of Luther. But Calvin demurs to just this opinion with great violence and bitter contempt. He feels that any denial of the continued existence of the immortal soul in death—hence the title of his polemical study[1]—calls in question the truth of eternal life generally. Hence the doctrine of the immortality of the soul has special significance for Calvin and his eschatology.

1. DEATH AS SEPARATION OF THE SOUL AND BODY

First, we must expound Calvin's own doctrine of death as the background to his doctrine of immortality.

We have seen already in Part 1 that for Calvin the endeavour to reach eternal life is primarily an aiming at death. And this is so because death is for him the dividing line between present and future (heavenly) life; less an end of this wretched life than a beginning of that blessed life beyond. Hence the Christian *meditatio mortis* is predominantly a joyful aspiration towards death rather than the fear of death like the gloomy *memento mori* of the heathen. " No one rejoices in death or the cutting off of his lifetime in and for itself; but when we think of the heavenly glory and bliss which beckon to us on the other side then not only do we go obediently to death but hasten gladly towards it as to a goal to which we

[1] *Psychopannychia* means not the sleep of the soul but the watchfulness of the soul ($παννυχίζω$ to be awake the whole night); cf. Zimmerli, *op cit.*, p. 10.

are summoned by faith and hope."[1] The life to come begins already with death because then the soul freed from the body enters the sphere of blessedness. Thus the Christian life of hope or the Christian pilgrimage finds in death a goal (even though provisional). The journey is ended, the course is run, the struggle has been fought out and endured to the end. A Christian " considers death as nothing because it spells for him not annihilation but only the separation of soul and body ".[2] As such, death is for Calvin the end of the struggle between spirit and flesh—a struggle which lies at the root of our life in regeneration or sanctification, the life of the *mortificatio* and *vivificatio* in the *communio cum Christo*, the life of the *tolerantia crucis*. Death is the final slaying of the flesh and the full vivification of the spirit.[3] " As soon as we cast off this burden of the body this strife of spirit and flesh ceases. Therefore the slaying of the flesh releases the spirit into life." Death is thus the end of the fight for believers, " because when they are freed from the body they no longer have to struggle with the desires of the flesh but stand as it were outside the scene of combat ".[4]

Thus for Calvin this mortal body is to be equated with the sinful flesh. Again and again he identifies the anthropological difference of the soul and body with the theological opposition of σάρξ and πνεῦμα (in the Biblical-Pauline sense) although as an exegete he is well aware that these two antitheses are not the same. " To attempt to refer the guilt of sin to the body in the usual sense would however be foolish. On the other hand neither does the soul bear such life in itself that it might be called life in the true sense."[5] What Paul describes as the body of this death is the sinful mass or material of which the lump of humanity is composed and which holds us in its bonds. " For Paul sees the origin of sin in the fact that man

[1] On Luke 12:50; *C.R.* 73, 682.
[2] On 2 Tim. 4:6.
[3] " . . . ubi molem hanc corporis abicimus, cessare pugnam illam spiritus adversus carnem et carnis adversus spiritum. Denique mortificationem carnis esse vivificationem spiritus." (*Psy.* 54;196; here and in the following passages quoted according to Zimmerli's edition and *C.R.* 33.)
[4] On Phil. 1:6; *C.R.* 80, 9 f.
[5] On Rom. 8:10 f.; *C.R.* 77, 145.

fell away from the law ordained for him in creation and thus became fleshly and earthly ... and we may add that his soul in so far as it became itself unfaithful was assimilated to the body. Man has lost the superiority of his spirit and has become like the beasts."[1] And in the *Psychopannychia* we find: " When Paul writes—the spirit lusteth against the flesh (Gal. 5:7) he does not mean that the soul wars against the flesh or reason against desire, but that the soul itself, in so far as it is ruled by the spirit of God, strives with itself in so far as it is empty of the spirit of God and is governed by its own desires ".[2] Calvin bases his phraseology on the theory that πνεῦμα and ψυχή, or *spiritus* and *anima*, are frequently used *promiscue* in Holy Scripture. " Often the soul is also called spirit, and although these two words when they are juxtaposed are of different meaning yet spirit when occurring singly means the same as soul."[3]

But it is questionable whether this partial promiscuous use of *spiritus* and *anima* is systematized in Scripture and may legitimately be made an equation as happens in Calvin. In any event Luther was more aware of the fundamental character of the Biblical antithesis of flesh and spirit (as distinct from that between body and soul) and brought it out in his theology. We may adduce for example his exegesis of 1 Cor. 15:44 f.: " The same distinction is made by Christ in John 3 when He says ' What is born of the flesh is flesh and what is born of the spirit is spirit ' etc. For by flesh He means the whole man as naturally born with body and soul, reason and senses; such human nature unchanged does not belong to heaven. If it is to come to heaven it must be born again of the Spirit and become spiritual both in body and soul, and thus become quite a different life from the natural one, although the same body—the same human person—remains outwardly unchanged."[4]

Calvin represents death as the separation of soul and body in a whole series of metaphors. It is the final homecoming of the earthly pilgrim from foreign lands to his father's house.

---

[1] On Rom. 7:24; *C.R.* 77, 134 f.
[2] *Psy.* 25:180.
[3] *Inst.* I, 15, 2; *O.S.* 3, 174.
[4] *W.A.* 36, 665.

THE IMMORTALITY OF THE SOUL 59

" Paul says . . . that we are travellers in foreign lands, far from the Lord, so long as we remain in the body. But when souls are divested of their bodies they retain their essence and share in blessed immortality. . . . It is quite enough for us to be rescued from our travels by the common Father of all believers." [1] Death is the departure of the guest from that tent of the body which is constructed only to be broken up. " Scripture compares the body with a tabernacle (2 Cor. 5:1) which we are bidden to leave when we die, for the Bible interprets us by that part of our being which distinguishes us from the common animals . . ." [2] It is only a question of man's departure from his earthly abode. " If a departure is in question then it is understood that we do not perish utterly in death, since the soul merely departs from the body. Hence we draw the conclusion that death is nothing but an exodus of the soul from the body. Thus this text contains a testimony to the immortality of the soul." [3]

But Calvin also employs once the comparison, so dear to Luther, of death and baptism, which according to Romans 6 implies a dying of the whole man. " He (Christ) compares death with a baptism. For the dissolution of the body signifies for God's children that for a period they are as it were immersed and soon surge up again into life so that death for them is nothing other than a path through the waters." [4] But Calvin mostly uses for death the image of emancipation from prison: the immortal soul is freed from the house of bondage of the mortal body. " We are shut up in the disciplinary house of the flesh as slaves . . ." [5] As long as we journey on earth we must aspire to death as the sole means by which our disgrace can be ended. . . . As long as they dwell in the flesh, believers can never fully attain the end of righteousness . . . until they depart from the body." [6] " Death is the redemption from the slavery of sin and the transition into the kingdom of heaven." [7] " If

---

[1] *Inst.* III, 25, 6; *O.S.* 4, 442.
[2] *Loc. cit.*
[3] On 2 Tim. 4:6; *C.R.* 80, 389.
[4] On Luke 12:50; *C.R.* 73, 682.
[5] On 1 John 3:2, *C.R.* 83, 330.
[6] On Rom. 7:24 f. *C.R.* 77, 135 f.
[7] On Phil. 1:23; *C.R.* 80, 18.

emancipation from the body leads to true freedom—what is then this body but a prison?"[1] This characterization of the body signifies a strong devaluation of it as compared with the soul. It is merely the perishable form of an imperishable content which it simply fetters. " If the body is nothing but the prison of the soul, which is cramped in its earthly tabernacle, what is then this soul when freed from its prison and delivered from its bonds?"[2] Almost no word is strong enough for Calvin in order to express this his disesteem, indeed contempt of the body. In his sermons he often calls it " *charongne* "—a rotting carcase. " We are developed from our bodies which are but dung."[3] Yet at the same time he can speak of the body in the highest terms : " However much our bodies may be but wretched dung, they do not cease to be the temple of the Holy Ghost, and God wishes to be honoured therein."[4]

It is a question whether these ideas are scriptural. For the Bible, especially for the Old Testament, man is a creaturely unity whose life as such is corporeal. But if the body is but the material envelope of a spiritual essence then it is properly superfluous: it is not necessary to the life of the soul, which rather only begins truly to live when it is divested of the body. Calvin's point of departure is not a pessimistic contempt of the body but rather a high esteem of the soul which unlike the transient body is unquestionably immortal. But in Scripture the body is not thus devalued, because it is not viewed in this exclusive opposition to the soul. Certainly Paul describes this his present life as standing as a whole both under the sign of the flesh, that is, of sin and death, and under that of the spirit, as a temporal tabernacle which is to be dissolved in death; but he says this by way of comparison with the eternal structure of the new body which awaits him. (Cf. 2 Cor. 5 and 1 Cor. 15.) The Pauline-Lutheran *simul justus et peccator* is necessarily bound up with a hope that is totally orientated

---

[1] *Inst.* III, 9, 4; *O.S.* 4, 174.
[2] *Psy.* 54; 196.
[3] " Nous sommes enveloppés de nos corps, dit-il, qui ne sont que charongnes ". *Sermons sur le livre de Daniel*, C.R. 69, 459; quoted after E. Doumergue, *Jean Calvin*, III, 311.
[4] *Sermons sur le Deutéronome*, C.R. 55, 19 f.; quoted after E. Doumergue, *op. cit.*

towards the resurrection. It must be asked whether Calvin does full justice to either aspect of the antithesis. We have already seen in his doctrine of sanctification that instead of a *simul* he suggests rather a *partim-partim* : in progressive regeneration the remnants of the flesh are more and more overcome by the spirit, and this spirit is seated pre-eminently in the soul which on its separation from the body in death is completely freed from the fetters of the flesh and attains heavenly perfection. This question was in a way implied by the objection of the Baptists, who as against Calvin's doctrine of immortality brought into the field of discussion the totality of human sin. He answers it with his doctrine of the spiritual death of the soul, which we shall have to expound in its right place.

Calvin with his habitual sobriety gives us no further detail as to how he conceives the separation of soul and body. What man sees in death is only the mortal body; the soul is essentially invisible. But Calvin accepts the Biblical image of breath for the soul, and quotes in defence of his doctrine of immortality texts of Scripture which speak of a breathing out of the soul and a giving up of the ghost. " Scripture says that the soul departs by the same mode of speech as that in which we say popularly that the soul is breathed out. Thus of Rachel : As her soul was departing (for she herself died) she called the name of the boy Ben-Oni (Gen. 35 : 18). We know that the spirit is breath and wind and thus it was often described by the Greeks as πνοή." [1] " Thus for example Solomon speaks about death and says ' then the spirit returns to God who gave it ' (Ecc. 12 :7). Also Christ commends His spirit to the Father (Lk. 23 :46) just as Stephen does to Christ (Acts 7 :58) and thereby nothing else is to be understood but that when the soul is freed from bondage to the flesh, God is ever its Guardian and Keeper." [2]

2. THE BEING OF THE IMMORTAL SOUL

(a) *The independence of the soul*

In order rightly to understand Calvin's doctrine of immor-

[1] *Psy.* 25 : 179.
[2] *Inst.* 1, 15, 2; *O.S.* 3, 175.

tality we must study more closely his doctrine of the soul which he develops in his theological anthropology. Calvin considers that the soul of man is a substance independent of the body with its own life and being (*essentia*). It is his chief reproach to the Libertines that they refuse to admit this. " But we insist that it is itself a substance and that it continues truly to live after the dissolution of the body, gifted with reason and perception and that according to the clear testimony of Scripture." [1] " The soul or the spirit of man is a substance distinct from the body." [2] Whereas the body is indirectly created through generation and birth, the soul is directly created by God at the same time as the appearance of the body. " When God has created a human being in the body of its mother, it has as yet no soul : on the other hand we know that while the creature is shaped in the maternal body God breathes into it a soul; it is certain that then a seed of life is extant." [3] Thus Calvin teaches with Augustine and Roman dogmatics the doctrine of creationism while Lutheran dogmatists teach that of traducianism—the creation of the soul in and with the emergence of the body in the sense of *creatio continua*.[4] Luther himself does not speculate further on the point but here too sees soul and body in their unity. " For who can adequately praise or even conceive the divine work of creating body and soul out of nothing . . . ? " [5] The difference between Calvin and the Lutherans at this point is in a sense analogous to their differences in the matter of the Eucharistic controversy. In both cases Calvin shows a spiritualizing tendency. The real action of God is completed in a special spiritual event to which the human corporeal act merely runs parallel.

For Calvin the body is from below, the soul from above. The body is formed from the loam of the earth; the soul

[1] *Psy.* 23; 177.
[2] *Psy.* 32; 184.
[3] " . . . quand Dieu a mis une créature humaine au ventre de la mère, il n'y a point d'âme; au contraire, nous savons quand la créature est conceuë au ventre de la mère, que Dieu y inspire une âme, il est certain que voilà une semence de vie." *Sermon on Job.* 3 : 16; *C.R.* 61, 162.
[4] Cf. A. Vilmar, *Dogmatik*, I, 348 ff.
[5] *W.A.* 31, I, 407, 21.

springs to life from the living breath of God. "The soul of man (unlike that of animals) is not of the earth, but flows from the Word of God, that is, from a secret power."[1] The body came from the earth and must return again to earth; but the soul is of God and must return again to God. Body and soul are as different as heaven and earth. "As far as the heaven is from the earth, so far removed is the heavenly soul from the earthly body."[2] The fact that man is composed of body and soul makes him the representative of a middle term between purely heavenly and purely earthly creatures, between angels and animals. He is both a visible and invisible being in this his dualism of body and soul, which Calvin sees more as a tension than as a unity. For the soul is the really good, better and nobler part of man.[3] The body is only its despicable abode, a rotten vessel.[4] "He (Job) does not call man a worthless vessel but says that he inhabits a worthless vessel. The body is formed of the mud of the earth and as such is destined to pass away in dust and ashes. That must make man humble." For it would be unreasonable for a creature to boast of his pre-eminent position who not only dwells in a mud hut but even is himself partly of dust and ashes.[5] But Calvin again tries to qualify this sharp depreciation by adding immediately: "Of course God has condescended to vivify this earthen vessel (ensoul it) and has ordained it as the dwelling place of an immortal spirit. Adam could rightly boast of such generosity on the part of his Creator".[6] But this our earthly body is only an animal body animated by the soul. Only in the resurrection do we receive a spiritual body.[7] But that too is really only an appendage of the redeemed soul. At the same time the body must not be denied its share in

[1] *Psy.* 28; 181.
[2] ". . . quantum distant coeli a terra, coelestem animam a terreno corpore discernerent." *Psy.* 55: 197.
[3] "Quasi bona pars hominis (quae est anima) domicilio illo terreno continatur." *Psy.* 31; 182. Cf. the definition in the *Institutes*: "atque animae nomine essentiam immortalem, creatam tamen intelligo, quae nobilior eius pars est." *Inst.* I, 15, 2; *O.S.* 3, 174.
[4] *Psy., loc. cit.*
[5] *Inst.* I 15, 1; *loc. cit.*
[6] *Loc. cit.*
[7] *Psy.* 64; 202.

heavenly glory in so far as it is an appendage of the soul.[1]

The soul is for Calvin the real man. He thinks to find this opinion also expressed in Scripture in texts where the word soul means man. "These texts . . . to be sure quite plainly distinguish the soul from the body, in fact they describe man as soul and thus clearly show that the latter is the most important part."[2] Calvin forgets that both *nephesh* in the Old Testament and ψυχή in the New mostly denote the man as a whole, as a living being, although he does recognize the equation soul = life. But he counters this objection, which the Baptists already made, by expressing the fear that in such a case the soul might be viewed merely as a power breathed into the body and disappearing with it. "It is a beastly error to make of the spirit which is formed after God's own image a passing breath which receives form and substance only in this frail earthly life."[3]

Calvin thinks that this pre-eminence of the soul is based on the fact of creation. The soul is the real image of God in man. In the *Psychopannychia* he even asserts that it is exclusively so. "Sacred history reminds us of God's decision in creating man to form an image and a likeness of His own self (Gen. 1:26). These words can in no way be related to the body."[4] Even though as a marvellous work of God he is to be preferred to other creatures, yet he cannot be God's likeness since God is spirit and cannot be represented by any bodily image. God's image must be purely spiritual. In the latter editions of the *Institutio* Calvin—corresponding to his exegesis of the creation story in his commentary on Genesis—has somewhat modified his opinion in favour of the body. "Certainly in the external side of man there also is reflected the divine glory; but the real seat of that likeness lies certainly in the soul."[5] In so far as the form of man is different from the animals—we are thinking especially of the upright march and the raised head which enables him to look towards heaven—

---
[1] On 1 Pet. 1:9; *C.R.* 83, 215.
[2] *Inst.* I, 15, 2; *O.S.* 3, 176.
[3] *Inst.* III, 25, 6; *O.S.* 4, 441.
[4] *Psy.* 26, 180.
[5] *Inst.* I, 15, 3; *O.S.* 3, 176.

the body too may be reckoned as part of the image of God. " Only it must be firmly asserted: the image of God which shines forth in such outward marks, is essentially spiritual." [1]

We meet here as often elsewhere the humanistic bent of Calvin; he strongly and repeatedly emphasizes the difference between man and the animals: but man is distinguished above all from the rest of creation by his special relation to God. At the same time therefore his spiritual bent shows itself and it is closely connected with the former: man's special relation to God is rooted in the original analogy with God in which he was created and in accordance with the being of God this analogy must be a spiritual one. In this connexion " spiritual " means for Calvin—as moreover in the German of Luther (and in modern Dutch: *geestelijk*)—both pertaining to the spirit (the Holy Ghost) and intellectual (pertaining to the mind of man). The spiritual element in man or the soul stands for him in a special analogy to God and His spirit, at least originally. Thus Calvin can say in express contradiction to Scripture (cf. 1 Cor. 6) that the soul or the spirit of man is the temple of the Holy Ghost " in which the divine most strongly radiates ".[2]

But Calvin bases the pre-eminence of the soul as of the true image of God in us not only on the fact of creation but also and even more on that of redemption; that is, on the restoration through Christ of the divine likeness which has been obscured or destroyed through the fall. " The aim of the new birth consists in the fact that Christ restores the divine image in us." [3] According to the New Testament witness this is shown above all in spiritual and intellectual gifts such as insight, righteousness, and holiness (Eph. 4:24 and Col. 3:10) radiating from the prototype of the new likeness: Christ. He is the " most perfect image of God " and as such " the second Adam " (1 Cor. 15) in whom our corrupted nature is renewed and made more splendid than it was originally.

Calvin comprises under the idea of the image of God every-

[1] *Loc. cit.*
[2] *Inst.* III, 25, 6; *O.S.* 4, 441.
[3] " . . . hunc regenerationis esse finem, ut nos Christus ad imaginem Dei reformet." *Inst.* I, 15, 4; *O.S.* 3, 179.

thing "that is related to spiritual eternal life".¹ It is significant that Calvin relates mainly and almost exclusively the mind or the soul and its gifts to eternal or future life, and equates spiritual and eternal life without making any distinction between life flowing from the spirit of God and the life of the human spirit in man. He also assumes this identification of the soul and life in God in Adam as he existed before the fall, for he concludes from the nature of the restored image to its original character in creation, " There is no gainsaying the principle : what stands first in the restoration of the divine image must also have been the essential thing in its original creation ".²

Hence Calvin has no doubt that man from the start was made for heavenly life. " Without any doubt man was created to aspire to heavenly life." ³ The *meditatio futurae* or *coelestis vitae* is thus necessary, not simply for the reason that our actual life has been corrupted and ruined, nor has it become a possibility only through the promise of redemption, but is rather to be considered as the proper, original and normal relation of man to God. And, further, the seed of it is implanted in the soul itself, which is gifted with reason and will and by its aspiration to heaven is able to recognize and fulfil the will of God. " It exercises its pre-eminence in that it guides man's life." ⁴ Calvin finds in man traces of this his original relation to God even though it has been reversed through sin. There is intrinsic to the soul of man itself a seed of religion (*semen religionis*) and this consists above all in an original knowledge of heavenly life. It is the most splendid endowment of human reason and the chief power of the soul to be aware of blessedness which is perfected in union with God. To aim at this blessedness is the most important thing for the soul; and the reasonableness of the humanity of man is shown most decisively in the degree to which he aims at " coming nearer to God ".⁵

Calvin's anthropology is thus to be understood less against

---

¹ *Inst.* I, 15, 4; *O.S.* 3, 180.
² *Loc. cit.*
³ *Inst.* I, 15, 6; *O.S.* 183.
⁴ *Loc. cit.*
⁵ *Loc. cit.*

the background of creation than against that of redemption and eschatology. Man's being is orientated towards the new creation in Christ; this is especially true of his soul, and his earthly life from the beginning is destined to eternity. In regeneration through Christ this destiny of man made in the likeness of God comes to its fulfilment—a fulfilment which has its beginning here and now but is completed only in the sphere of heavenly glory. "The likeness to God is thus the original pre-eminent endowment of human nature which shone forth clearly in Adam before the fall; later, however, it was so spoiled and indeed destroyed that from the wreckage only what was confused, distorted, and stained survived. It is just this divine likeness which is now partially visible in the elect in so far as they are born again of the Spirit, and which will attain its full splendour in heaven." [1]

Calvin expresses himself in greater detail about the difference between the first and the second creation, especially as regards the soul, in his exegesis of 1 Cor. 15:45 ff. where Paul contrasts the first Adam as a living soul with the last Adam as a life-giving Spirit. Here again Calvin interprets ψυχή as *pars pro toto* and indeed as *praecipua pars*: "The creative power of the soul made the lifeless stuff of the body a living man. Now the body hides living power or, better, essential life." Here he concedes that there is a certain analogy between man and the animals, for in the creation story from which the Pauline expression stems it is said of the animal that it "is" a living soul (not merely has). In regard to animals Calvin understands "soul" only in a partial sense. In every creature the soul has a different stamp and thus we must admit that "in spite of the general similarity of living essences the soul of man received a peculiar and special endowment". This is "the light of the understanding" and the powers of reason, but especially "essential immortality". But the text compels Calvin to grant that the life of the first Adam was natural and earthly because the first man was of the earth (v. 47); only with Christ, the last Adam, the man from heaven, does spiritual life arise. Yet for him the earthiness of the first

[1] *Inst.* I, 15, 4; *O.S.* 3, 180.

Adam is conditioned only by his earthly body which then—obviously Calvin is here contradicting his statements in the *Institutio*—determined the nature of the original man more than his heavenly soul. "Although the first man possessed an immortal soul which was in no sense derived from the earth," yet his action and endeavour was tied up with the earth from which his body sprang and on which he had to live his life.

Thus we can understand the expressions of Calvin in regard to the original orientation of man's being towards heavenly life only in the sense of something potential, which was not realized in the first creation but becomes a full reality only in the new creation. " Christ has brought to us from heaven His life-giving spirit by which we are born anew to a better life transcending all earthly aims; . . . in fine, Paul wishes to say : the state into which Christ introduces us is far more splendid than the state of the first man." [1] Cf. also Calvin's interpretation of Gen. 2, 7 : "In Adam the perfect state was not yet reached. By the work of Christ we are born again into heavenly life, whereas Adam even before the fall had an earthly and perishable life." [2]

(b) *The two-fold basis of immortality*

For Calvin the immortality of the human soul is closely bound up with its independence. We have already seen in expounding Calvin's view of the soul as an independent entity over against the body that he constantly relates the special pre-eminence of the soul to the fact that it is essentially immortal. This he bases mainly upon the facts of creation. The immortality of the soul is bound up with its nature as made in God's own image, of which such immortality is a necessary corollary. In his commentary on Genesis Calvin represents the creation of man in three stages, of which the last and highest is its endowment with the divine likeness and at the same time with immortality. "Three stages can be distinguished in the creation of man : from the earth a lifeless body was formed, then a soul was given to it whence it received life and move-

---

[1] On 1 Cor. 15:45 ff.; *C.R.* 77, 558 ff.
[2] On Gen. 2:7; *C.R.* 51, 36.

ment, then God stamped upon the soul His own image from which immortality flowed."[1] Because the soul stems from the word and spirit of God it shares in divine immortality.

Of course it is not simply an outflow of the divine being. To assert that, as Servetus and the Manichaeans have done, means to efface the indissoluble distinction between the Creator and the creature. In that case the being of God would be, like our own, subject to change and to the passions which agitate our own soul. For we know that the soul itself is " a sink and a receptacle of all filth ".[2] It is noteworthy that in this connexion Calvin does not specifically mention the fact of sin as the root of the soul's corruption, but emphasizes only its creaturely status as opposed to divine being. " Although the divine likeness is impressed upon the soul, yet it is created like the angels. But creation is not emanation (of the divine being) it is rather the beginning of a new being springing from nothing."[3] In this respect Calvin sharply differentiates his own doctrine of the soul from the Platonic or neo-Platonic theory of emanations. He calls the latter a devilish error which results in " crude and disgusting nonsense ". The fact that the soul comes from God and returns to God when it leaves the body does not mean that it is a part of the divine substance (*substantia*). Again Calvin explains from the New Testament witness to the renewal of man in Christ how the divine image may be rightly understood. Man is made analogous to God not by an emanation of the divine substance but by grace and the power of the divine spirit. For Paul says that in proportion as we contemplate the glory of Christ we are by the spirit of the Lord changed into the same image.[4] " Just as little as the being of the human soul is an emanation of the divine, is the immortality of the human soul the same as divine immortality."

Calvin knows, it is written, that God alone has immortality (1 Tim. 6:16). God is immortal by nature because He alone

---

[1] *Loc. cit.*
[2] " . . . animam ipsam scimus sordium omnium lacunam ac receptaculum esse. " *Inst.* I, 15, 5; *O.S.* 3, 181.
[3] *Loc. cit.*
[4] *Inst. loc. cit.*, p. 182.

is from everlasting. But the soul of man is not immortal in itself any more than are the created heavenly spirits, the angels. "For everything which has a beginning can also have an end, can perish."[1] God has eternal life within His power and with supreme disposal imparts it to angels and men. It inheres in these His creatures only in so far as He breathes upon them His own life. "If this divine power which is inbreathed into men is taken away, then their immortality vanishes and the same can be assumed with regard to the angels."[2] In spite of the corruption of man by sin, God continues to impart to him immortality. "He does not cease to endow us with immortality since He has once breathed life into men whom He created."[3] That is no reason for our glory, but for His. If God did not bestow immortality upon us our death would not be in any way different from that of any other animal. "For we are not worthier and nobler intrinsically but we only become so by the fact that it has pleased God to give us this peculiar privilege of being immortal." But then it should be remembered that true immortality consists in obedience to God. "For there is survival even for the devil and the damned, but it is of another kind: it is life in the knowledge that they have God opposed to them and are rejected by Him."[4] There is true immortality only in God and in the longing for His kingdom. This is restored to man in Christ and primarily in the life of the soul.

Before we pass to consider this second foundation in Calvin for man's immortality, viz. in the fact of redemption, we must —by way of an excursus, and before leaving the thought of its foundation in the fact of creation—make reference to Calvin's hypothesis of a universal human consciousness of immortality. Calvin rests his doctrine of the soul's immortality as based on the order of creation not only on Scripture but also on experience, even though he does so only incidentally.

---

[1] "Vray est donc, que les anges sont esprits immortels, que ceste qualité aussi convient à nos âmes, mais cela n'est point de nature: car tout ce qui a eu commencement, peut avoir fin, et peut . . . voire perir . . ." Sermon on 1 Tim. 6:15 f.; C.R. 81, 619 ff.
[2] Commentary on 1 Tim. 6:16; C.R. 80, 532.
[3] Sermon on 1 Tim., *loc. cit.*
[4] *Loc. cit.*

In spite of the obscuring of the human mind, which is too much concerned with earthly things and is hardly in a position to conceive a life after death, man has even so preserved a last faint idea of immortality.[1] One proof of that is above all the conscience. "For conscience, which in its distinction between right and wrong corresponds to the tribunal of God, is an unambiguous sign of the immortality of the human soul." The sense of something akin to guilt before God and the sense of God generally which Calvin clearly presupposes to exist in all men sufficiently shows that spirit, which is thus capable of transcending the world, is immortal, "because no unspiritual power could thus penetrate to the source of all life". Calvin speaks here even of a knowledge of God. "The high gifts of the human personality are for him plain indications that something divine is implanted in man and these gifts are as a whole signs of his immortality." Unlike that of animals, the thinking and feeling of man transcends the bodily sphere, and the human spirit seeks to fathom the mysteries of heaven and earth, nature and history, and to systematize their inner connexions. The spirit or the soul of man can even by its reason conceive God and the angels; this the body cannot do. Even sleep is for Calvin a clear token of immortality because in dreams it gives us the possibility of picturing what has not yet happened and of divining the future. Here Calvin points out specifically that even heathen authors can speak of these things, although with exaggeration. "For the pious of course the mere mention will suffice."[2] But that does not prevent him from occasionally adducing such heathen philosophers in support of his doctrine of the soul and immortality.

We come here upon the question of natural theology in Calvin. In the doctrine of the soul as the true image of God we have already met the Calvinistic idea of the seed of religion (*semen religionis*) implanted in man. There again we found in the main only positive expressions about this general consciousness of God and immortality. But it must be borne in mind that Calvin is thinking of the original creation and

---

[1] *Inst.* 1, 15, 2; *O.S.* 3, 175.
[2] *Loc. cit.*

state of man whose nature is now terribly distorted by the fall but whose divinely bestowed gifts so remind him of his once happy condition that he remains inexcusable before God (*see* Rom. 1). " We consider it indisputable that the human spirit possesses by natural intuition a feeling for the divine. For God Himself has imparted to all men an awareness of His divinity so that no one might plead the excuse of ignorance." [1] But this original awareness of God is suppressed by man and turned into idolatry. " Some lose themselves in superstition, others depart from God intentionally and with an evil mind; but all deviate from the true knowledge of God." [2] Thus in fact man comes to God not otherwise than through God's unique revelation in Jesus Christ as attested in Holy Scripture. " Whoever wishes to attain to the knowledge of God the Creator must have Holy Scripture as his guide and teacher " is Calvin's heading for the 6th chapter of the 1st book of the *Institutio*. " In the eternal word of God attested therein (in Scripture), in Christ, is revealed for faith the Creator and Redeemer " (Peter Barth).[3]

Thus for Calvin the knowledge of immortality is decidedly not to be gained from the surmises of the heathen and the speculations of philosophers, but first and last from the Bible alone and its testimony to creation and redemption. " It would be foolish to take the advice of the philosophers on the being of the soul, for apart from Plato almost none of them has recognized its immortality." [4] Still more definite is the rejection of philosophy in the *Psychopannychia*, in the case of which, however, as the first theological writing of Calvin a humanistic-philosophical influence is rather to be presumed : " Let us here set aside all that springs from human wisdom,

---

[1] *Inst.* I, 3, 1; *O.S.* 3, 37.
[2] *Inst.* I, 4, 1; *O.S.* 3, 41.
[3] *Das Problem der natürlichen Theologie bei Calvin*, p. 26. Cf. also Peter Brunner, *Allgemeine und besondere Offenbarung in Calvins Institutio*, " Ev. Theologie ", 1934, 5. Further, G. Gloede, *Theologia Naturalis bei Calvin*. With some reason he mentions the question of immortality as the " historical starting point " for Calvin's natural theology (p. 88). But he does not make clear the fact that Calvin centres immortality in Christ and he does not sufficiently note that Calvin essentially recognizes the *imago Dei* through its renewal in the Incarnate.
[4] *Inst.* I, 15, 6; *O.S.* 3, 182.

which no doubt has speculated much concerning the soul but has grasped nothing rightly. Away with the philosophers, who with their habit of making baseless distinctions in almost everything here dispute so much that you will hardly find two witnesses who will lead you to any sort of satisfactory conclusion. In many passages Plato has discussed excellently the capacities of the soul, but it was Aristotle who did so most acutely. But what the soul is and from whence it comes you will in vain ask them and all the sages, although they considered themselves cleverer and clearer thinkers than those who glory in being the disciples of Christ." [1]

By contrast Calvin wishes to base his teaching of the immortality of the soul on " the illuminating testimony of Scripture ".[2] For a genuine knowledge of this immortality arises not from the soul of man himself. " No human spirit has conceived this knowledge, but it springs from the revelation of the Holy Ghost. Hence believers alone possess it." [3] The knowledge of the heathen is uncertain; hence they cannot rest any confidence in it. " Only believers can freely and frankly confess what God's word and spirit testifies to them." [4] And that is then for them no general conviction but a firm personal faith—faith in the immortality of the individual soul.

The question nevertheless remains whether in fact Calvin, in spite of his fundamental rejection of philosophy, does not develop a doctrine of the soul which is more philosophical than theological and which does not accord with Biblical anthropology. His basing of the immortality of the soul on the fact of creation (or the story of creation) is in any case exegetically questionable, because his interpretation of *nephesh* does not do justice to Biblical linguistic usage, and because in Scripture it is nowhere expressly stated that the soul as a part of human nature is created immortal.

What is the situation with regard to Calvin's foundation of his doctrine on the fact of redemption? Calvin here adduces his proof of immortality from the communion with Christ

[1] *Psy.* 23; 178.
[2] *Loc. cit.*
[3] On 2 Cor. 5:1; *C.R.* 78, 60.
[4] *Loc. cit.*

which believers enjoy. By their incorporation into the body of Christ which takes place through faith His members are endowed with the Holy Ghost and receive eternal life here and now, of which death can no more deprive them. The body still dies, but the soul which has been awakened through the Holy Ghost from the death of sin and born anew by judgment and grace can no longer die, but on its separation from the body in death already enters the sphere of heavenly felicity where it is fully united with Christ. Fellowship with Christ cannot be suspended by death; not even temporarily. " To have fallen asleep with Christ means to remain in communion with Christ in death, for he who by faith is made a member of Christ must also die with Him in order to be able to live with Him." [1] Believers only attain the end of regeneration " when they are freed from the body and fully incorporated into Christ." [2] The soul is for Calvin in this connexion that part of man which is born anew by the Holy Spirit, and in general he insists on interpreting in this sense most of the passages of Scripture which speak of the Spirit. " Most frequently what is called spirit is that which is born anew in us of the Spirit of God ",[3] " The spirit is that part of man which is born again in us spiritually . . . his better half which is held in bondage to the fetters of the flesh but is freed by death." [4] Although, following Paul, Calvin is aware of a struggle between the flesh and spirit in the soul,[5] he permits himself this simplifying identification of the soul and spirit which modifies the Pauline contrast of $\sigma\acute{a}\rho\xi$ and $\pi\nu\epsilon\hat{v}\mu a$.

Of course Calvin realizes the sinfulness of the soul and grants that it too must in a certain sense die. But this death is a spiritual death. In this way he seeks to counter the theologically important objection of those critics who reminded him of the curse of death which sin implies and under which

---

[1] " Dormire per Christum est retinere in morte coniunctionem quam habemus cum Christo; nam qui fide in Christum inserti sunt, mortem cum eo communem habent, ut sint vitae socii." On 1 Thess. 4:14; C.R. 80, 165.
[2] On 2 Pet. 3:14; C.R. 83, 477.
[3] Psy. 25; 179.
[4] Psy. 50:194.
[5] Cf. Psy. 25. See above, pp. 57 f.

man, as a whole, stands. " They object that the soul, although endowed with immortality, yet has fallen into sin as a result of which its immortality has been destroyed. This was appointed and declared to the first parents as their due punishment for sin: 'Ye shall die' (Gen. 2:17). And Paul says that the wages of sin is death (Rom. 6:23). And the prophet exclaims: 'Every soul that sinneth, it shall die'" (Ez. 18:4).[1] As a reply Calvin declares that the death of the soul is something other than the death of the body, and is in fact the judgment of God, whose severity the sick soul cannot endure; so that it becomes utterly despairing, collapses, and dies (*dispereat*). Thus Scripture teaches us and this has been experienced by those whom God has shattered by those terrors. Calvin is here no doubt thinking of his own sudden conversion (*subita conversio*) which he touches on in his preface to his commentary on the Psalms,[2] and which was characterized by the awareness of the judging and annihilating majesty of God. Spiritual death is the experience of the wrath of God in the conscience. " Do you wish to know what the death of the soul is? To be without God, to be forsaken by God, to be abandoned to oneself." [3] To lose the presence of God means to lose life, because God is the true life and light of men.[4]

Man is not only alienated from God by judgment, but he is so already by sin, by his defection from God, the source of life, as a result of which he is surrendered to death. That in itself implies a dying of the soul; a death in sin. " As the spiritual life of Adam consisted in the fact that he was united with his Creator and remained in fellowship with Him, so alienation from Him means the ruin of the soul." [5] This applies also to our individual sins. " Thus we die unto God in so far as we are enslaved by the desire which lives in us ... We are a living death, i.e. we die eternally " (I Tim. 5:6) [6]

[1] *Psy.* 65; 203.
[2] *C.R.* 59, 21.
[3] " Vultis scire quae sit animae mors? Deo carere, a Deo desertam esse, sibi relictam esse." *Psy.* 68; 204.
[4] *Loc. cit.*
[5] *Inst.* II, 1, 5; *O.S.* 3, 232.
[6] *Psy.* 51; 205.

Thus as a result of sin we are doomed to be estranged from God and to eternal death. Calvin here means what the orthodox dogmatists later, with their fine distinctions, called "*mors spiritualis infidelium*" leading to "*mors aeterna*". In contrast stands the "*mors fidelium*"—what Calvin represents as real spiritual death without clearly distinguishing it from the former. The death of the soul which believers undergo—Calvin points this out above all in commenting on the Psalms—is the awareness of the death in which all men live through their separation from God. It is the terror of this spiritual and eternal death which makes bodily death—in itself already an evil—still more terrible. " We teach: Although by death is often denoted the break-up of this present life and by hell the grave, yet in Scripture these terms are also much used to suggest divine anger and rejection so that to die and go down into hell or to live in hell is said of those who are alienated from God, are plunged into ruin by the divine judgment and are torn asunder by his hand." [1] " I ask, will a believer call simple and natural death God's anger and terror? I think that these critics are not so shameless as to dare to assert so much." [2] " *In summa*: I grant that death is in itself an evil, since it is the curse and punishment of God, and as in itself it is full of terror and the sense of abandonment, it casts all the more into the extremity of despair all those who feel that thereby they are struck down by God who is angry with them and is punishing them." [3]

But there is a Saviour from this death of the soul, and that is He who has suffered it for us to its bitter end: Jesus Christ. " Whatever be the implications of this death of the soul, Christ has overcome them for us." [4] By this Calvin means not merely the death on the cross in itself, but the descent into hell, which is essentially bound up with it and which in the first instance he understands in a spiritual sense, although he accepts also the theory of the descent into the kingdom of

---

[1] *Psy.* 97; 223.
[2] *Psy.* 100; 226.
[3] *Psy.* 101; 226.
[4] *Psy.* 69; 205.

the dead and makes use of it at appropriate points.¹ Christ has suffered for us not only bodily but also spiritual death. "In truth He must have felt the whole weight and severity of the divine judgment in order to avert God's wrath and to make satisfaction to His just judgment." ² Thus—from the wrestling in prayer of Gethsemane to the complete abandonment by God on Calvary—He suffers the death which the anger of God brings upon evil-doers. Not only did He surrender His body but surrendered His soul in that He suffered "the most terrible torments of a lost and reprobate man." ³ In so doing He has in our place gained the victory over "a natural and spiritual death. Had it not been that His soul bore the punishment also, He would certainly be the Saviour of our body only." Thus as our Leader (*Princeps noster*) He has vicariously fought out for us the struggle with death and the devil.⁴ Now we are freed from the judgment of God, and hell or eternal death have no more claim upon us. "His soul was harried with fear and terror so that ours, emancipated from all fear, should gain peace and rest." ⁵

Of course believers in a certain sense also experience spiritual death when they recognize their sin and become saddened about it in their soul; but just in that situation they are made alive by Him who through His death has taken away from them the guilt of their sin; and upon whom they learn to place all their trust when they despair of themselves. "He (God) frees the heart-broken and despairing and raises them to hope." ⁶ His anger brings death, His mercy life. This applies also and precisely to the trials of the soul in bodily death. "There is a medicine which alleviates its bitterness; to recognize in the midst of such fears that we have God as Father and Christ as Leader and Companion

¹ Cf. on the contrary Luther's understanding of the *descensus ad inferos* as a beginning of the *exaltatio Christi*, as a triumph of the Lord over the devil and his kingdom, according to Eph. 4:8–10; cf. among others *W.A.* 37, 63. This interpretation affirmed itself against other views in Lutheranism; cf. F.C. IX, *Bek. Schr.* 1049 ff.
² *Inst.* II, 16, 10; *O.S.* 3, 495.
³ *Loc. cit.*
⁴ *Inst.* II, 16, 11/12; *O.S.* 3, 497.
⁵ *Loc. cit.*, p. 499.
⁶ *Psy.* 102; 227.

in our destiny. But for such as have not this medicine, death brings destruction and eternal damnation."[1]

Christ has died for us that we might live. But He Himself did not fully perish in death although He really died. He is Himself life. "Thus Christ has life in Himself, i.e. fullness of life by which He Himself lives and makes His own to live... Faith makes us certain of this, that Christ could not be overcome by death, nor even His humanity. And although He was truly and naturally given over to death, to which we are all subject, He nevertheless always preserved that gift of the Father."[2] It is His soul which on its separation from the body in death did not lose this life in God. "The soul never lost its life which was given to it, by the Father and thus could only be blessed.... For His soul was strengthened by divine power so that it should not suffer corruption but His body was kept in the grave until the resurrection. All this has been summed up by Peter in the word: Christ could not be holden by death..."[3] Thus Calvin connects this testimony of the first Pentecost not with the resurrection of Christ of which Peter is there expressly speaking (Acts 2:31) but rather with the immortality of the soul of Christ which he simply takes for granted and which is the basis of our own. But in his subsequent arguments he admits that this should comfort us less than the fact of the resurrection of Christ. "Moreover our comfort is not so much that Christ our Head did not perish in the shadow of death, for to this certainty is added that of His resurrection by which He is established as the Lord of death and rescues us from death."[4]

For Calvin the communion between Christ and His elect is so inward that a total dying of believers means for him a threat to the life of their exalted Lord; likewise also even the sleep of death which for him is equivalent to complete death. "If the life of Christ is ours, then he who would have our

[1] "Unum est condimentum, quod tantam acerbitatem temperet, inter eius angustias cognoscere deum sibi esse patrem, Christum habere ducem ac comitem. Hoc condimento qui carent, habent mortem pro confusione et perditione aeterna." *Psy.* 101; 226.
[2] *Psy.* 47; 192.
[3] *Loc. cit.*
[4] *Psy.* 49; 193.

life end in death draws Christ from the right hand of the Father and plunges Him into a second death; but if there is no limit to His life then our souls which are incorporated into Him cannot be destroyed by any sort of death; . . . thus we tear the members of Christ from Him when we wish to deprive them of life." [1]

By total death the progress of our regeneration would be interrupted and generally called in question. What happens —particularly in our soul—through the slaying and making alive wrought by the Holy Spirit is our renewal, our transfiguration into the likeness of Christ, and it is a process which takes place stage by stage, and daily progress; in death it reaches only a provisional completion when the soul through its separation from the body is transplanted into a blessed immortality. " We only began in our regenerate life to adopt the image of Christ; day by day we are more and more transformed into His likeness." [2] But Christ already lives in the soul, and eternal life—the kingdom of God—begins. This new life, Calvin thinks, would by a death or sleep of the soul be destroyed. " O that we were able to apprehend in true faith the real nature of the kingdom of God which lives in believers even during this present life. Then it would be easy to grasp the fact that eternal life has here and now begun. . . . But if the transition to eternal life has already taken place, why will one insist that death interrupts it ? " [3] That would mean for Calvin that the continuity of the new life is broken and also its progressive character. " If souls are constantly growing until they see God, and through this growth proceed to the vision of God, how then can these people suppose that they become buried in the comatose condition of sleep? " [4] Just as little as the spirit of Christ was

---

[1] " Si vita Christi nostra est, qui vitam nostram finire vult morte, detrahat Christum e dextera patris et in secundam mortem deturbet. Si mori ille potest, certa mors nos sequitur; si nullum habet vitae finem, neque animae nostrae, quae illi insitae sunt, finiri ulla morte possunt . . . Avellamus ergo a Christo membra sua, si volumus ipsis vitam adimere." *Psy., loc. cit.*
[2] On 1 Cor. 15:49; *C.R.* 77, 560.
[3] *Psy.* 50; 194.
[4] *Psy.* 52; 195.

overcome by death—He who descended into hell to preach to departed spirits and hence did not sleep, while His body rested in the grave—will our soul which has been quickened by His spirit pass away or sleep in death. Calvin thus understands the descent into hell described in I Pet. 3:19. The apostle Peter shows no less clearly that souls will be freed from death and will live, since he tells us that "Christ preached to the spirits who were in Hades and not only announced to the spirits of the pious their forgiveness and sanctification but also to the spirits of the impious their damnation.... It can surprise no one that the holy patriarchs were so to speak shut up in prison, since they were still awaiting the redemption of Christ." [1] Thus the life of departed souls has only through the advent of Christ been transformed into blessedness and only thereby has their immortality been made their salvation.

Calvin also uses Christ's ascent into heaven as a basis of his doctrine of immortality. Because the head has ascended into heaven He attracts the souls of his elect thither. While in the *meditatio vitae coelestis* we found that this was expressed only in the sense of *sursum corda*, here there is taught a literal ascent into heaven of souls separated from their bodies; the ascent of Christ produces an ascent into heaven of believers. Calvin argues thus not on his own initiative but adduces a supposed saying of Augustine with which he obviously agrees: "But elsewhere he teaches that after the ascent of Christ the souls of those ascend into heaven to whom Christ is life." [2] Thus it should be clear that this teaching has no scriptural basis, but it is thoroughly in accord with the rest of Calvin's teaching about the soul, for the Christological basis of which the ascension into heaven is better adapted than the resurrection, which however—as we saw—he also brings forward (even though only by way of completion or correction). For him just in this connexion the spiritual resurrection of the soul from the death of sin is more important, for as a result of it

---

[1] *Psy.* 36; 185.
[2] *De ecclesiae dogmatibus*, c. 46; a pseudo-Augustinian writing; cf. Zimmerli, *Psy.* 84.

THE IMMORTALITY OF THE SOUL 81

the soul receives eternal life [now already] so that on separation from the body it enters into a blessed immortality and eternal glory. " The death of the soul is alienation from God. Hence those who believe in Christ, although formerly they were dead, begin to live, because faith is the spiritual resurrection of the soul and in a certain sense quickens the soul itself so that it lives in God." [1]

Calvin's founding of the immortality of the soul on the fact of redemption has a real theological justification in the idea of the indestructibility of the communion of Christ. But it is a question whether its continuity through death is dependent on the nature of the soul and its progressive glorification. The sureness and eternity of fellowship with Christ rests not upon us but upon Him alone. The testimony of Holy Scripture to our eternal life in Him is not dependent on any dualistic anthropology even if it employs the terminology of the latter at times. The question of death as imperilling our communion with the living Lord is completely resolved in the New Testament by reference to His and our bodily resurrection, and that is its sufficient answer.

3. THE STATE OF THE SOUL AFTER DEATH
(a) *Provisional Blessedness*

Calvin teaches that man's soul, which is immortal in essence, does not perish nor sleep in death but in so far as it is born again in Christ already enjoys heavenly peace in the expectation of the resurrection of the body, which will bring it consummate blessedness; but the souls of the impious will be held imprisoned in terrible expectation of their final condemnation.

The state of redeemed souls is considered by Calvin to involve a two-fold and plainly contradictory aspect. On the one hand the position of the soul after its emancipation from

---

[1] " Nam mors animae alienatio a Deo. Ergo qui in Christum credunt, quum prius mortui essent, incipiunt vivere, quia fides spiritualis est animae resurrectio et animam ipsam quodammodo animat ut vivat Deo secundum illud: ' Mortui audient vocem filii Dei et qui audierint, vivent ' (John 5:25)." On John 11:25; *C.R.* 75, 262.

the body is described with the utmost fervour as the goal of all our hopes; on the other hand it is depicted as a yet incomplete state. It is at one and the same time already blessed and not yet so. This contradiction can be traced in all Calvin's statements about the intervening state of souls at rest, but the first aspect clearly predominates.

(i) *The rest of the soul*

The souls of the saved attain eternal peace in death. They are in Abraham's bosom; they are already with God and Christ. " Let us consider here the rest of souls which have been delivered from the body in assured faith in the promises of God. By the bosom of Abraham the Scriptures mean to symbolize that state of peace." [1] It is the grace of God which delivers us for such rest out of the body of this death through Jesus Christ our Lord.[2] Calvin accepts as denoting this rest the Biblical name sleep; but he protests sharply against the " hypnologists ", his Baptist opponents, who, he thinks, misunderstand it and misuse it. " In the main, like them, we call this rest sleep. And we would not be at all afraid of the word sleep had it not been corrupted and sullied by their lies." [3] Hence Calvin wishes to confine its use to the rest of the mortal body in the grave. A sleep of the soul such as the Anabaptists assert would mean the death and complete ruin of the soul because only in a waking condition can the soul display its capacities, especially reason and will, to the honour of God, and thus live out its true life. " Then is the soul truly spiritual when, casting aside all earthly filth, it is at one with the will of God and no longer feels the tyranny of the flesh which is its enemy, and thus now rests in peace and thinks only of God. And is it then to sleep when, no longer crushed under any weight, it can soar? Is it then to snore when it can apprehend so much with its intellectual powers and is no longer held up by any obstacles ?"

Nor is that alone their error; it is due also to their malicious

---

[1] *Psy.* 41; 188.
[2] *Psy.* 82; 214.
[3] *Psy.* 41.

envy of God's works and powers which are reflected in the lives of His saints, as Scripture declares. We recognize God to be the secret life which comes to birth in His elect and increases daily, as the sage teaches us, " The path of the just shineth more and more unto the perfect day " (Prov. 4 : 18). And the apostle confirms this : " He who has begun the good work in you will also perfect it unto the day of Jesus Christ " (Phil. 1 : 6).[1] The progressive work of regeneration must in no way be suspended in death. Such a pause would not simply be retrogression but final dissolution. " These men do not just interrupt the work of God for a period, but also quench it." [2]

The rest of the soul is no idle leisure. From the living progress of renewal through Christ and the spirit there cannot be a lapse into lazy inactivity. " Shall those who formerly went from strength to strength and already enjoyed a foretaste of felicity in their aspirations towards God, now be snatched away from faith, virtue and the contemplation of God and lie idly and sleepily on cushions? " Here no scorn is bitter enough for Calvin : " How do they wish to explain this progress? Do they suppose that the soul would be perfected if it wallowed in sleep? " In that case souls will present themselves to God in a glutted state when He sits in judgment.[3] Since Calvin understands the interim between death and the last judgment as a time period according to the measure of our time, there must be for him in this interim a continuation of the progress of the soul begun on earth and in fact an increase in its perfection. He sees this progress taking place in specific stages: from the peace of the soul with God already received in this world but still obscured in the flesh by the struggle with sin, through the higher peace after deliverance from the body, to its consummation in a blessed resurrection. In support of his conception Calvin calls to mind the ladder of the soul's progress visualized by Augustine—a scheme of ideas which he does not altogether adopt, but the fundamental justification of which he recognizes. " It does not displease me to see that

[1] *Psy.* 54; 197.
[2] *Psy.* 55; 197.
[3] *Loc. cit.*

for the purposes of instruction he somewhere argues that there are stages in the life of the soul, provided that this is interpreted soundly and with restraint. . . . He insists as forcibly as possible that there is an evolution of the soul towards the ultimate end, the day of judgment."[1] Calvin's ethic of progress corresponds to a sort of eschatological progress.

The rest of the soul in the interval consists in peace of conscience. As the spiritual death of the soul is alienation from God and the experience of His judgment in the conscience, so its blessedness is the awareness of reconciliation with God through faith, bringing peace to the conscience here and now, although it is still engaged in a struggle with dispeace and only after death will become quite secure. " We understand by peace . . . the rest and security of the conscience which is ever connected with faith but is never completed unless it be after death."[2] Believers receive this peace of conscience through the gospel, as a result of which they learn to recognize God the Judge as their Father in Jesus Christ and become certain " that instead of being sons of wrath they are sons of grace."[3] Yet they possess this peace only at the heart of the warfare of the Christian life and in conflict with the surviving traces of the flesh. For so long as we bear the flesh with us we have the enemy in our own house. But amid all the pressure of the world and the flesh, God Himself is already the peace of the soul even in the face of the attacks of the enemy. But when in death we lay aside the flesh, then in truth we attain full peace of conscience. " Death increases this peace and leads to a better one, thus bringing to the very centre of peace those who are released and as it were dismissed from the warfare of this world."[4] So long as we live in the body, in this muddy prison house of the flesh, we live in the hope of faith which is not yet sight.[5] The eyes of our spirit are still buried in the flesh and therefore their sight is not sharp

[1] *Psy.* 85; 216.
[2] *Psy.* 41; 188.
[3] *Psy.* 42; 188.
[4] *Psy.* 45; 191.
[5] *Psy.* 81; 279.

enough. "So soon, however, as we get rid of this eye disease, so to speak, our faith will be crowned in sight and we shall fully enjoy peace."[1] The true peace of believers was already in the conflict here below the eternal peace of God, and to the full enjoyment of that eternal peace He brings His own when they die. "Because their peace was in God even when they were engaged in warfare with the world He leads them to the final stage of peace . . . Only then will they truly be at rest and dwell with God."[2]

This rest in God is for Calvin the same thing as the bosom of Abraham (Lk. 16). As in the parable the poor Lazarus at his death is borne by angels into the bosom of the patriarch, so Calvin sees the souls of all the redeemed united in death with the Father of all the faithful. This parable of Jesus concerning the rich and the poor occupies an important place in Calvin's arguments about immortality. He vigorously disputes the idea that it is only metaphorical in its import, and asserts that it is a true story or a series of symbols setting forth actual relations as do the parables of Jesus generally.[3] Abraham himself is the prototype of the faith which hopes, since he trusts in the promises of God although he walks without sight, and expects the promised seed with such assured confidence "that he as it were clasps it with his hands and grasps it with all the senses of his soul and body."[4] Hence Christ said that Abraham rejoiced to see His day (Jn. 8). This vision of God in Christ is the rest of the soul which after death it enjoys in a supreme degree with the spirits of all just men made perfect. "What more pleasant can the conscience have, how can it more securely rest than in this peace which discloses the treasures of heavenly grace—the sweet chalice of the Lord from which it drinks with rapture?" Calvin opposes this felicity to the drunken sleep of his opponents—those who long for sleep and proclaim its necessity. "When one hears of drunkenness does not one think of dizziness,

[1] Loc. cit.
[2] Psy. 42; 189.
[3] Psy. 38 ff.; 187 ff.
[4] Psy. 43; 189.

reeling gait, and your gross fleshly sleep?" The elect who rest in Abraham's bosom are with him in the " seat of peace " and " enjoy the vision of God without satiety." [1]

This quiet of the soul in the vision of God is already the heavenly Jerusalem, the vision with which the God of peace blesses the peacemakers according to the promise of Christ (Matt. 5).[2] There the Lord satisfies His own with His riches. There the soul is completely and without distraction concentrated in attention to its Lord, seeing Him directly and not merely through the mirror of the Word as now in this earthly pilgrimage. " Our eye of faith sees God only from a distance . . . but when we reach our journey's end in God, then we shall behold Him face to face with full manifestation. . . . Although we attain the full vision only on the day of the Lord's appearing, yet already in death, which releases our soul from the fetters of the flesh, we are drawn nearer to the vision of God; then we need no external word, no makeshift supports." [3] In the peace of the soul which has been delivered from the body we become aware of the presence of God; we live no longer in faith but in sight, for we are relieved of the burden of this earth which crushed us and " like a barrier separated us from God and removed us far from Him." [4]

The souls of the redeemed therefore essentially enter into eternal blessedness when they die. " Scripture teaches us that Christ is present to them and that He receives them in paradise." [5] Jesus' word to the thief is for Calvin a text of capital importance : " If souls when they have laid aside the burden of the flesh did not retain their own identity and become partakers of blessed immortality, then Christ would not have said to the thief : To-day shalt thou be with me in paradise " (Lk. 23 : 43).[6] Calvin specifically rejects an exegesis

---

[1] *Loc. cit.*
[2] " Est inquam, requies illa coelestis Jerusalem, hoc est visio pacis, in qua deus pacis dat se videndum suis pacificis iuxta Christi promissum (Mt. 5)." *Psy.* 43 f.; 190.
[3] On 1 Cor. 13 : 12; *C.R.* 77, 514 f.
[4] *Psy.* 53; 196.
[5] *Inst.* III, 26, 6; *O.S.* 4, 442.
[6] *Loc. cit.*

which refers this text to the eternal presence of God before whom a thousand years are but as a day.[1] " They forget that as often as God speaks with man He adapts Himself to human modes of apprehension. And in the Scriptures we do not read that a day stands for a thousand years." The text quoted by Calvin's opponents (2 Pet. 3:8) has reference merely to the delay in the parousia which is there being discussed. Calvin's view is that the thief on that very day—the day of his death— is rescued from the misery into which Adam fell and as a result of which he transgressed the commandment of God. " Thus immortality was restored to the thief." [2]

(ii) *The waiting of the soul*
Calvin qualifies this strong emphasis on the blessedness of the souls of the redeemed in the intervening state by referring to the provisional nature of their felicity, and his thought here derives from the centrality of the resurrection in the Scriptures. The delivered soul that is conscious after death still awaits its consummation on the day of judgment. No doubt the soul already enjoys heavenly communion with Christ and in the blessed company of elect spirits in the bosom of Abraham, for it receives the fruition of its faith, and only in the fellowship of fathers and brothers, i.e. in the church, the body of Christ, can we be perfected and become fully united with the Head; " since we cannot be members of Christ without growing up into His stature." [3] That is the nearer goal of our journey and it is reached already in death. But Calvin thinks that alongside it is a further goal, the true consummation. Meanwhile Scripture admonishes us to hold fast to the expectation of the advent of Christ, and the crown of glory is held up until then. Thus we must not wish to know more than God indicates concerning our state after death, and ought not to attempt to go beyond the bounds of His word. " When the souls of the pious have endured the trials of earthly warfare they enter into a blessed rest where with joyous

[1] *Psy.* 57; 199.
[2] *Psy.* 59; 200.
[3] *Inst. III*, 25, 6; *O.S.*, 4, 442.

peace they await the promised glory; so everything remains in the balance until Christ appears as Redeemer." [1]

In contrast with other expressions which referred to an utterly unsurpassable joy in God, here his theme is expectation. Calvin attempts to resolve the contradiction by saying that the felicity of the soul after death consists precisely in this expectation which is no longer based on faith but on sight. Souls await indeed what they have not yet, but they are nevertheless happy because they both realize their adoption in God and see their future reward, resting in assured hope of the blessed resurrection.[2] " Thus already they enjoy the vision of God and of Christ, though not yet perfectly." The last judgment increases their happiness in degree only and hence can have for Calvin only the significance of completing the process.

Calvin accepts the term sleep, as already indicated, to denote this state of assured but not yet fulfilled expectation. He points out that in Holy Scripture the peace of the conscience, according to Hebraic usage, is often suggested by the image of sleep and rest in a somewhat familiar manner (*familiariter*), e.g.: " I will rest and sleep in peace " (Ps. 4:9); but this does not imply any shadowy condition but the peace of an assured trust in God in expectation of the ultimate peace—a trust which here on earth is already a calm and clear-eyed aspiration towards the promised but still invisible inheritance. It is a yet imperfect peace which, however, in death is brought to a provisional state of perfection.[3] " Yet these souls who sleep in full consciousness still lack something which they desire to see,

---

[1] " Interea quum Scriptura ubique iubeat pendere ab exspectatione adventus Christi, et gloriae coronam eousque differat, contenti simus his finibus divinitus nobis praescriptis: animas piorum mitiae labore perfunctas in beatam quietem concedere, ubi cum foelici laetitia fruitionem promissae gloriae exspectant: atque ita omnia teneri suspensa donec Christus appareat redemptor." *Loc. cit.*—In his study *The Dispute Concerning the Beatific Vision of God.*, (1331–38), G. Hoffman, p. 779, remarks that this expression of Calvin is most closely connected with the teaching of Pope John XXII, which he so sharply criticizes (cf. *Inst.* IV, 7, 28). Hoffman points out that the reformer was but imperfectly acquainted with the views of the pope and the turns of the debate in question.

[2] *Psy.* 81; 213.

[3] *Psy.* 44; 190.

viz. the supreme and perfect glory of God for which they constantly strive. Although their longing is not impatience, their rest is not yet perfect and completed.[1] "Our own felicity will be brought to its fullness only when the glory of God is finally and perfectly disclosed. This consummation takes place on the day of judgment. Then that word is fulfilled: "When I awake, I shall be satisfied with the sight of Thy countenance" (Ps. 17 : 15).[2]

At appropriate points Calvin can very vigorously emphasize the ultimate orientation of hope towards the resurrection, and in so doing he again partly contradicts what he previously said about the felicity of the immortal soul after death. "If we rightly consider the teaching of Scripture, then in fact a continued life of the soul without the hope of the resurrection is a sheer illusion. For God does not say that the soul survives death as though it immediately attained the glory and blessedness of the end, but He refers its hope to the Last Day." [3] The life of the soul is in so far not independent of that of the body inasmuch as its immortality without the prospect of the resurrection of the flesh is questionable and in point of fact falls to the ground. "According to Scripture the life of the spirit is inseparable from the resurrection, and souls that are delivered from the body await the day of resurrection; thus he who rejects the resurrection at the last day deprives the soul of its hope of immortality." [4] What is striking is how frequently and emphatically Calvin in this connexion refers to Scripture as the decisive norm of his doctrine. He allows his personal leaning towards a doctrine of survival and immortality to be checked by the command of the Bible and its message of resurrection. This applies even to the *Psychopannychia* where his spiritualizing tendency is in other respects most apparent: "Thus we are of all men most miserable if

---

[1] *Psy.* 45; 191.
[2] *Loc. cit.*
[3] "Et certe, si probe expenditur scripturae doctrina, animae vita sine spe resurrectionis merum erit somnium. Neque enim Deus pronuntiat, animas a morte esse superstites, quasi iam praesenti perfecta gloria et sua beatitudine fruantur, sed earum spem in ultimum usque diem suspendit." On Matt. 22 : 23; *C.R.* 73, 106.
[4] *Loc. cit.*

there is no resurrection, for although prior to the general resurrection we are already blessed, yet we are not so apart from the fact of resurrection. The spirits of the righteous are at peace in that they rest in the hope of the resurrection, without which their whole blessedness would vanish." [1] So even here he brings to a climax his teaching about progressive sanctification or regeneration in the resurrection of the re-created body on the second coming of Christ. " The kingdom of God does not yet exist, not for the reason that it is not yet accomplished . . . The kingdom of God is within you (Lk. 17:21). Already God reigns in the lives of His saints whom He guides by His spirit . . . But His kingdom will wholly appear when it is fulfilled. And it will be fulfilled when the glory of His majesty is fully disclosed. . . ." [2]

The kingdom of God begins for Calvin in the life of Christians who stand in faith and obedience under His rule and so reign with Him. " That kingdom consists in the structure of the church and the growth of the faithful, who, as Paul says, from stage to stage grow up into the perfect man " (Eph. 4:13). Despite these visible beginnings, we must direct our faith to the manifestation in the resurrection of the new life which is yet hidden in Christ (Col. 3 quoted again here by Calvin). " The apostle indeed admits that we have this hidden life in Christ our head and with God; but the disclosure of the full splendour of it will not be until the day when the glory of Christ is manifested—Christ who because He is the head of the church draws to Himself His own as His members." [3] The δόξα of Christians will not be disclosed and perfected apart from the δόξα of Jesus Christ, which will not be until His visible second coming to summon us to our bodily resurrection. Our perfecting does not anticipate that of the revelation of the Lord. The blessedness of the departed soul is only its beginning. " There is fulfilled in the body what has begun in the soul; or rather there will be perfected in both soul and body what has only begun in the soul." [4]

[1] *Psy.* 88; 218.
[2] *Psy.* 79; 212.
[3] *Psy.* 80; 212.
[4] *Psy.* 71; 206.

THE IMMORTALITY OF THE SOUL

In Calvin's polemic against the Anabaptists, in addition to proof from Scripture, a considerable if subordinate part is played by his reference to the Fathers, and this applies also to this question of the relationship between immortality and resurrection. " The ancient Fathers taught that souls are indeed in paradise and in heaven, but that they have not yet attained their glory and reward. For Tertullian says: ' Both recompense and judgment are linked with the event of the resurrection' (*Liber de resurrectio carnis*, 21). Yet he also teaches that the souls of the departed are with God and live in Him. Elsewhere he calls the bosom of Abraham a temporary refuge for the souls of believers."[1] Among other teachers of the early church Calvin also quotes Chrysostom, who says of the departed: " They have gone before us in the struggle, but they have not anticipated us as far as the winning of the crown is concerned; for a time is appointed for decorating the victor with his garland" (*Hom.* 28 in *II ad Hebraeos*). Nor must Calvin's crowning patristic witness be forgotten, namely Augustine, who writes in a letter to Jerome: " After the death of the body souls will be at rest and finally the body is received into glory" (*Ep.* 166 c.2).[2] It does not occur to Calvin at this point to subject the church tradition to a critical examination, as he did very energetically in regard to those points which were vital for the reformation; just here he sees no discord between Scripture and tradition, and so in this matter as in others he gladly refers to the consensus of the opinion of the Fathers—in whose theology he is excellently versed—the more so as (like Luther though in different ways) he lays stress on the communion of our faith with the ancient church, indeed with the church of all times and places in so far as in the essential things of the faith he is at one with it. There we see Calvin's catholic tendency clearly reflected.[3]

We will sum up two particularly fine passages from the

[1] *Psy.* 83; 215.
[2] *Psy.* 84; 215.
[3] Cf. on the whole problem, J. Koopmans' *Het oudkerklijk dogma in de reformatie, bepaaldelijk bij Calvijn*, Utrechter Dissertation, 1938.

polemical writings of Calvin: " But even though departed souls are conscious they still lack their consummate glory . . . for our blessedness is always at stake until that day which will finally terminate our course; thus it is a question of holding in view the ultimate glory of the elect and the goal of all our hopes—that day when all will be fulfilled. For we are all agreed that there can be no fulfilment of blessedness and glory unless we are perfectly united with God. To that end we all aspire and hasten, to that all the texts and promises of God point us." [1] " Jerusalem is not yet builded, the chief city and the seat of rule of the kingdom (Cf. on the other hand p. 86.) As yet Solomon the king of peace does not govern all things with the sway of his sceptre. Therefore only the souls of the departed are in peace, for they have escaped from the hand of the enemy. They are in a kingdom of which it is said: They go from strength to strength. But as soon as the heavenly Jerusalem will have arisen in all its glory, and the true Solomon, Christ the king of peace, shall have come, then He will sit exalted upon the throne and the true Israelites will reign with Him." [2]

(b) *Provisional damnation*

While at death the souls of the elect enter the blessedness of Abraham's bosom or paradise, thus enjoying the first fruits of their eternal salvation, the souls of the reprobate, dissociated from the body and unable to die, are held prisoner and fearfully await the torments of eternal damnation. " The reprobate will undoubtedly have the lot which Jude allots to

---

[1] " Atqui etiamsi vigilent, carere possunt gloria . . . beatitudinem nostram semper in cursu esse usque ad diem illum, qui omnem cursum claudet et terminabit, ita electorum gloriam et ultimae spei finem ad eum ipsum diem spectare, ut impleantur. Nam hoc satis inter omnes convenit, nullam esse vel beatitudinis vel gloriae perfectionem nisi perfectam cum deo coniunctionem. Huc omnes tendimus, huc properamus, huc omnes scripturae mittunt et dei promissiones." *Psy.* 77; 211.
[2] " Sed nondum erecta est Jerusalem, caput ac sedes regni. Nondum Solomon, rex pacis, sceptra tenet omniaque moderatur. Sunt ergo sanctorum animae post mortem in pace, quae extra manum hostis evolarunt. Sunt in opulentia, de quibus dictum est: Ibunt de abundantia ad abundantiam. Ubi vero surrexerit in gloriam suam coelestis Jerusalem et verus Solomon Christus, rex pacis, sublimis sederit in tribunali, regnabunt cum suo rege veri Israelitae." *Psy.* 82; 214.

the devils: they will be bound in chains until they are taken to the punishment to which they are condemned" (Jude 6).[1] Thus they suffer a foretaste of the fire of hell.

Here too Calvin opposes the doctrine of the soul's sleep. For there is no rest in death to the impious. Their souls are agitated with terrible fear of the judgment which awaits them. The spirit of a reprobate man while expecting a terrible judgment is tortured by that foreboding which Paul described as terrible φοβεράν (Heb. 10:27). The unquiet spirit of the impious which cannot find God in this world then seeks Him in vain, because he has neglected the offer of the word and spirit of God. "He seeks to delve into the abyss of the divine mysteries, although it was sufficient to learn what the Holy Ghost the divine Teacher had adequately taught. His word is: Hear me and your soul shall live."[2] The impious have remained in the spiritual death of sin and alienation from God and they only realize this when it is too late; their terrified conscience does not allow them to attain peace in death, so that death is something quite different for them from a gentle sleep. "When you hear that the godless sleep, do you imagine a sleep of the soul which can have no worse torture than the bad conscience by which they are tormented? How is sleep possible amid such terrors? . . . There is no peace for the wicked, says the Lord" (Is. 57)[3] It is just by contrast with the terrible plight in which the souls of the damned find themselves after death that the blessedness of pious souls in heavenly rest becomes plain to Calvin. "If the former plight is so terrible then the latter is, to be sure, rightly to be called joyous and blessed."[4]

The souls of the godless after death are now already as much tormented as are the fallen angels in their hellish dungeon. But this torment reaches its climax only when they enter the eternal fire at the last judgment. "For even if it is certain that evil spirits are now tortured, as Peter assures us (2 Pet. 2:4), it is also said that that fire in which the damned

---

[1] *Inst. III*, 25, 6; *O.S.* 4, 442.
[2] *Psy.* 60; 201.
[3] *Psy.* 55; 207.
[4] *Psy.* 81; 213.

are cast on the judgment day is prepared by the devil. Both thoughts have been expressed by the author who wrote that they were kept in eternal bonds until the judgment on the great day (Jude 6). He means by their bondage the punishment which they do not yet feel, by their actual chains that which they already endure." [1] But it may be questioned whether this passage and its parallels in 2 Peter, both of which expressly speak of the demons, ought to be referred to the souls of godless men. The third quotation of Calvin, Heb. 10:27, means unequivocally the expectation of a hopeless eternal future which must already be the lot of converts who have lapsed from the faith.

In this matter Calvin bases himself particularly on Augustine, whose eschatology has influenced his own in more than one respect. Augustine teaches that the souls of the pious and impious are found after death in a state of expectation and that in the underworld the kingdom of the dead is divided into a place of joy and a place of sorrow (Lk. 16): while some are in Abraham's bosom, others are already in a sort of vestibule to hell and their terrors will be further increased in the eternal fire, just as the blessedness of ransomed souls will be enhanced in eternal life.[2] He too compares the place in which reprobate souls are guarded with a dungeon and indeed with a place of visitation, whilst the repose of the pious is presented by him more as a blessed dream; but occasionally he suggests that they are already in paradise and goes beyond Lk. 16 in asserting that the saints, especially the martyrs, already reign with Christ. Eger (*loc. cit.*) comes to the conclusion that Augustine hovered between " the spiritualizing eschatological line of tradition which puts the start of heavenly bliss immediately after death and the tradition which is eschatological in the narrower sense as it connects bliss with the last judgment, although in fact the latter view is more in accordance with his interpretation as a whole. . . . But the spiritualizing tradition has the popular

---

[1] *Psy.* 85; 216.
[2] Cf. Hans Eger, *Die Eschatologie Augustins*, 1933, pp. 24 ff.

faith on its side, and Augustine again and again surrendered to it at the expense of his own teaching ".[1]

Although with Calvin regard for the popular tradition does not play such a part, yet a similar dualism is to be observed in his work and is rooted in his keen concern for the immortality of the soul.

Calvin's teaching about the condition of the soul after death (and about immortality in general) is the fundamental problem of his eschatology. We have so far repeatedly alluded to the contradiction which runs through the whole of his exposition of the state of departed souls. Every expression suggesting the felicity of eternal life in the vision and enjoyment of God is employed with reference to the state of the soul after death, but it is then added that this bliss is consummated only at the general resurrection. However, in this connexion it is not clear in what this enhancement produced by the consummation of communion with God consists. For the reunion of the soul with the body is not specially stressed when the resurrection is mentioned from this point of view. The vision of God is and remains for Calvin essentially spiritual or intellectual—a point which will specially concern us when we deal with the parousia of Christ. On the other hand, by the stress on the intervening period as a time of waiting, the Biblical tension between faith and sight is eluded; between the experience of communion with God or Jesus Christ in this world and the next, here entirely conditioned by hope, there entirely fulfilled, there comes as the mediating stage that state of expectation where faith is surpassed though hope still remains, where there is vision but not the beatific vision, and the tensions of earth are partially resolved.

In spite of his many allusions to the Bible, Calvin fails to convince us that his teaching about immortality and the state after death is consonant with Scripture. The Old Testament, in which Christian eschatology is rooted much more than is commonly supposed, shows absolutely no knowledge of the

[1] *Op. cit.*, p. 36. E. Dinkler comes to the same conclusion, *Die Anthropologie Augustins*, p. 213: " But this being in death in the separation of body and soul is of less importance for Augustine. What concerns him far more is . . . the question of the resurrection of the flesh."

Calvinistic distinction between body and soul, although it asserts a sort of survival of the dead in Sheol, while the New Testament hardly considers the state of souls after death, because it sees death wholly in the light of the resurrection. Hence it calls death a sleep, and not by way of euphemism as in heathendom, but as expressing the sure hope of the resurrection given us in the promise which is rooted in the resurrection of Christ and was formulated by Himself. " Whoever has received God's promise is not dead but only sleeps; such a one lives in virtue of his relation to God (Lk. 20:38 par.). Only he is dead who stands not under the promise but under the shadow of judgment. This sleep of the just is not something different from the death of other men, but describes the same state as that of the natural man, though here the sleep is conditioned by the promise of the ἀνάστασις τῶν νεκρῶν."[1] Through the witness of the cross and resurrection appropriated in faith we receive eternal life also, of which death cannot deprive us and which will be fully manifested when we rise again at the last through Christ. Hence in death we only fall asleep. " The new factor in the Christian message about them that are fallen asleep lies in the reality which comes to birth in Christ " (J. Schniewind).[2]

Only in the word of promise, that is to say, in the last resort in Christ Himself, is continuity effected between the new life which begins here and is consummated above. Any other kind of continuity between this life and the next suggests that the latter is merely the endless persistence of this our unredeemed life in time, and is thus no comfort. The discontinuity which is implied by the New Testament emphasis on the resurrection of the dead marks the life in Christ as a veritable new creation. Hence the New Testament does not speak about immortality. " Doctrines of immortality are always in some sort an attempt to think of eternal life as continuous with our life here and now." [3]

Of course man does not simply perish in death. The

---

[1] O. Michel, *Die christliche Hoffnung*, 1936, p. 27. Cf. there also the exegetical sketch on pp. 37 ff. on κοιμᾶσθαι and καθεύδειν.
[2] Quoted after O. Michel, *op. cit.* p. 39.
[3] E. Thurneysen, *Christus und seine Zukunft*, 3rd edn., 1931, p. 206.

resurrection is not of course a new creation out of nothing, but a reawakening. " According to Scripture man is never dissolved into nothing." [1] But no details are given about his state in and after death because the attention of the Biblical witnesses is concentrated on the hope of eternal life. (Isolated indications offer no basis for the structure of detailed teaching concerning the state after death.)

This exegetical state of affairs is better followed by Luther than Calvin. Luther's eschatology is governed more strongly than that of Calvin by the thought of the resurrection of the dead. This is shown for example by his sermons on 1 Corinthians 15. Although he too distinguishes body and soul and sees the beginnings of renewal in the life of the soul, he stresses more plainly than Calvin that it is a question of a renewal of the whole man who as such will be raised again on the last day. Then only does eternal bliss begin for him; at present we apprehend it only by faith. Hence his hope is wholly orientated towards the end. " Thus thou seest how we must bend every effort to make secure this article of our faith; for if that becomes unsteady and insecure then all the rest avails nothing because everything has taken place for the sake of the resurrection and eternal life; it is for that that Christ has come and has set up His kingdom in the world. Where then this—the foundation and basic reason and end of all the articles of faith—is overthrown or taken away, all else collapses with it, hence it is of vital urgency that this article should be well fixed and confirmed in our minds. . . ." [2] Eternal life in all its reality begins now for Luther and the immortality of the soul is for him a present fact hinging on faith in Christ. " For sin is forgiven and effaced by Christ, God's wrath and hell are blotted out, and the Christian lives already in and with Christ, sharing in virtue of his better part, which is the soul, in eternal life, hence death has no more hold over him; only what remains of the old man—the old skin flesh and blood—must yet pass away so that the body may be renewed and follow in the wake of the soul; otherwise we have already

[1] O. Michel, *op. cit.*
[2] Sermon on 1 Cor. 15; *W.A.* 36, 605.

G

entered into life because Christ and my soul are no longer held in the bands of death."[1]

But flesh and blood for Luther, as Scripture teaches, are not simply the same thing as the body but imply rather the whole man so far as he is still under the rule of sin.[2] " Paul means here by flesh and blood nothing other than evil lust and desire such as we inherit from Adam in our flesh and blood, viz. our sinful mortal existence...."[3] Hence all the evil which clings to our flesh and blood must now pass away so that we rise new and pure on that day in body and soul."[4] For Luther, the resurrection is the restoration of the unity of body and soul in a newer higher form. " We shall all rise again in body and soul but with a new structure of the body and its members."[5] He turns sharply against all spiritualism which he sees operative here as in the question of the sacraments, attempting to dissolve the reality of the divine promises. In this connexion he warns us against the confusion of spirit and soul. " So learn then according to the Scripture how to distinguish the terms natural and spiritual, not that the body is to be distinguished from the soul—for that is the thought in our minds when we hear the word spirit or spiritual—but rather that the body must become spirit or live spiritually, as we have already begun to do in our baptism, as a result of which we live spiritually and God views our body as spiritual . . . for we are baptized not merely in our souls; the body also is baptized. Thus too the gospel is preached and we are blessed not merely in the soul but also in the body, since it is the whole man that is the aim. Again not only the soul but also the body receives the body and blood of the Lord; so that in the sacraments it should accompany the soul to that sphere where we are judged on the last day."[6]

Because the resurrection thus occupies the central place in

---

[1] *W. A.* 36, 581.
[2] E. Schott shows in his work *Fleisch und Geist nach Luthers Lehre* . . . , 1928, that for Luther both spirit and flesh are comprehensive ideas and realities determining the human personality as a whole. Cf. pp. 50 ff.
[3] *W. A.* 36, 629; cf. also 665.
[4] *W. A.* 36, 629.
[5] *W. A.* 36, 653.
[6] *W. A.* 36, 665 f.

Luther's hope, the state of souls after death is for him of no importance. Hence he affirms with Scripture that death has become a mere sleep. " For what previously apart from Christ was a real eternal death is now, after Christ has passed through death and is risen again, no longer death but simply a sleep, so that Christians whose bodies lie in the grave are not dead but are said to sleep as those who certainly will rise again . . . in Christ it is only a question of a night after which He will wake us from sleep." [1]

The sphere of this sleep is for Luther the word. It is the word of God's promise which is also His creator word and makes us live as it raised Christ from the dead. " For no one could understand nor conceive that Christ would live on the third day, and in the whole world there was not a spark of wisdom which knew anything of it; yet the Word is there which declares Him alive while He yet lies in the grave, and as it gives utterance so must it come to pass although the sense and reason of the world and all things are contrary thereto. So then it is with us: there lie the dead under the earth long rotted or consumed by worms and all sorts of vermin or scattered in dust; but in the Word which we believe and confess they are alive and risen. The world cannot understand it; but the Word can bring it to pass and therefore it must be; for it is the working of God's own power and might." [2] In Him we live even in death.

Since the word of God is, lastly, Christ Himself, Luther can describe the place of our rest as the bosom of Christ where we sleep as gently as a child in the cradle. " We must accustom and discipline ourselves to despise death in faith and to regard it as a deep, strong, and sweet sleep. We must consider the coffin as nothing more than the bosom of our Lord, or paradise, the grave as nothing more than a downy bed on which to lay ourselves. As in fact it is before God, for Christ says: Lazarus our friend sleepeth (Jn. 11:11). The maid is

---

[1] *W. A.* 36, 547 f.; cf also *W. A.* 37, 151: "We must sleep until He comes and knocks at our little grave and exclaims, ' Dr. Martin, get up! ' Then in the twinkling of an eye I shall rise again and will rejoice with him eternally."

[2] *W. A.* 36, 496 f.

not dead but sleepeth (Mt. 9:24). Death and grave mean nothing more than that God neatly lays you as a child in his cradle or soft little bed where you sweetly sleep until the day of judgment." [1]

This sleep implies no loss of the new life, but rather effects precisely its continuation and completion, because it spells hiddenness in Christ who will make it corporeally plain at His future coming.

Luther's teaching about the sleep of death and the state of the departed is by no means consistent.[2] How sleep is to be conceived, whether unconscious or in some way consciously expectant, remains vague in his writings; likewise it is not clear whether the souls of the pious sleep in the grave with the body or whether carried aloft by angels they already rest in the bosom of God in heaven.[3] But Luther does not mean that the soul lives while the body is dead. Against that view his well known Table Talk is emphatic: " *Quidam dicunt eas (animas) statim postquam evolarunt e corpore mortali, in coelum transmigrare, sicut Christus dicebat: Hodie mecum eris in paradiso. Respondebat:* What does *hodie* mean? It is true: *Animae audiunt sentiunt vident post mortem,* but how it happens we do not understand.... Christians *expectant resurrectionem mortuorum et mortui et vivi. Item Abraham vivit. Deus est Deus vivorum.* If you wish to suppose: *Anima Abrahae vivit apud Deum, corpus hic jacet mortuum,* the distinction is absurd. I will contest it. The meaning must be: *Totus Abraham,* the whole man shall live. But you want to tear off a part of Abraham and say: that lives. Thus the philosophi talk: *Postquam anima ex hoc domicilio emigravit* etc. That is fantastic, the

---

[1] *W. A.* 35, 478, 12, and *W. A.* 22, 102, 1.
[2] Cf. the controversy of C. Stange and P. Althaus about Luther's attitude towards the immortality of the soul, especially in regard to the decision of the Fourth Lateran Council; see the essays of Strange and Althaus on this question in the *Zeitschrift für Syst. Theologie,* 1929 ff. as well as Althaus, *Unsterblichkeit und ewiges Sterben bei Luther,* 1930, and *Die letzten Dinge,* 1933.
[3] Cf. Art. Schmalkalde " Concerning the invocation of saints; ... for where there can no longer be any question of utility or help, the saints should be left in peace, whether they be in the grave or in heaven ... "; see the Latin text, " sive illi sint in sepulcris, sive in coelis." (*Bekenntnis Schrift,* 1930, p. 425.)

soul in heaven would miss its body." [1] The difference between Luther's and Calvin's conception is especially plain here. Luther realizes more keenly than Calvin the wholeness in which man, according to Scripture, stands in the presence of God, and he is more acutely aware of the contrast between this Biblical anthropology and philosophical dualism. He still uses the body-soul scheme of thought of the latter, but more clearly than Calvin he modifies it in a Biblical theological sense.[2] The "soul" is the whole man as addressed by God who is thus rendered undying and appointed to eternal felicity or damnation. " Whoever or with whomsoever God speaks, be it in wrath or grace, such an one lives eternally. The person of God who thus speaks and the word He utters show that we are such creatures as God wills to address eternally." [3] Hence for Luther it is a question of the whole man who is to be resurrected either to eternal life or to eternal damnation.

Because Luther sees death in such close connexion with the general resurrection, the interval separating our end from the end of all things shrinks for him: between the day of our death and the last judgment lies only the short interval of our sleep, from which we shall be so joyfully awakened at the last that it will seem as though we had fallen asleep only yesterday. This interval stands for Luther wholly in the light of eternity and its utterly other dimension. " In this connexion we must put earthly time completely out of our minds, for in that world there is neither time nor hour but all is one eternal now." [4] For this reason Luther does not enquire much as to the condition of the departed after death.

In this Luther again coincides with Calvin, who, as everywhere in his theology, here also discourages idle speculation which cannot serve to promote the interests of the faith. Calvin repudiates all clever questions about the condition of the soul after death as illegitimate and unfruitful. Nor does he

---

[1] *W.A. Tr.* V, 5534. *Clemen*, 8, 320 f.
[2] F. Blanke says that "Luther gave to the Greek formula a Christian content." See his essay. *Die Bedeutung von Tod und Unsterblichkeit bei Luther,* " Luther ", *Vierteljahrsschr. d. Luther-Ges.,* 1926, pp. 49 ff.
[3] *W.A.* 43, 481.
[4] *W.A.* 10, III, 194.

consider as such only the question as to the locality of departed souls: "for we know that the soul has not dimensions like the body".[1] But he also disallows detailed consideration as to "whether they already enjoy heavenly glory or not", although, as we saw, he gives a quite detailed answer to this very question. "But it is foolish and presumptuous to institute deeper investigation about unknown things which God has not permitted us to know." Hence Calvin limits himself to the most essential pronouncements as to the fact of a provisional completion of the elect and reprobate, in so far as he thinks Scripture indicates. "So let us be content with the limits which God has prescribed."[2] Thus Calvin himself calls in question his own doctrine of the immortality of the soul, which emerges so strongly into the foreground of his eschatology that it necessarily diverts our view from the centre of the Christian hope; which is the final consummation, as the apostolic message suggests, to the question of this problematic interval. "The apostle intentionally gives no detailed information about the state of souls after death because it would not help our piety to know anything about it."[3]

4. THE QUESTION OF PURGATORY

Although Calvin teaches that there is a special state of the soul between death and the general resurrection, and that it is one of partial consummation, he very vigorously contests the possibility of a decision of our eternal destiny after death or of any modification of it by influences from this world. Hence he rejects the Romish doctrine of purgatory, which makes possible our purification after death through penal suffering, and at the same time all prayer for the departed which is connected with it.

Calvin's first argument against the doctrine of purgatory is this: that it does not spring from the Word of God—Holy Scripture. It has been devised in audacious presumptuous conceit, and then to support it Bible texts have been misused and

---

[1] *Inst.* III, 25, 6; *O.S.* 4, 442.
[2] *Loc. cit.*
[3] On 1 Cor. 13:12; *C.R.* 77, 515.

distorted. In this regard Calvin points to the fact that the Word of God expressly forbids us to enquire more closely into the fate of the departed, and he cites the prohibition of all questioning of the dead in Deut. 18:11. But the chief argument against this devilish error, which is based on deceitful revelations brought about by the craft of Satan, is that it negates the all-sufficient unique atoning work of Christ and thus divorces faith in the forgiveness of sins from its true basis in the perfect penal suffering of the Saviour. " The doctrine of purgatory is a ruinous device of the devil; it renders vain the cross of Christ, it is an unbearable insult to the mercy of God, it dissolves and uproots our faith." [1] For it is impossible that we ourselves should make satisfaction for our sins. Rather the blood of Christ is the sole satisfaction for the sins of the faithful; the one atonement, the one purification.[2] " Therefore to assert the doctrine of purgatory is a terrible blasphemy against Christ and a source of impiety."

The Roman text-proof for the doctrine is first and foremost 1 Cor. 3:12-15. Unlike most of the church Fathers, who relate the fire of which it is spoken here to our being tested by the cross of suffering, Calvin understands by it—obviously catching the meaning of the apostle—our being tried by the Holy Spirit, who more than once in Scripture is compared with an illuminating but purifying and judging fire. In this text it is a question in the first instance of the testing of the work of the apostle; that is, of his teaching and preaching. " Paul is speaking here of church teachers, without a doubt." [3] The whole thing is a parable about the discrimination between the true and the false elements in the doctrine of a preacher of the gospel—a process of testing which God performs and will perform. Now it is clear to everyone that such testing is carried out by the Spirit of God.[4] " With the true doctrine there may be mingled what is false, human, and not of God, and in

---

[1] "Clamandum ergo non modo vocis sed gutturis ac laterum contentione, purgatorium exitiale Satanae esse commentum, quod Christi crucem evacuat, quod contumeliam Dei misericordiae non ferendam irrogat, quod fidem nostram labefacit et evertit." *Inst.* III, 5, 6; *O.S.* 4, 138.
[2] *Loc. cit.*
[3] On 1 Cor. 3:15b; *C.R.* 77, 357.
[4] *Inst.* III, 5, 9; *O.S.* 4, 142.

judgment it must be cleansed of the baser element like all the works of the faithful. That happens by the grace and power of the Holy Spirit." [1]

It is especially interesting for Calvin's eschatology to note that the phrase of v. 13 is differently interpreted: "the day will bring it to light". Consistently with Biblical usage as a whole and with the thought of the apostle Calvin calls this day the "day of the Lord". In his commentary on 1 Corinthians he interprets this as the last judgment day, when all our works must be brought before the judgment seat of Christ. "Of what sort each work is, will one day be disclosed, even though for a time it remain concealed. . . . When all darkness and mist will have been dispersed and the truth will shine forth in its own light, then the day will dawn and on that day all liars and deceivers must be unmasked. As long as the obscurity of night remains, which hides both good and evil, the faithful servants of the Lord cannot always be distinguished from false workers; but the night does not last for ever. . . . For so soon as that day dawns all work which has not found the approval of the Lord will completely disappear." [2] On the day of Jesus Christ all must pass the critical test of His Holy Spirit, and even apostles and teachers of the church will be able to sustain it only by the mercy of Him who purifies their works, and especially their teaching, from all false accretions. In contrast with this we find a different understanding of this text in the *Institutio*. There the day of the Lord is for Calvin the judgment which confronts men when they become aware of some special revelation of the divine presence. "This testing by the Holy Spirit is described by Paul as the 'day' of the Lord in accordance with the customary terminology of Holy Scripture. For whenever the Lord in some way reveals Himself to men, then Scripture describes it as the day of the Lord." [3] Calvin quotes no specific texts in support of this. The idea which stems from the Old Testament is, however, thoroughly eschatological and is understood as the breaking

---

[1] *Loc. cit.*
[2] On 1 Cor. 3: 12 f.; *C.R.* 77, 355.
[3] *Inst., loc. cit.*

forth of the coming reign of God or of the Messianic kingdom which begins with the advent of the Servant of the Lord; in the New Testament it connotes the day of Christ and His judgment.

In this connexion we find in Calvin the thought of a dual judgment which renders intelligible the contradiction in his exegesis of this text. He knows not only the last judgment of the end of the world but also the divine judgment confronting man in this his present life in the sphere of conscience (cf. Calvin's doctrine of spiritual death).[1] " God's judgment is on the one hand the verdict which in this life every man feels to be passed on him in his conscience, but also the last judgment which is openly manifested at the general resurrection." [2] Since Calvin describes both as the day of the Lord, he arrives at a dual eschatology: the ἀποκάλυψις and the judgment of the Lord takes place already here and now wherever men are convicted in their consciences of the presence of God in His word (by the light of divine truth).[3] But it only becomes ultimate and plain to all on the day of the appearing of Christ.

Thus Calvin represents both "axiological" and "teleological" eschatology—if we may borrow the distinction of Althaus. For him these offer no contradiction, but necessarily belong together in accordance with the close connexion of faith and hope which he teaches on the basis of Scripture.

Calvin rejects not only purgatory but prayer for departed souls, condemning it also as unbiblical; nor does he limit his rejection to prayers for their release from purgatory. Age-long use is no proof of its justification. Although human inclination towards it is natural and understandable, yet it is not right. "It is always to be held as an infallible rule that we have not the right to introduce what we will into our prayers, but we must rather remember that our wishes are to be subordinated to the word of God; for it belongs to His judgment to prescribe what we are to include in our prayers to Him." [4] Of course prayer and sacrifices for the dead among the

---

[1] See above, pp. 74 ff.
[2] *Inst.* III, 5, 7; *O.S.* 4, 139.
[3] *Inst.* III, 5, 9; *loc. cit.*
[4] *Inst.* III, 5, 10; *O.S.* 4, 145.

heathen give evidence of an awareness of life after death, " of the insight that death means not a passing away but the transition from this life to another ".[1] But the devil has perverted this correct principle into a lie to deceive men and thus seduced them into superstition. Faith in a future life thus corrupted makes the heathen inexcusable before God: " this superstition itself will convict the heathen of guilt before God's judgment seat because they have neglected to concern themselves about this eternal life in which they confessed their belief ".[2] Once again we meet here Calvin's idea that there exists in all men a dim surmise of immortality or eternal life, which however in itself does not produce a true aspiration towards the life of heaven, but, on the contrary, through Satan is made an occasion for sin.[3] As against this error Calvin points to the comfort of the word of God. Christians must not suppose that they have to compete with the heathen in veneration of and intercession for the dead, for they have a true hope of the beyond. " In the Romish religion the most marked piety consists in seeking to alleviate the penal sufferings of the departed. Scripture gives us another far better and stronger comfort by its witness: 'Blessed are the dead which die in the Lord' (Rev. 14:13). Also it adds the reason: ' For they rest from their labours '. But we must not indulge our love to the extent that we introduce into the church a perverse type of prayer." [4]

For Calvin, with death the gate is decisively opened either to eternal blessedness or eternal damnation. Afterwards there is still of course an ultimate consummation, but no possibility of changing the verdict that has been passed. Again in this opinion he refers to Augustine[5] in spite of the fluctuations in the latter's attitude towards purgatory and his expressions in favour of prayers for the dead: " He teaches that all await the resurrection of the flesh and eternal glory, but that the rest which follows death is received by every one who is worthy

---

[1] *Loc. cit.* p. 144.
[2] *Loc. cit.*
[3] See above, pp. 70 ff.
[4] *Inst., loc. cit.*
[5] Cf. *Eger, op. cit*, pp. 37 ff.

of it in the very moment of death. He declares therefore that all the pious, no less than prophets, apostles and martyrs, enjoy the rest of the blessed immediately after death." [1] In these sentences Calvin's teaching concerning the destiny of the soul in death is precisely summed up.

Although Luther would not absolutely forbid prayers for the dead—largely on pastoral grounds—he repudiated the doctrine of purgatory as unchristian just as decisively as Calvin. The special reason which he gives for rejecting it is the character of decision which marks the whole of our present life in time: each hour may be the hour of our death and therefore we must decide for faith here and now and constantly live in the hope of the hereafter.[2]

---

[1] *Inst., loc. cit.*
[2] " Christians should be taught as Christ and St. Paul teach, that after baptism or absolution they should behave as those who are at every moment ready for death awaiting the ultimate manifestation of the blessedness they have already received; by the doctrine of purgatory they are brought to trust in a false security so that they think they can put in store their salvation and delay things until the day of their death: then they try to assume repentance and sorrow and escape purgatory by means of covenants, masses for the soul, and testaments; but doubtless they will then discover the truth." *W.A.* 10, I, 1, 111, 22.

3
THE GENERAL RESURRECTION[1]

THE special eschatological chapter of the *Institutio* bears the characteristic title *De resurrectione ultima* (III, 25). Although the immortality of the soul is so important for Calvin he insists, consonantly with the Bible and the confession of Christendom, on placing the resurrection of the dead in the centre of the Christian hope.[2] The article about the resurrection of the flesh is for him no mere appendix of Christian doctrine but the culmination to which all proceeds and which is integrated with the most central things; hence Calvin treats of the final resurrection and sets it in the light of the resurrection of Christ and the spiritual resurrection of believers, both of which converge on this ultimate event. The general resurrection forms the conclusion of the work of Christ, he adds, on His second coming. The parousia of Christ and the awakening of the dead through Him are for Calvin quite synonymous. Both ideas imply one and the same goal of our hope, which is orientated towards the One Jesus Christ who is also to come. Thus an exposition of the eschatology of Calvin in the narrower sense might be headed: The future coming of Jesus Christ.

It is significant for the difference which divides the reformer from his successors in the period of orthodoxy that with him eschatological events are not classed in chronological succession under their respective headings (*de novissimis* or *de glorificatione*).[3] In Calvin's scheme we do not find eschatology completely summed up at any one point, but the theme of the last things is appropriately developed in the course of expounding the creed and exegesis of Scripture and becomes a moving

[1] "Ultima resurrectio", cf. *O.S.* 4, 432 ff.
[2] Whereas in the first *Institutio* (1536) eschatology is treated only quite briefly, in the second edition (1539) Calvin goes into the matter more fully; here he himself emphasizes the opposition between the Christian hope of resurrection and the philosophical doctrine of immortality.
[3] Cf. H. Schmid, *Die Dogmatik der ev.-luth. Kirche*, 1863, and H. Heppe, *Die Dogmatik der ev.-ref. Kirche*, new edition, 1935.

testimony to the Christ who finishes His saving work and whose actions form in the last resort one unique event. This event takes place on the border line between the old and the new aeon; it is the breaking in of the future of God which cannot be included in the span of world time. Hence Calvin here sketches out no great apocalyptic picture in terms of which the ultimate event could be mythologized. (One might well ask whether his horror of fanatical excesses did not at some points make him too cautious in face of the Biblical picture of the future.) But if we present in a certain pattern the thoughts of Calvin which circle round the parousia of Christ we do so only for the sake of clarity in exposition; we shall attempt in so doing to keep well in view the central (Christological) standpoint.

1. THE VISIBLE PRESENCE OF CHRIST

In accordance with the literal sense of the word παρουσία, Calvin characterizes the second coming as the presence of Christ by distinction from the hiddenness of the exalted and ascended Lord following which He has become invisibly omnipresent. " He has departed from us in order that He may be present to us in a way that is far richer in blessing than was possible during His incarnate life, when He was yet confined to the humble abode of the flesh. . . . He has been received into heaven and has thereby withdrawn from our gaze His bodily presence. But His purpose was not to withdraw His help from the faithful who are yet pilgrims on the earth but in order to govern heaven and earth with more effectual power." [1] He has been raised to the right hand of His Father that in His name He may exercise dominion over the world —a dominion which is yet hidden but which on His second coming will be gloriously manifest. Then He will be visibly present and in fact differently from the manner of His presence in the humility of His first coming. " Christ bestows upon His own clear proofs of His effectual present power. But His kingdom is in some sense concealed upon earth by the frailties of the flesh and so faith is rightly called upon to consider that

[1] *Inst.* II, 16, 14; *O.S.* 3, 501 f.

visible presence of Christ which He will disclose at the Last Day. For He will visibly come again from Heaven just as He was seen to ascend thither " (Acts. 1:11; Mt. 24:30).[1] Calvin emphasizes the bond between the ascension and the return of Christ as the two decisive appearances of the Lord by which the life of the Christian and the church is determined in this intervening period between the epiphany and the parousia. In the first part we have shown in detail what the centring of hope upon the future coming of Jesus Christ implies. Here our task is once more to stress the element of expectation and now the expectation of the Last Day.

(a) *The expectation of the second coming*
It is typical of Calvin that he is less concerned with the imminency of the New Testament hope than with its witness to the hiddenness of the Day of Christ.[2] He goes so far as to assert that even if Paul had known by a special revelation the date of this Day, he would still have had to affirm to his flock human ignorance of it, to guard them from a sense of false security and unholy curiosity and to awaken in them a true aspiration. His precise concern is to see that believers are always ready[3] and stand constantly " in a state of tense expectation like a soldier at his sentry duty ".[4] Because the day will dawn suddenly as a thief in the night, catching the godless unawares and finding the godly in a state of preparedness " it is foolish to attempt to determine the time by calculation from prophecy ".[5]

Calvin attempts to solve the problem presented by the expectation of an imminent end by reference to 2 Peter 3. " The solution is simple : The day is near, looked at from God's point of view, for whom a thousand years are as a day. But we must

---

[1] " Non obscura quidem praesentissimae virtutis documenta praebet suis Christus: sed quia sub carnis humilitate quodammodo in terris delitescit eius regnum, optimo iure vocatur fides ad cogitandam visibilem illam praesentiam quam supremo die manifestabit. Visibili enim forma e caelo descendet qualis ascendere visus est (Act. 1; Matth. 24.) ". *Inst.* II, 16, 17; *O.S.* 3, 504.
[2] See above, pp. 26 f.
[3] On 1 Thess. 4:15; *C.R.* 80, 166.
[4] On 1 Thess. 5:1 f.; *C.R.* 80, 168.
[5] *Loc. cit.*

await it with vigilance without calculating in advance any specific period." [1] Thus Calvin here makes use of the *nunc aeternum* conception which he rejected in regard to the state immediately after death. " The time seems to us so long because we try to measure it by the standards of this transient life. If we were able to grasp the eternal duration of the future life, then many centuries would appear to us as a moment as 2 Peter 3:8 teaches." [2] The ultimate aeon has already begun with the first coming of Christ. " Hence the saints felt obliged hourly to expect the dawn of the last day." [3] Essentially we ought to do the same. " As Christ has now appeared, no other attitude is possible for believers but to await constantly in keen vigilance His second coming." [4]

Thus the last day is for Calvin indeed a day in time, but as the last day of this time world it is also the dawn of quite another aeon, of the new world and time of God to which our time measurements are no longer applicable and which is thus essentially beyond all human calculation. This stress on the necessity of constant preparedness may endanger the element of pure expectation. It can eliminate the mood of expectation. In spite of the centring of his whole theology on hope, no direct expectation of the end is to be found in his work such as we find in that of Luther, who very concretely hoped to experience " the dear Last Day ". For Calvin on the contrary the characteristic note is rather one of longing for redemption—a longing that is satisfied in the prospect of provisional personal salvation in death. In this regard his prayers are especially typical as we meet them in connexion with his lectures, for although they have mostly an eschatological ring the emphasis is on the imminent blessed rest in heaven, which is to be regarded as the centre of our hopes and which, as we saw, implies the rest of the soul after death.

Yet at the same time death is always for Calvin the gate through which we pass into future glory as a whole. " It is Thy will that we should live as strangers in this world until

[1] On 2 Thess. 2:2; *C.R.* 80, 196.
[2] On 1 Pet. 4:7; *C.R.* 83, 274.
[3] On 1 Cor. 15:52; *C.R.* 77, 562.
[4] On 1 Pet., *loc. cit.*

Thou dost call us to Thy peace. Grant then, almighty God, that we direct all our thoughts and effort and action to that eternal inheritance and home. May we so walk on earth that we become not inconstant or stray from the true path. May we always keep well in view the goal which Thou dost set before us and remain on our right course until the race is run and we come to that glory which Thine only begotten Son has purchased for us by His own blood." [1] The blessedness of the soul that is saved determines Calvin's personal expectations. This is clear from his letters, e.g. in that to Farel about the death of his own wife. Here he speaks of the day when she gave her soul to the Lord, and reports her last words, which significantly express rather the hope of future resurrection. (She came from those Anabaptist circles which Calvin opposed on account of their doctrine of the sleep of the soul and total resurrection). ". . . she uttered a word from which it was plain that her heart had already soared high above this world. This was her expression: 'O glorious resurrection! O God of Abraham and all our fathers! For centuries all believers have hoped in Thee and none has ever been deceived; so then my trust is in Thee.'" But Calvin on the other hand speaks to her a few words about the grace of Christ, the hope of eternal life, about our tent of pilgrimage in this world and our return home.[2]

In the well-known letter to Luther, Calvin expresses the hope that he will soon be united with him in the kingdom of God, so as there to experience in faith that personal fellowship with the much venerated father which he now so sorely misses; by this he obviously means the encounter of their souls in heaven after death.[3]

(b) *The signs of the second coming*

Calvin's expectation of the end is a waiting for the day of

---

[1] Prayer on Ezekiel 12:1-7; see J. Calvin, *Gebete zu den Borlesungen über Jeremia und Hesekiel*, translated by Werner Dahm, 1934, p. 42. These prayers have been incorporated in the *Corpus Reformatorum* only to a small extent.

[2] C.R. 41 no. 1171, quoted after R. Schwarz, *Calvins Lebenswerk in seinen Briefen*, no. 259.

[3] Cf. A. Lang. *J. Calvin*, p. 67; C.R. 40, no. 605.

death as the moment which, as it were, embodies the Last Day for him personally. Unremitting watchfulness for the second coming of Christ is in fact identical with preparedness for death. Calvin entertains no specific expectation of the parousia such as is characteristic of the New Testament hope. "The expectation of coming judgment and of the new world of God is the fundamental thing in the preaching of Jesus as of the first church, and the expectation of an imminent end flows from it" (J. Schniewind).[1] This distinguishes the primitive Christian eschatology from all false apocalypticism. Calvin is so horrified by the apocalyptic fanaticism of his time that he himself does not dare to preach any such hope of a near end. For this reason the signs of the times or of the end which are so closely connected with Biblical apocalyptic play hardly any part in his eschatology viewed as a whole. Yet he considers them in detail in his exegesis of the relevant Scripture passages.

In the exegesis of 1 Thessalonians 5 he emphasizes principally the lack of any time-indication. "There is no question here of any obvious signs which might foreshadow the coming of the future world."[2] From this he draws the conclusion that it is foolish to attempt to determine the date of the end by calculations in advance. But he does not conceal from himself the fact that Paul names such a sign in 2 Thessalonians 2. "Here the apostle prophesies to the Thessalonians (2 Thess. 2) the coming devastation of the church which will precede the return of Christ."[3] But he also points out that the statements of the apostle preclude here too any unlawful attempt to calculate the time of the parousia. "It is seductive to assert that one knows in advance the day of redemption. Satan exploits the curiosity of folk in order to make them waver in faith afterwards. How necessary then was the warning of the apostle."[4] Calvin associates the prophecy of Paul in this chapter with the great apocalyptic discourse of Jesus in Mt. 24 ff. In both instances he sees as the sign of the end the testimony to the outer and inner disintegration of the church as a result

[1] *Das Evangelium nach Markus* (in "Das N. T. Deutsch"), p. 115.
[2] On 1 Thess. 5:2; C.R. 80, 168.
[3] On 1 Cor. 15:52; C.R. 77, 562.
[4] On 2 Thess. 2:1; C.R. 80, 195.

H

of persecution and defection. Because of this the suffering of the church generally and in all periods acquires for Calvin an eschatological significance. On its long path of suffering through the world the church draws nearer and nearer to the end, the ultimate consummation. Every outstanding stage in this path of suffering becomes therefore a foreshadowing of the final redemption. It is the will of God that a development of the kingdom should precede the blessed peace of consummation. But now, as formerly, the disciples of Christ want to enjoy " the fruit of hope " without the cross of pain and warfare.[1] They must be content to receive now only a foretaste of future good and to endure in hope.

Calvin thinks that it is a great mistake to suppose that the promises of the gospel must be fulfilled at one stroke, whereas the whole gospel suggests rather a progressive growth. The full manifestation of the kingdom will only come after the Lord has first tested His church by severe temptations.[2] The special signs of the end in the world of nature are dependent on this development of the church in the fire of suffering; the signs in heaven will not begin until the church has filled up the cup of its sorrows.[3] Here again the significance of the thought of progress in the theology and especially the eschatology of Calvin becomes plain. The end is the ripe fruit of a growth which has reached its term, and not an abrupt outbreak from the beyond; but God only knows when this process will attain its completion because He Himself is guiding and fulfilling it. Hence Calvin's interpretation of the signs of the times is more a philosophy of church history than in the true sense an eschatological interpretation of the end.

Closely connected with this development of the church is the course of the gospel through the world, the completion of which, as Mt. 24 : 14 suggests, is a special sign of the coming of the end. Calvin thinks that the mission of the church consists in the fact that the gospel must be preached to all peoples throughout the world before the end is ripe. " Christ says . . .

[1] On Matt. 24 : 3; C.R. 73, 649.
[2] On Matt. 24 : 14; C.R. 73, 657.
[3] On Matt. 24 : 29; C.R. 73, 666.

that this gospel which now seems so crushed in its home in Judah must be carried before His return to the uttermost ends of the earth." [1] He compares the preaching of the joyful message of the Kingdom of God with the Biblical picture of the seed for whose ripening unto harvest the sowing flock of Christ must wait. "We learn that the preaching of the gospel is to be regarded as the sowing of seed. Therefore we must wait patiently for the time of harvest." [2] In this connexion the spread of the Word encounters increasing opposition in the world. "The more closely God comes to the world in His gospel and invites men into His kingdom, the more impudently will men in general spew forth the poison of their ungodliness." [3] Despite this survey of far-off horizons, Calvin sees the gospel rapidly spreading at least in apostolic times. "When we think of the marvellous rapidity with which the gospel has hastened on its course through the world, we have before us an illuminating token of the power of God. For it is not by the power of men that the gospel has shot through the world like a lightning flash : rather it is Christ who here evinces authoritatively His heavenly splendour." [4] For Calvin refers the lightning flash—here obviously erroneously—with which Jesus compares the sudden breaking forth of the Son of Man in the future, to the wider expansion of the kingdom of Christ emerging suddenly and unexpectedly and whose path is the path of lightning, for Christ is " sent as the Saviour who does not confine the process of redemption to any one corner of the earth but suddenly when least expected pours out His grace over the whole world ".[5] Here Calvin's horror of apocalypticism plainly leads him astray from the text and meaning of Scripture. The statements of Jesus about His second coming are referred back to His first, or to the rise and spread of the

---

[1] C.R. 73, 656.
[2] On Matt. 24:4; C.R. 73, 649.
[3] On 2 Pet. 3:3; C.R. 83, 473.
[4] " Atque haec admirabilis celeritas, qua evangelium per omnes mundi partes volitavit, illustre fuit divinae potentiae testimonium. Neque enim humana industria fieri poterat, ut lux evangelii instar fulguris, simul ac emicuit, ab una mundi plaga usque ad oppositam penetraret: ideoque Christus non temere hac circumstantia coelestem suam gloriam commendat." On Matt. 24:26; C.R. 73, 665.
[5] Loc. cit.

church, not without some contradiction also to the reports of the apostles; although the latter speak of the victorious march of the gospel they also say that the consummation of the church and its mission depends on an abrupt irruption of the Lord.

Romans 11:25 ff. teaches that the evangelization of the world will culminate in the conversion of Israel, which thus becomes a sign of the end. Here again Calvin warns against the relation of the event to a specific point in time. " Paul refuses to give a specific period of time after which the hardening of the Jews will cease." [1] He insists on interpreting the phrase " until the fullness of the Gentiles be brought in " as meaning only " that they may come in ". Likewise he rejects the interpretation of " all Israel " as referring to Jewry in its entirety. " Many suppose that the apostle wants here to hold up to the Jewish people the prospect of a restoration of its former conditions of religious life. But by Israel I understand rather the whole people of God." [2] Thus here again Calvin interprets in a spiritualizing sense: he is thinking of the spiritual Israel, the church as composed of Jews and Gentiles. God has not hardened the whole of Israel but has chosen a tiny remnant to serve as the seed of the future. "The Lord wills always to have a certain remnant of Jews as seed." [3] The real conversion of the Jews will follow only after the conversion of the heathen. " When in fact the heathen have been gathered into the kingdom of God, and also the Jews returning from their apostasy will have recovered the obedience of faith, then the entire holy people of God, which He wills to compose of both elements, will have reached its goal yet in such a way that the Jews as the first born of the family of God claim the leading position." [4]

The preaching of the gospel throughout the world is always accompanied and imperilled by the appearance of erroneous doctrines and anti-Christian movements which as the end approaches, so Scripture teaches, become especially menacing

---

[1] On Rom. 11:25; C.R. 77, 226.
[2] Loc. cit.
[3] On 1 Thess. 2:16; C.R. 80, 153.
[4] On Rom. 11, loc. cit.

and produce a great falling away from Christ and His true church. All this culminates in the appearance of Antichrist and his temporary triumph over Christendom. Here Calvin explains the relevant New Testament texts partly with reference to church history and partly with reference to the end of history, because he takes them as the word of God for himself and his time. He underlines both the consoling and the admonitory character of this message of the Bible. " The apostle (John) enheartens the faithful against vexations which might bewilder them." But he does not simply endeavour to protect the faithful against the possibility of wavering; rather he uses all his arguments for another end. He reminds them in point of fact that it is already the last hour and so he admonishes them to increase their vigilance. Heresies as foreshadowing the second coming and the final victory of Christ acquire a positive significance for the church. " It is as though he said : when all sorts of heresies emerge you must not allow yourselves to be horrified but rather aroused to greater attention. For from all that you should conclude that Christ is no longer remote. Therefore let us be attentive to expect Him so that He does not suddenly take us unawares." [1] Calvin applies this directly to his own flock. " Likewise to-day we must be alert to grasp in faith the imminent return of Christ, especially when Satan throws everything into confusion in order to upset the mind of the church. For that is a sign of the last hour." [2] Thus as a result of his experience of severe conflict with his Romish and other fanatical opponents the reformer comes to take in all seriousness and very concretely the Biblically attested signs of the second coming. He disposes of the objection that the parousia has been delayed for centuries by referring to the eternity of God's kingdom. The whole span of time subsequent to the epiphany of Christ, however protracted it may be, is the last hour. We must firmly believe that the apostle characterizes that time as the last time in which things have gone so far that nothing remains but the final revelation of the Christ." [3]

[1] On 1 John 2:18; C.R. 83, 320.
[2] Loc. cit.
[3] Loc. cit., p. 321.

However, Calvin does not merely consider in a general way that erroneous teachings indicate apostasies which foreshadow the end but that such phenomena are massed together in the shape of a single power of seduction, in which he sees in his own time already the embodiment of Antichrist; and with Luther he identifies this power with the papacy (not with the pope as a specific individual). Since he leaves the Revelation of John out of account he disallows the scriptural allusion to Nero and the Roman empire as Antichrist. Also he refers the plurality of αντιχρίστοι mentioned in 1 John to the one great kingdom of Antichrist. "Of course it is a mistake to suppose that there will be only one individual person as Antichrist. But in thinking of the coming apostasy, Paul (2 Thess. 2) clearly shows that it will be a question of one unified body and a single kingdom. This is not contradicted by John, who merely wishes to show that in his time already particular sects are emerging which are a prelude to the defection which is yet in the future. Cerinthus Basilides, Marcion, Valentinus, Ebion, Arius, and others were already members of the kingdom which the devil will later set up against Christ. To be precise, Antichrist did not then exist but the mystery of evil was secretly stirring."[1] "Even then Christians were summoned to be watchful against the approach of the enemy and to look out for his signs; how much less is there now time for sleeping when he holds the church crushed under his cruel tyranny and openly mocks Christ."

Calvin considers that the danger threatening the church from the beginning has in the meantime become acute and above all in the papacy as the personification of a whole system centred in Antichrist. "All the signs by which the spirit of God denotes Antichrist are to be found clearly in the papacy." A more detailed basis for his view he finds in the Pauline vision of Antichrist in 2 Thess. 2 : "Firstly Paul predicts the apostasy which will infect the whole church so that in a sense it is a common evil; then he evokes as the head of this apostasy the figure of Antichrist who will sit in the temple of God and will arrogate to himself divine being and

[1] *Loc. cit.*

honours ".[1] It will not be any sort of fissiparous tendency in the church, but a mighty convulsion of the whole of Christendom by a terrible corruption of the church; of course in all the crises which come upon the church as a result of false doctrine and false teachers is to be seen a defection from Christ because such sectarianism destroys the unity of the church, as is clear for example from Mohammed and his following, which seduced or overcame by force one half of Christendom. " All that was wanting was that Antichrist should corrupt the remaining part of Christendom by his poison." [2] This came about through the establishment of the papacy in the church itself. For as a result of this the prophecy of Paul was truly fulfilled; here the terror took form and shape in that Satan set up his monstrous throne in the midst of the temple of God.

Although Paul expressly declares that " the man of sin, the child of iniquity or the evil one " will be revealed, Calvin rejects the suggestion that an individual man is meant and thinks the early Christian thesis about an allusion to Nero unconvincing. Calvin thinks that Antichrist implies a kingdom, the rule of Satan's representative in the church, who will usurp the authority of God. " Paul sums up this sphere of atrocity and horror under the name of a person." [3] Antichrist in the true sense of the word is for Calvin enmity to Christ within the church of Christ itself. All the features of the picture which Paul draws he sees plainly fulfilled in the papacy. Where a man claims divine honours in the temple of God, there a kingdom is set up in opposition to the kingdom of Christ, which, like the latter, aims at spiritual power. " Thus Antichrist exercises authority over souls by his godless doctrines, he even performs apparent miracles and imitates Christ the better to combat Him." " Thus Antichrist is the precise antithesis of Christ[4] and his kingdom the perversion of the kingdom of Christ." [5] He usurps the authority of God and thus becomes contemptuous of religion. All the power and honour that in

---

[1] *Loc. cit.*
[2] On 2 Thess. 2:3; *C.R.* 80, 197.
[3] *Loc. cit.*
[4] On v. 4; *loc. cit.*, pp. 198 f.
[5] On v. 9; *loc. cit.*, p. 202.

Scripture is ascribed to God, he claims. "Now any one who has an exact knowledge of Scripture and knows what is becoming to God and then compares the claims of the pope, will without much trouble recognize Antichrist."[1] By the abuse of conceptions of the divine he deliberately falsifies the whole of religion. Antichrist becomes so impudent that he even wants to sit upon the throne of God Himself and tries to rob Him of His honour in the midst of His sanctuary. The church in which that happens can hardly be still described as the church of Christ, but yet it remains Christ's property. "I would thus be prepared to admit that it is the temple of God in which the pope reigns although it is desecrated by countless outrages."[2] "It is not just recently that this horrible corruption has appeared in the holy place, for it is but the development of an ancient evil in the church. The kingdom of Antichrist covers many generations. As long as Satan has not enough power openly to crush the church he carries on his work in secret and in all silence."[3]

It is the testimony of the apostle that something is there which still checks him. Calvin does not altogether dispute the justification of referring this mysterious κατέχον to the Roman empire, but it is significant that he himself thinks that it implies the preaching of the gospel. "The light of the gospel must shine over the whole earth before God gives Satan a free hand ... I think I hear Paul speaking of the calling of all peoples and declaring that the grace of God must be offered to the whole earth so that the impiety of men should stand out clearly." Antichrist will not come until humanity through the rejection of divine grace has become ripe for judgment.[4] "Thus the appearance of Antichrist means the end of the preaching of the gospel and its succession by a real divine judgment on godless humanity which in its ingratitude has refused the gospel." Paul testifies that Antichrist is the executioner of God's just judgment and punishment on all those

---

[1] On v. 4; *loc. cit.*
[2] *Loc. cit.* Cf. also *Inst.* IV, 2. 12; "traces of the church" are still to be found there. *O.S.* 5, 41.
[3] On 2 Thess. 2:7; *C.R.* 80, 200. Cf. also *Inst.* IV, 7, 25; *O.S.* 5, 128 ff.
[4] On 2 Thess, 2:6; *loc. cit.*

THE GENERAL RESURRECTION

who, called to salvation, have despised the gospel and have preferred to turn to impiety and error.[1] In their lot is God's eternal rejection of them already visible, and Calvin does not shrink from declaring that all who surrender themselves to the fantastic superstitions of popery must belong to the number of the damned; for the fact that in face of the truth they remain unseeing can only be because "God has struck them with blindness".[2]

In all this there is obviously confusion between a purely eschatological interpretation of Antichrist and one which is based on a reading of church history. On the one hand he is to emerge only after the preaching of the gospel is completed; on the other he is already incarnate in the papacy, and subjection to his dominion is shown precisely in a hardening of heart against the preaching of the gospel, the essence of which has been newly clarified by the reformers. These thoughts can be properly co-ordinated only if with Luther we see in the Reformation the last great offer of God to the world, and thus our own time as the immediate last time. The seriousness with which Calvin takes the papacy as the embodiment of Antichrist with which men stand confronted involves in itself this consequence.

But Calvin thinks that the victory over Antichrist is not directly bound up with the advent of Christ and the end, although he realizes that it is possible to interpret thus Paul's testimony to the conquest of evil, as indeed the phrasing of v. 8 suggests. But he prefers to see here a reference to the hoped-for triumph of the gospel over the Papacy. Paul does not believe that Christ will accomplish this work of destruction in a moment. Rather it is that by the beams which precede His second coming He will dispel the darkness in which Antichrist reigns, just as the sun before it shines upon us in all its radiance puts to flight by its rays the shadows of the night. In such a manner the Word

---

[1] "... In summa, testatur Paulus, Antichristum iustae Dei vindictae ministrum fore adversus eos, qui ad salutem vocati evangelium respuerint, ac potius adiecerint animum ad impietatem et errores." On 2 Thess. 2:10; C.R. 80, 203.
[2] On v. 11; loc. cit., p. 204.

will be victorious over the world; for the spirit or breath of the mouth (of Christ) means nothing other than the Word. ... Thus true and healthy doctrine suffices to overcome all godlessness and will always remain victorious in the face of all the crafts of Satan[1] " because in it Christ Himself is already at work ". " The light which streams forth from Christ will disperse the darkness of Antichrist. So long as the power of Christ remains hidden, so to speak, Antichrist is able to exercise his dominion. The presence of Christ alone is able to protect the elect from the devices of Satan." [2] Thus Calvin sees in the reformation a kind of revelation of Christ destined to precede His final appearance. It is the dawn of that day which will pierce and overcome the darkness of the anti-Christian papacy.

Luther too, with whose Antichrist opinions those of Calvin largely coincide, views the reformation as a victory of the Word over the forces of Antichrist, but for him it is only a foreshadowing of the real victory of Christ over His opponents—a victory which will not fully operate until the time of His imminent advent. The latter Luther expects with increasing longing and certainty. " *Acceleretur dies ille Christi destructurus Antichristum istum* " (1522).[3] " *Veni Domine Jesu ... Veni etiam illustratione adventus tui. Amen* " (1540); " May it be God's good pleasure to bring to pass the last day, in accordance with my hopes " (1541).[4] The shining of the light of the gospel in the time of the reformation is only " a sure token of the glorious future of Christ like the first gleam of dawn before sunrise ".[5]

(c) *The event of the parousia*

The future advent of Christ means His renewed and final appearance on the earth, no longer in humility but in the splendour of His divine power which He already has but which will then be unambiguously revealed to all men by His

[1] On v. 8; *loc. cit.*, p. 201.
[2] *Loc. cit.*
[3] *W. A. Br.* 2, p. 567, 36.
[4] *End.* 13, 227, 29 and *End.* 14, 89, 31.
[5] *W. A. Tr.* 1169. Cf. Hans Preutz, *Die Borstellung vom Antichrist im späteren Mittelalter, bei Luther und in der konfessionellen Polemik*, 1906,

visible presence. " To all He will appear in the ineffable glory of His kingdom, in the radiance of eternity, and in the boundless might of divine majesty accompanied by the army of angels." [1] The future coming of Christ implies the effective establishment of His kingdom—of the rule of God. " His first coming does not mean at all that He wills to set up His kingdom." Hence His disciples must hope and wait for His second advent. " For although He has begun to establish His kingdom on earth and now sits at the right hand of the Father in order to exercise dominion over heaven and earth in the fullness of His authority, men cannot yet see the throne from which His divine majesty on the last day will radiate with quite other splendour." [2] Then our eyes will behold what we now apprehend only by faith. The fact that Christ as the Son of Man will appear on the clouds of heaven is a plain indication that His divine glory and the glory of His kingdom will be no earthly phenomenon, as the disciples had supposed. " He who in His incarnate life had hidden His heavenly majesty under the form of a servant will then be manifest with all the tokens of the power of that kingdom which is from heaven because it is the kingdom of God."

Calvin stresses the heavenly glory of the second as opposed to the first advent of Christ. " Here Jesus distinguishes still more plainly between the present state of His kingdom and its future glory. As long as the darkness of suffering lasts, the power of Christ is hidden, so that at any rate the fleshly understanding does not grasp the redemption which He has effected. Hence the Lord testifies that He wills to reveal Himself on His second coming so that all eyes may be turned towards Him as the One who is equipped with heavenly power like a streaming[3] uplifted banner." His coming will also be accompanied by extraordinary signs in the whole cosmos. Here again Calvin tries to spiritualize the apocalyptic traits of the Biblical picture of the parousia. " The fact that the stars fall from heaven is not to be understood literally, but as an image adapted to our

---

[1] *Inst.* II, 16, 17; *O.S.* 3, 504.
[2] On Matt. 25:31; *C.R.* 73, 686.
[3] On Matt. 24:30; *C.R.* 73, 667.

capacities of understanding." This theory of accommodation is often used by Calvin to render intelligible Scripture statements which seem to him too crude. " Thus the convulsion of the foundations of the earth will be so violent that even the stars will seem to fall." But in the last resort Calvin here again submits to the mystery of the word which allows us to see only in a glass darkly until the time of the final revelation (1 Cor. 13). " We do not know how we should picture the darkening of the sun; we shall discover that only when Christ Himself comes." [1]

On that day the whole creation with manifest signs will enter the service of its Lord who is becoming fully disclosed. "The point of these various wonders is that all creatures in the heights and in the depths as heralds will summon men before that judgment seat which until the very last they have constantly despised." [2] But for the gathering together of the faithful Christ uses above all the creatures of heaven, those special servants of God, the angels. " In order to suggest the plenitude of His authority Christ points to the fact that He will send His angels to assemble His elect." This is a strong comfort for His people. " In order that our faith in these promises may surmount all obstacles, we are reminded of the power of the angels; Christ refers to them in order to lift our thoughts far above man and human means." [3] The angels are the most powerful sign of the divine authority of Christ. In appearing with Him they reveal to all the world that all power is given to Christ in heaven and on earth, and that He is the Lord of all creation through whom it was brought into being. " Thus Paul places the Son of God upon a very exalted seat of honour so that He may stand at the head of angels and men and have all creatures under His authority in heaven and on earth." [4] In this connexion Calvin emphasizes that Christ has entrusted to the angels the special protection of His church. They do not serve Him alone but for His sake and in His honour they care for the whole body of the church whose

---

[1] On v. 29, *loc. cit.*
[2] *Loc. cit.*
[3] On v. 31; *loc. cit.*, p. 668.
[4] On Col. 1:17; C.R. 80, 86.

Head Christ is.[1] " In redemption Christ breaks down[2] the barrier which sin has created between angels and men, and this becomes plain at the consummation of redemption at the last day when by the angels and at the behest of Christ the church is assembled from the ends of the earth in order with them to serve Him in the kingdom of God." However much the elect may be scattered, they must be gathered together again so as to be united under their Head in eternity.[3]

The advent of Christ will spell for all those who are not with His church equipped to meet it, a terrible surprise. They are so deeply involved in the affairs of the world that the day of judgment will overtake them as it were in a sleep. " When the Lord speaks of the cry which arises at midnight, the picture is intended to suggest the suddenness of the advent. . . . Indeed the Lord cries out even now that His advent is near, but then the whole world will echo the cry and His terrible majesty will so fill the heavens and the earth that it will arouse them that sleep and call the dead from their graves." [4] But believers are in need of constant admonition not to fall into the sleep of this world, especially as they cannot escape the toils of earthly cares. Therefore Christ in the parable of the ten virgins spurs on His disciples to live in constant expectation of His future coming. " In order to press on with the zeal to walk in holiness and righteousness believers must look with the eye of faith towards the life of heaven which, now hidden, will be manifest when Christ comes again." [5] In representing the last things Calvin never confines his attention to purely eschatological events but always shows the relation of eschatology and ethics. Just at this point he is not interested in pure speculation, but is concerned to challenge us to a life in faith and hope.

The parousia is not only the manifestation of the glory of Christ but as such it is also the revelation of the glory of God.

---

[1] On John 1:51; C.R. 75, 37.
[2] " Significat nos angelis associari . . . quum per evangelium ad se Christus vocat." On Heb. 11:23; C.R. 83, 183.
[3] On Matt. 24:31; C.R. 73, 668.
[4] On Matt. 25:5; C.R. 73, 684.
[5] On Matt. 25:31; C.R. 73, 185.

God is certainly glorious in Himself, and even here and now there are not lacking reflections of His glory, but the glaring brilliance of the world so dazzles the eyes of men that they are blind to it. " For so long as the glory of the world strikes our eyes it blinds them so that the glory and majesty of God, however much they are daily reflected in His works, vanishes." On the Last Day all that is changed at a stroke. " When Christ returns He will break through all these worldly powers and scatter them as a fog, so that henceforth nothing more darkens the splendour of His glory or diminishes its greatness." [1] This δόξα Χρίστου is thus the δόξα θέου which on His appearance He conveys to His chosen ones. At some time in the future God will radiate the plenitude of His glory so that His elect may share it. " The revelation of this divine glory takes place in the person of Christ." [2] Christ as *Dei loquentis persona*, as Calvin likes to call Him, proves Himself such too in His second coming. We shall have to speak later of the special Christological problem presented by the eschatology of Calvin.[3]

None of the saving mysteries is presented by Calvin without his at the same time pointing out its fruits in the life of faith. This applies also to his doctrine of the second coming of Christ. It has for him a two-fold significance : on the one hand it is the advent of the Lord to judge the godless, but on the other and above all the ultimate redemption of the faithful by their Saviour. The presupposition for both is the resurrection of the dead which He effects on His return.

2. THE RESURRECTION THROUGH CHRIST

The second coming and the final resurrection are closely linked for Calvin. The hope of the second coming is for him essentially a resurrection hope. " For of what use would it be for us to remember the second coming unless it directs our faith and hope to that blessed life of the world to come which

---
[1] On Tit. 2 : 13; *C.R.* 80, 424.
[2] " Gloriam Dei interpretor, non tantum qua in se gloriosus ipse erit, sed qua tunc se quaquaversum diffundet, ut omnes suos electos eius faciat participes. Paulus de revelatione gloriae magni Dei loquutus mox Christum adiunxit, ut sciremus, in huius (Christi) persona fore illam gloriae revelationem." *Loc. cit.*
[3] See below, pp. 166 ff.

is at present hidden from us? "[1] This implies also that this general resurrection is bound up with another one. The resurrection of the flesh, in so far as it is blessed, is the consequence of spiritual resurrection (in the faithful) and the latter again is rooted in the resurrection of Christ. The resurrection of the flesh is " a fruit of spiritual living ".[2] As we have repeatedly learnt from Calvin, in the general resurrection it is a question of our new life flowing from the Holy Ghost and now hidden in Christ, and which when He comes again will be gloriously manifest as resurrection life.

The resurrection is the presupposition underlying the completion of our communion with God in Christ. Such perfected communion with God is the highest good of man. The philosophers know nothing of this, with the exception of Plato; but even he could say nothing about the mode of this union with God " because he had heard nothing about the holy bond effecting this fellowship, i.e. because he did not know Christ ".[3] But as Christians we know something of this unique and perfect blessedness, and we aspire to it day by day until at some future time we are permitted fully to enjoy it. Hence Calvin says that " only he can profit by the benefits of Christ who lifts up his heart to the (future) resurrection ".[4] The latter is the ultimate object of our faith. With the resurrection stands or falls our whole life as Christians—so Calvin testifies with St. Paul (1 Cor. 15). Not in vain does St. Paul assert that the whole gospel is vain and false if the dead rise not."[5] With the gospel our salvation would collapse. Hence Calvin calls this article of the faith by far the most serious. Thus all his arguments about the appropriation of salvation in the 3rd book of his *Institutio* culminate in the chapter " concerning the general resurrection " which he himself specifically stresses. We must tirelessly concentrate our hopes on this : " As a result of this consideration I have reserved until now what is briefly

---

[1] On 2 Thess. 1:10; *C.R.* 80, 192.
[2] On 1 Cor. 15:21; *C.R.* 77, 546.
[3] *Inst.* III, 25, 2; *O.S.* 4, 433.
[4] " Ideo dixi ex Christi beneficiis fructum non percipere nisi qui ad resurrectionem animos attollunt." *Loc. cit.*
[5] *Inst.* III, 25, 3; *O.S.* 4, 434.

to be said on this point, so that my readers after accepting Christ the Giver of full salvation now further learn to soar higher and to know that He has become clothed with heavenly glory and immortality, so that the whole body should be conformed to its Head ". Calvin admits that the resurrection of the body is more difficult to believe than the immortality of the soul of which the human wisdom of philosophers can also speak. " Accordingly many philosophers have affirmed that the soul is immortal; only few have recognized the resurrection of the flesh." [1] It is so difficult for our intelligence to grasp because it far surpasses the capacity of our mind. Calvin thus admits that the doctrine of the immortality of the soul is not properly speaking a truth of revelation and faith, as is the specifically Biblical message of the resurrection of the dead which he here characterizes in the most emphatic terms as the content of the Christian hope.

(a) *The dual foundation of the resurrection*

As with the immortality of the soul, Calvin adduces a twofold proof for the resurrection in his first and second articles; only here in the reverse order. " That faith may overcome such great difficulties Scripture offers us two chief means; the first is the prototype of Christ, the second lies in the almighty power of God." [2]

The resurrection of the dead is grounded in the resurrection of Christ. That is the clear witness of the New Testament. " The hope of our resurrection is based on the resurrection of Christ." [3] As the head of the church He has gone before us and thus has given to all those who are or who will become His own the firm promise that they too shall rise, and in fact as corporeally and as gloriously as Himself. " Christ rose again in order to make all those who are His members sharers of His glory." [4] Incorporation by faith into the body of Christ is for Calvin the decisive and most secure foundation of the hope of the resurrection. Christ has given us His spirit in order that

[1] *Loc. cit.*
[2] *Loc. cit.*
[3] " Christi resurrectionem hic commemorat, in qua nostrae resurrectionis spes fundata est." On 1 Thess. 1:10; *C.R.* 80, 145.
[4] *Loc. cit.*

He may make alive what in us is mortal.[1] " That is the very spirit of God through which Christ Himself was raised up." Thus Christ has risen again in order that we may participate in His life in eternity.[2] " His resurrection loses its meaning if we do not also rise with Him and through Him." Hence Paul thinks that Christ's resurrection would have been in vain if as the Redeemer He did not return in order to give to the whole body of His church the benefits of that power which was manifest in Him.[3] Not for Himself but for us and with us did Christ die and rise again. " He died with us and in consequence we shall rise again with Him."[4] His death is the basis of our reconciliation with God, His resurrection that of our ultimate glorification. In His resurrection He gives us a certain pledge of life for that resurrection and discloses to us what His death has gained for us.[5] The resurrection together with the death of Christ is the heart of that glad gospel message which according to apostolic testimony would be utterly valueless without it. " If this essential content vanishes, all the rest has no value. Our faith too would be vain, for on what can it securely rest if it provides no hope of eternal life?" "Whether our faith has power, whether the gospel has a real content, whether our hope has secure foundations "[6] depends entirely on the resurrection of Christ and our own resurrection which the former implies. Because Calvin takes so seriously the communion of believers with Christ, the resurrection of the Head and that of the members are fused for him into one eternal fact, so that his statements about it can often be taken as relating to the one or the other aspect indifferently.

In this matter resurrection is for him no mere idea or symbol but a living bodily fact. " The resurrection is not a metaphor but a palpable reality." For a spiritual resurrection cannot be seen. For this reason Calvin seldom calls regeneration a spiritual resurrection, because he wishes to confine the term

[1] *Inst.* III, *loc. cit.*, p. 436.
[2] *Loc. cit.*
[3] On 2 Thess. 1:10; *loc. cit.*
[4] On 1 Cor. 15:3; *C.R.* 77, 538.
[5] On Rom. 4:24 f.; *C.R.* 77, 86 f.
[6] On 1 Cor. 15:14 f. *C.R.* 77, 542 f.

resurrection to the raising up of Christ and the final resurrection of the dead. With regard to the truth of the Lord's resurrection as the basis of our hope he gives detailed proof from Scripture. Here again the testimony of the word of God is of decisive importance for him. His arguments take the form of an apology for the Biblical accounts of the resurrection. The latter are often scorned as legendary and incredible; "what sort of importance can be attached to a message brought by a lot of terrified women and then confirmed by despairing disciples?" We should prefer a testimony from Pilate or the soldiers guarding the grave. But Calvin sees precisely in the weakness of the testimony given by these people whose credentials from the worldly point of view are so doubtful, a sign of the marvellous providence of God. The fearful despairing disciples, who at first refused to give credence to the information brought by the women, are later convinced by what they see and hear at the tomb from the mouth of the messengers of God. But to the unbelieving the vision of Christ was refused. Yet against their will the latter must give evidence of the Lord's resurrection. "Thus Pilate by his seal in reality sealed the resurrection of Christ, and the soldiers who had been stationed to guard the tomb by their silence or lying became in truth heralds of the resurrection."[1] But the decisive factor is the testimony of Christ Himself. Several times He appears to His disciples even after His ascension—above all to the apostle Paul—and the outpouring of the Holy Ghost which He had promised is a special proof of the fact that He lives and reigns. "If we refuse to believe so many and such credible testimonies, then it is due not merely to a lack of faith but to sheer wicked and irrational perversity."[2] By these arguments Calvin wishes to facilitate and strengthen not merely faith in the resurrection of Christ but also faith in our own resurrection.

But the resurrection of the dead is further grounded by Calvin in the facts of creation and the omnipotence of God. The resurrection is a paradoxical event. It mocks all the con-

[1] *Inst.*, *loc. cit.*, p. 437.
[2] *Loc. cit.*

cepts of our reason that rotting corpses should again be made to live, and that in a new and higher state. " Nothing seems to men more incredible and contrary to our human intelligence than the idea of resurrection. Hence Paul aims at dispelling all doubt by reminding us of the unfathomable power of God. For in these matters doubt and disbelief arise because we apply the inadequate measure of our understanding." [1] The apostle does not simply say that God can make all things subject to Himself, but he deliberately speaks of His effectual working which has shown itself in the " transfiguration of the body of Jesus Christ ". If we assent to God's *creatio ex nihilo* then the *resurrectio mortuorum* must also be credible to us. " As soon as we remind ourselves of the fact that God who created all out of nothing can bid the earth and the other elements to restore what has been entrusted to them, then our mind will be able to rise to the firm hope and even the spiritual vision of the resurrection." [2] This almighty power to raise the dead God has entrusted to His Son; it is part of the kingly office of the Mediator and Redeemer. "What glorious evidence of the divine majesty of the Christ! We infer from it also that the world was created by Him. For the Creator alone can make all things subject to Himself." [3] Calvin considers that in Christ consists the unity of the first and second creation. By the creative word we are called into this life and by the same word awakened to life eternal. Thus for Calvin the omnipotence of God becomes manifest in the saving power of Jesus Christ.

Calvin also finds evidence of the divine power to raise the dead in the Old Testament. Although prophetic texts which allude to resurrection may be explained as referring to the liberation and restoration of Israel, yet it is characteristic that just this metaphor is used to express the idea. " Holy men seek their comfort solely in the image of resurrection." The prophet Ezekiel by this means encourages the people to hope for their return; but he derives the ground of this hope from the fact

---

[1] On Phil. 3:21; *C.R.* 80, 57.
[2] *Loc. cit.*
[3] *Loc. cit.*

of resurrection—" the most striking image for acts of deliverance which believers experience in this world." [1] Here Calvin is thinking above all of the spiritual resurrection by the quickening power of the gospel, which has its foundation in the resurrection of Christ and its ultimate goal in our bodily resurrection.

Alongside of, or better, included in these scriptural witnesses to the resurrection, Calvin with Paul thinks of evidence of God's power in the world of nature to raise the dead again to life. Of course resurrection is an unheard-of miracle of God which cannot be comprehended by the criteria of nature. " Hence there is nothing more unfitting than to consider here what might happen according to the course of nature, when we are faced by a miracle that is unthinkable and that in its colossal dimensions surpasses our capacities of comprehension. In spite of this, Paul brings forward a proof from the world of nature in order to refute the nonsense of those who deny the resurrection." [2] The resurrection is indeed the most offensive of the articles of the faith for the natural reason of man, which finds it impossible and repugnant. To apprehend it rightly it is necessary to see it in the divine illumination of faith. " Only he who is enlightened by God can grasp the fact that bodies decaying in the ground or burnt by fire or torn by wild beasts can be not only restored but transformed into a far more glorious state." [3]

We can prove to no one the fact of the resurrection on the basis of reason. Yet after the example of the apostle we may point to the tokens of the divine creative power in nature. Paul " observes that so far from contradicting the course of nature it is rather that nature itself daily presents to us the pattern of resurrection." [4] Taking the example of the seed, he gives us a parable of the resurrection. The seed bears fruit only after it has died in the ground. " But, if its death is the

---

[1] *Inst.* III, 25, 4; *O.S.* 4, 438.
[2] *Inst., loc. cit.*, p. 437.
[3] " Quis enim, nisi solus Deus, persuadeat, corpora, quae nunc corruptioni subiecta sunt, ubi computruerint aut igni consumpta fuerint, aut a bestiis discerpta, non modo in integrum, sed in naturam longe meliorem restitutum iri? " On 1 Cor. 15:35; *C.R.* 77, 555.
[4] On 1 Cor. 15:36; *C.R.* 77, 556.

secret source and ground of a new birth, we have there a prototype of the resurrection. What perverse ingratitude it is then not to be willing to acknowledge God's omnipotence, reflections of which we see daily." [1] We only have to acquire the right depth of vision to see the wonders of creation which surround us on every hand.[2]

Calvin here simply repeats the testimony of Paul, without noting that such vision is only granted to the eye which is first illuminated by the word and brought to faith in the Father of Jesus Christ. But indirectly he attests this when he says that " only he is truly convinced of the resurrection who gives due honour to the power of God." [3] He knows that in the last resort it is a question of submission to the majesty of God, and this happens only when we have true faith and thus trust in the divine power to bring to pass what is unfathomable to our intelligence; for what we think impossible is very easy to God.[4]

(b) *The mode of the resurrection*

(i) *Bodily identity*

The resurrection is a raising up again of this our body. Calvin, in spite of his preference for the idea of the immortality of the soul, emphasizes this thought as against all Manichaeanism, old and new, which would regard the body or the flesh as anti-spiritual and unworthy of resurrection. It is as though he were aware of the danger which his own dualistic anthropology spelt for him, and therefore opposed this error with special determination. In this connexion he plainly stresses the totality of man's corruption by sin and at the same time the totality of the promise of grace which is valid for both soul and body. " As though there were no uncleanness in souls " he exclaims to those who consider that the body is impure by nature and regard it as devilish. He confronts them with his pointed thesis : " I will just call attention to the fact that

[1] *Loc. cit.*
[2] *Inst., loc cit.*
[3] *Inst., loc. cit.,* p. 438.
[4] On 1 Cor. 15, *loc. cit.*

everything which in us is at present unworthy of heaven does not of itself preclude the resurrection." [1]

Always in the Gospel it is a question of the renovation and redemption of the whole man. Thus for example Paul reminds us that we are to praise God with both our body and soul because both belong to Him (1 Cor. 6:20). He will not allow us to relegate to eternal corruption what we are to preserve before God as holy.[2] In this dispute Calvin is quite specifically concerned about the "resurrection of the flesh which we bear about with us." Here again what is at stake for him is the continuity between the regenerate man in this and the future life, but now in regard to the body rather than the soul He refers in this connexion above all to 1 Cor. 15:53 and lays stress on the fact that it is here plainly a question of a putting on: "only as with a garment is our flesh invested with this new glory." [3] If the continuity of the body is challenged, then at the same time the identity of the individual in this world and the next is called in question. We must at some time give an account to God about our life in this body, according to the declaration of Paul. "But that would not be possible if we appeared before the judgment seat of God in new and different bodies." [4] Of course Calvin considers that on the Last Day there is simply a resurrection of the body, not of the soul. "Are we to suppose that souls were resting in the tomb to hear the call of Christ from thence? Must we not rather assert that at His bidding bodies regain the power which they have lost?" Here again Calvin is concerned to maintain the indissolubility of the communion of Christ. "If we are to be endowed with new bodies what then happens to the parallelism between the Head and the members?" Christ at His resurrection received the same body which He had before His death. If as disciples we now follow Christ in His death through our suffering and bearing of the cross, then in the future our resurrection will be like His own. "For nothing is more improbable than that our flesh, on which are imprinted the marks of the

---

[1] *Inst.* III, 25, 7; *O.S.* 4, 445.
[2] *Loc. cit.*, p. 446.
[3] On 1 Cor. 15:53; *C.R.* 77, 563.
[4] *Inst., loc. cit.*

dying of Christ (2 Cor. 4), should be robbed of the glory of His resurrection." [1]

The adversaries with whom Calvin is here in dispute did not deny a corporeal resurrection in general, but merely asserted that on the Last Day men would rise with newly created bodies. Calvin thinks that this evinces an unbelieving state of mind which cannot trust God to be able to restore dead bodies to life. " But, on the contrary, the Spirit of God in Scripture exhorts us constantly to cherish the hope of the resurrection of our flesh." [2] The Bible testifies that Baptism and the Lord's Supper together with their promises are related to this body of ours. " The holy communion . . . invites us to have confidence in our future resurrection, for we receive the signs of spiritual grace with our mouths." Thus Calvin understands the " *manducatio oralis* " and its eschatological significance. The Word also summons us to place all our members in the service of Christ " who wills to quicken again our mortal bodies ". Of what use would it be then to commit our feet, hands, eyes and tongues to obedience to God if the former were not to share in the ultimate reward? [3] Here Calvin emphatically declares that according to apostolic testimony the body of him who is a member of Christ is a temple of the Holy Spirit.

A special though subordinate proof of the resurrection of this very body of ours is, for Calvin, the ancient custom of burial, which was known already to the heathen and was practised with particular emphasis by believers of the Old and New Covenants. Epicurean and Sadducean unbelief, which utterly denies the resurrection and holds that death is the end of all things, since it rejects even the immortality of the soul, cannot plead as an excuse that it is entirely without instruction in these matters. Men have " from a natural impulse always had before them a symbol of the resurrection ".[4] By this Calvin means the sacred and inviolable custom of burying the dead. He sees in that a plain indication and pledge of resurrection to a new life. (He applies the same terms to the resur-

---
[1] *Loc. cit.*
[2] *Inst.* III, 25, 8; *O.S.* 4, 448.
[3] *Loc. cit.*
[4] *Inst.* III, 25, 5; *O.S.* 4, 439.

rection of Christ.) In this custom we have to recognize an ineffaceable surmise of eternal life which God has given to the heathen. " God willed that this same custom should persist among the heathen (as among the holy patriarchs) so that there should be always before them a symbol of the resurrection to arouse them from their melancholy." [1]

Calvin sees in the custom of burial of the dead a plain insight among the heathen into the truth of resurrection, even though it remained without bearing fruit in faith and conviction. Thus, like the perverted heathen knowledge of God in general, it serves only for their greater condemnation—a thought which we have already found several times in Calvin (see for example pp. 71 f.). What is to be found even among the heathen is still more the case with pious men and the patriarchs of Israel. In Israel the custom is to be classed as one of the outward signs of the law by which they were schooled in the life of faith, even though it was a question of types and shadows only, prefiguring the saving doctrine which now is proclaimed brightly and clearly by the word of the gospel. " What was the point of this custom of burying the dead except to make men understand that a new life was being prepared for the buried bodies? " [2] All the ceremonies bound up with this cult, such as the strewing of sweet-smelling plants, were so many symbols of immortality pointing to the hope of resurrection. Careful burial was thus a matter of the first importance to our forefathers, for it was for them an extraordinary and precious auxiliary to faith.

Nor is this custom suspended by the coming of Christ. Rather He praises such a service to the dead as something of quite special importance. Calvin here alludes to the anointing of Jesus in Bethany before His death, by means of which the woman prepared His body for the burying (Mt. 26:12). He thinks that Christ praised this service " because it diverted men's glance from the spectacle of the grave, which consumes

---

[1] " Neque excipere licet, ex errore hoc esse natum: quia et sepulturae religio apud sanctos Patres semper viguit, et Deus apud Gentes manere voluit eundem morem, ut obiecta resurrectionis effigies, earum torporem expergefaceret." *Loc. cit.*
[2] *Inst.* III, 5, 8; O.S. 4, 449.

and effaces all, and raised it to the idea of renovation ".[1] But Jesus further praises the act of anointing as an allusion to His Messianic kingdom, which is consummated precisely through suffering and death.[2] Finally Calvin recalls the early Christians' favourite description of the places of burial as places of sleep (*coemeteria*) and the description of death as a sleep, which for him concerns only the body and also implies that the resurrection of the body is a resurrection of this particular body. The very word sleep, which can only be applied to bodies, suggests the same thing. Not least the words resurrection and raising up express clearly enough that it is not a question of a complete new creation out of nothing. As Calvin says, they make this plain " even to children ".[3]

Calvin's defence of the resurrection as a resurrection of the flesh (=of this our earthly body) is calculated to preserve the realism of the Biblical resurrection message. At this point he is himself in conflict with the spiritualizing tendencies of the ecstatics and fanatics. But he incorporates the truth of their contentions by suggesting that our body will be glorified on the Last Day.

(ii) *The newness of the risen body*

Just as certainly as it is the same bodies which rise again, so is it sure that they do so in a new and glorious form. Calvin here adopts the Augustinian distinction between the substance (*substantia*) and the character (*qualitas*) of the body. Although in the resurrection the body is substantively the same, it is qualitatively transformed.[4] " As far as the basic substance of our body is concerned we shall rise again in the same flesh. But its character and capacities will be other." Here again Calvin derives his chief proof of this from the resurrection of Christ. His risen body is the same as that in which He was crucified for us, as the remaining marks of His wounds show. It is the body which He offered in sacrifice for us. Otherwise

[1] *Loc. cit.*
[2] Cf. J. Schniewind, *Das Evangelium nach Matthäus* (in " Das N. T. Deutsch ", p. 250.
[3] *Inst., loc. cit.*
[4] *Loc. cit.*

it would not help us, for the power of His death is effectual precisely in His resurrection. The power of the atonement would be called in question if He had received a new body and had cast off the body which He sacrificed on the cross.[1] " Yet the body of the Risen Lord has new qualities which it did not previously possess. His glorified body seems almost to be a new body. Although it was the very flesh of Christ, yet it is distinguished by quite other powers as if it had in fact become another flesh." [2]

At this point too Calvin adduces a further proof from the realm of nature, following the testimony of the apostle in 1 Cor. 15 : 35 ff. Although he is aware of the danger of losing oneself in too subtle and prolix discussions as to the " how " of the resurrection, yet he enters in some detail—at any rate in his exegesis—into the question of the character of the resurrected body. " Paul here speaks of a secret (1 Cor. 15 : 51) and thus admonishes us to be modest, restraining the immoderate inclination to philosophize too freely and subtly." [3] But Calvin sees in the arguments of the apostle about the examples of resurrection presented by the world of nature a permissible help to reason. " These illustrations are only intended to make intelligible to reason the idea of resurrection (in general)." [4] " It is not contrary to reason to suppose that our bodies will rise again in another form : for God causes to grow out of a single grain of wheat many pretty ears and new grains quickened by vital sap." " The glorified body which we shall receive at the general resurrection is not indeed so different from our present body that it does not retain anything more of the characteristics of the latter." [5] It is not a question of the creation of quite a new man composed of completely different constituent elements. " For God does not here summon new materials from the four elements in order to constitute a new man, but He summons the dead out of their graves." [6]

---

[1] *Inst.* III, 25, 7; *O.S.* 4, 447.
[2] *Loc. cit.*, p. 450.
[3] *Loc. cit.*
[4] On 1 Cor. 15:41; *C.R.* 77, 557.
[5] On v. 37; p. 556.
[6] *Inst.* III, 25, 7; *O.S.* 4, 446 f.

But the renewed body in spite of its continuity with our present one will be in its way plainly distinct from it. For as the bodies of men and animals are all composed of flesh and yet are very different from each other, so also in this sphere the same substance can be present in manifold and various qualities. Even the stars consist of the same material and yet differ in glory. Such varieties prefigure the resurrection. They illustrate the unity and the difference between the present and the future body. They also reflect the almighty power of the Creator, to whom it is a very little thing to renovate our body and transfigure its present condition.[1] " The transmuted state will be far more glorious, for in the resurrection we shall lay aside corruption and receive instead incorruption without its being necessary for our body completely to perish in the process." Since God holds in His grasp all the elements " there is no difficulty to prevent Him from bidding earth and water and fire from giving up what may seem to have been consumed by them ".[2] Despite these analogies, however, the resurrection is in the last resort an incomparable miracle of God.

This is above all plain in the decisive difference between the earthly and the heavenly form of the body : in its earthly form it is mortal, like all flesh, but in its heavenly form it is immortal. " Now our body is subject to death and hateful mortality; then it will be glorious and immortal." [3] Calvin following the pattern of Paul's thought sees all these differences summed up in the antithesis between the natural and the spiritual body. In this connexion he notes specifically that natural (ψυχικόν) here properly signifies " pertaining to the soul ", and he develops his exegesis of the text in accordance with a theological idea of the soul which stands in a certain contradiction to his own anthropological dualism, as it is notably expressed in his doctrine of the immortality of the soul. Our present body is shaped by the soul, our future body by the spirit. " Nature or the soul of flesh rules our present body, spirit or divine life-giving power will rule our eternal body." [4] The natural soul-

[1] On 1 Cor. 15: 39; *loc. cit.*
[2] *Inst.* III, 25, 8; *O.S.* 4, 450.
[3] On v. 43; p. 557.
[4] On v. 44; *loc. cit.*

body is characterized by the weaknesses of its earthly needs, such as eating, drinking and sleeping, whereas the spiritual body has laid all these aside. It is the body as animated by the soul which is subjugated by infirmity, sin and death and is consequently " flesh ".

Calvin here sees the soul not in antithesis to but in a special connexion with the flesh because he is employing both concepts in the spirit of Pauline theology. " Of course as long as it is the soul which animates our body we bear about with us the marks of our weakness . . . but when we are penetrated by the quickening power of the spirit, then we are perfect." [1] This is especially clear in the opposition of Adam and Christ which Calvin takes over from Paul and likes to make use of. " The one is only a living soul; the other is life itself and the source of all life." But we are now determined by both— children of Adam and children of God. " Thus it is true of us inasmuch as we are of Adam and have only a living soul (though Paul says : are) that the body is dead because of sin, so that in consequence we bear within us the seed of death. At the same time the Spirit of Christ dwells within us, because of which the Lord could not be conquered by death : this spirit is life and will one day wake us from the dead." [2] Calvin is here concerned, like Paul, about the superiority of the second creation over the first and especially about the far higher glory of the renewed and transfigured body. We shall also be—and indeed corporeally—changed into the image of Christ, the Risen One who has ascended into heaven. It is indeed true that flesh and blood cannot inherit the kingdom of God, i.e. man in his present sinful and mortal condition. " Our flesh will win a share in the glory of God, but as a renewed body quickened by the spirit of Christ." [3]

(iii) *The transformation*

Calvin also goes into the question of what will happen to those who are still alive when the Lord returns to raise up the dead.

[1] *Loc. cit.*
[2] On v. 45; p. 558.
[3] " . . . caro enim nostra particeps erit gloriae Dei sed innovata et vivificata a Christi spiritu." On v.50; p. 560.

He answers it in the Pauline sense: those who are still living will not have to die like the others, nor pass through any special state of transition, but they too will be changed because as they are they cannot enter into eternal life. Fundamentally therefore they have no advantage over the dead; in fact, the latter will precede the former in the order of the resurrection; the transformation of the living will take place after the raising of the dead. " Even though they do not die yet they must all be changed and freed from all that is mortal and transient." [1] Admittedly according to Heb. 9:27 it is appointed to all men once to die, but, since this transformation implies a putting off of the old man, it is a sort of death. " When nature passes through a process of transformation, then a sort of death takes place and that is the apt description of the process." [2] It is of course something quite different from the ordinary process of dying, because in this transmutation there is no separation of soul and body and therefore there cannot be any question of falling asleep, "since their soul does not flee from the body ".[3] Those who are still living at the return of Christ will suddenly be changed: " What is transient will immediately give place to blessed immortality ".[4]

It is significant that in this matter Calvin specifically mentions death as the common means of renewal for all, and not resurrection. " Thus it is thoroughly consistent that on the one hand all must be transformed by death and on the other that a separation of soul and body will not be necessary when that sudden transformation occurs." [5] Yet this transformation spells, in a certain sense, death. Hence the meaning of death is not absolutely the release of the enslaved soul from " the prison house of the body ". This latter conception is not the universally valid basis of redemption. The decisive experience for all is rather that of transformation in the narrower or wider sense, and this takes place through our being raised up by

---

[1] On v. 51; p. 561.
[2] *Inst.* III, 25, 8; *O.S.* 4, 450 f.
[3] On 1 Cor. 15:51; *loc. cit.*
[4] *Loc. cit.*, p. 562.
[5] *Inst., loc. cit.*

Christ. " All undergo a transformation of some sort, but the mode differs." ¹

The suddenness with which the living are changed is the special characteristic of the event of the general resurrection. It will happen " in a moment " because it is the act of the Son of God.

" In a moment the Lord can ... annihilate our mortal nature and by His power create a new (!) one." ² The advent of Christ for the general resurrection is proclaimed like the advent of a king, and in fact by the trumpet of God as a token of His divine majesty which is now to complete its work with full power and authority. Calvin prefers to understand the trumpet of the Last Day metaphorically. " Although the repetition of the word seems to suggest that we are meant to think here of a real trumpet, a metaphorical understanding of it is more to my taste." ³ In this connexion he points to the parallel afforded by 1 Thess. 4 : 16, in which it is a question of a battle cry and the voice of the archangel which he equates. " The archangel has the duty of a herald who summons the quick and the dead before the judgment seat of Christ." ⁴ In the last resort all this for Calvin is the voice of Christ Himself, which on His second coming is unmistakably audible to all men. " As a field marshal gathers his armies to battle by the sound of the trumpet, so Christ will summon all the dead with a voice that rings and resounds throughout the whole world. Moses tells us of the mighty sound of thunder which accompanied the law-giving on Sinai : but how will it be when not only a single people but the whole earth is to be summoned before the judgment throne of God, and when it is necessary not only to assemble the living but to summon the dead from their graves, and to command the withered bones—nay, the dust itself—that men may resume their former selves and regain their living breath in order to appear before the face of their Lord and Judge ? " ⁵ The whole picture drawn by the

---

[1] On 1 Cor. 15 : 52; *C.R.* 77, 562.
[2] On 1 Thess. 4 : 16; *C.R.* 80, 167.
[3] On 1 Cor. 15, *loc. cit.*
[4] On 1 Thess. 4, *loc. cit.*
[5] On 1 Cor. 15, *loc. cit.*

apostle is meant to impress upon us "the mighty and awful appearance of the Judge when we see Him face to face ".[1]

(c) *The universality of the resurrection*

Since Calvin, following Scripture, so strongly emphasizes the centrality of Christ as Saviour in the event of the resurrection, he here (like Christian eschatology in general) comes up against the problem of the resurrection of the godless; yet with the Bible and the whole church he teaches a general resurrection of all and not only of Christian believers. Calvin himself puts the question in all sharpness. " We know that in Adam all have been condemned to die; but now Christ has come, who is the resurrection and the life (Jn. 11)—but does this mean that He restores to life the whole race of men without discrimination? For what can be more pointless than that the godless in their stiff-necked blindness should attain what the pious worshippers of God receive only through faith? "[2] Or still more plainly in regard to communion with Christ: " How then shall the godless rise again, seeing that they have no part nor communion with the Son of God and are completely separated from His body? "[3] Yet Calvin holds fast to the common Christian doctrine and the witness of the Bible. " In spite of that we must steadfastly affirm that in the one case we have to do with a resurrection to judgment, in the other with a resurrection to life (Jn. 5) and that Christ will come in order to separate the sheep from the goats—(Matt. 25:32)."[4]

Again we find that here Calvin provides a dual basis for his arguments. On the one hand he bases the universality of the resurrection on the universality of divine grace which judges and saves, which is manifest in Christ and the rejection of which by the godless exposes them to judgment. Calvin sees a sign of this universality of divine grace in our daily experiences of the goodness of God with regard to our earthly life. " We know that in Adam we have lost our claim to inherit

[1] On 1 Thess. 4, *loc. cit.*, p. 166.
[2] *Inst.* III, 25; *O.S.* 4, 451.
[3] Sermon on Daniel 12:2; *C.R.* 70, 135 ff.
[4] *Inst., loc. cit.*

the whole earth, and that on equally just grounds our usual nourishment might have been withheld just as we were denied the fruit of the tree of life." [1] But God allows His sun to shine upon the just and the unjust (Mt. 5) and lavishes upon us in His mercy every good gift in our present life. " Hence we see without any doubt that what is the property of Christ and His members overflows also upon the ungodly—and that not in order that they might justly possess it, but that they might be so much the more without excuse." [2] In fact, God often pours out upon them more benefits than upon the godly; but just that proves their eternal undoing, for they do not receive these gifts gratefully as from His hand. Calvin compares the universality of the resurrection with such temporal gifts of God. But the resurrection of the godless is distinguished from their reception of earthly benefits, in that the judgment it brings is no longer indirect and hidden but immediate and manifest, involving them in the torment of eternal death. By their apostasy from God, the " source of life ", they have well deserved to be utterly destroyed, " but in God's marvellous counsel a middle position has been found for them, so that cast out of life they live in death." [3] This is no longer a blessing but an irrevocable curse, eternal death.

In addition Calvin bases the resurrection of the godless on the fact of the honour of Christ as Judge, who has the power to bring the enemies of God and His kingdom to condemnation and punishment. We find this argument used especially in the already quoted sermon on Daniel. Here he says: " While it is true that the resurrection to glory is by no means due to the unbelieving, it is necessary that the hand of the Lord should be outstretched upon them for their destruction." [4] Undoubtedly the return of Christ for the general resurrection, like the whole of His work, is properly intended to accomplish our salvation; but it has also the implication of intensifying

---

[1] *Loc. cit.*
[2] *Loc. cit.*
[3] *Loc. cit.*
[4] " Or il est vray que la resurrection de gloire n'appartienne point aux meschans, mais il faut que la vertu de nostre Seigneur s'estende iusques à eux pour leur confusion . . . " Sermon on Daniel 12, *loc. cit.*, p. 138.

THE GENERAL RESURRECTION 145

the punishment of unbelievers. " He comes to judgment. Certainly the grace of the Lord Jesus Christ is the source of the resurrection of believers . . . but His power extends much further and the godless will rise again by that power but to their greater damnation." " They must then appear before Him whom now they refuse to hear as Master and Teacher." [1] Pure annihilation in death would not be a severe enough punishment. They must be condemned by the Judge whose vengeance they have conjured up without measure or end.[2] " No doubt in the process their bodies too will be changed at the resurrection." " The godless too on that day will experience a transformation." [3] " But because they will stand naked before God in their shame they will not be clothed with the glorified body." [4] Calvin says nothing further about it because for him, as for Scripture and the creed of the church, it is more important to know that " Christ has really come not for the destruction but for the salvation of the world." [5]

3. THE JUDGMENT OF CHRIST

The return of Christ and the general resurrection which it effects have as their purpose judgment—the last judgment. That means the ultimate separation of the elect from the damned by the Saviour who is also the Judge of all mankind. " Hence we must await our Saviour on that day when He will divide the sheep from the goats, the elect from the damned (Mt. 25). Neither the living nor the dead will escape His judgment. For the sound of the trumpet will be heard to the ends of the earth summoning all men before His judgment seat." [6]

But the antithetic aspects of the judgment—corresponding to the dual resurrection—are not for Calvin of equal importance, any more than the two sides of predestination which is the ultimate ground of this last judgment. Although in his

[1] *Inst., loc. cit.*
[2] *Loc. cit.*
[3] On 1 Cor. 15:51; *C.R.* 77, 561.
[4] On 2 Cor. 5:3; *C.R.* 78, 61.
[5] *Inst., loc. cit.,* p. 452: " thus even in the creed the life of the blessed alone is mentioned ".
[6] *Inst.* II, 16, 17; *O.S.* 3, 504 f.

K

developed teaching on election his arguments about the eternal counsels of God might give the impression of such an even balance through his equal emphasis on both aspects, yet it is plain from his eschatological teaching that he is pre-eminently concerned about election and salvation in Christ. "Only in connexion with the accomplishment of the work of salvation was Calvin at pains to give expression to the problem of predestination as the mysterious background and basis of the former . . ." (H. Otten).[1] He brings out effectively the saving significance of the day and judgment of Christ. In comparison with this, the condemnation of the reprobate is but a shadow necessarily accompanying the light.

(a) *The judgment of grace*

The last judgment of Christ means, for the elect, ultimate redemption. Calvin prefers to use the idea of redemption for the consummation of the work of Christ, although he accepts it also for the foundation of that work in the atonement and for the saving work of Christ as a whole. Christ has been given to us to accomplish our redemption; in other words, " He redeems us from the bondage of sin and from all the misery which sin involves ".[2] This work is essentially accomplished by the sacrifice of Christ, but it is not yet consummated. " The sacrifice of the death of Christ must therefore bear its final fruit, our renewal and refashioning for the life of heaven; otherwise it would be fruitless and finally unavailing."[3] Thus the term redemption connotes the foundation and the culmination of our life which has been restored in Christ and is still at the last to be made new. This redemption in Christ stands at the beginning and also at the end of our new life. For until the day of the general resurrection we shall ever be found to aspire towards our ultimate redemption. " But Christ can redeem us because He has offered Himself as a ransom for us."[4] The day of judgment is called in Scripture too the day

---

[1] *Calvins theologische Anschauung von der Prädestination*, 1938, p. 22.
[2] On 1 Cor. 1:30; *C.R.* 77, 331.
[3] On Rom. 8:23; *C.R.* 77, 155.
[4] On 1 Cor. 1:30; *loc. cit.*

of redemption because " only then shall we be truly released from all our distress ".[1]

Calvin emphasizes this significance of the last day particularly in his *Sermon du dernier advenement de nostre Seigneur Jesus Christ*.[2] In it he calls the second coming one of the chief articles of our faith and represents it as the meaningful goal of the whole work of Christ because it properly consummates our redemption. Without it all that our Lord Jesus Christ has done and suffered would be ruined. " It is the sealing and ratifying of the whole work of Christ and thus the great hope for the future cherished by His own. He comes to rescue them from the hands of their enemies and to make manifest their glory, to reward them for their obedience and faith by His judgment which will be a judgment according to works. The Judge is the Saviour who has allowed Himself to die in our stead." He was condemned and cursed " so that we might be justified before the judgment seat of God and freed from the burden of all our sins."[3] " God has appointed this His Son whom for our sakes He delivered up to the punishment of Justice, to execute His ultimate righteous judgment." " We receive a wonderful comfort from the fact that the judgment lies in the hands of the Lord who has made us to be partakers of His honour in the judgment. Thus He will assuredly not sit in judgment to our condemnation. For how could He, the most merciful Prince, bring about the ruin of His own people? How could He the head destroy His own members? "[4]

The judgment of Christ is the final salvation of believers. " It gives us a wonderful sense of confidence to know that we are brought before no other judgment seat but that of our Redeemer from whom we are entitled to expect blessedness. Then most certainly will that promise of felicity be fulfilled which is now proclaimed to us in the gospel, and the fulfilment

---

[1] On Eph. 4:30b; *C.R.* 79, 212.
[2] Sermon on 1 Thess. 1:6–10; *C.R.* 80, 226 ff.
[3] *Loc. cit.*
[4] " Hinc egregia exoritur consolatio, quod penes eum iudicium audimus esse qui nos sibi in iudicando honoris consortes iam destinavit : tantum abest ut in condemnationem nostram tribunal sit conscensurus. Quomodo enim perderet populum suum clementissimus princeps? quomodo membra sua caput dissiparet? " *Inst* II, 16, 18; *O.S.* 3, 505.

will come to pass precisely through His pronouncing judgment."¹ The handing over of divine judgment to Christ takes place not only for the sake of the honour of the Saviour but also for the sake of us Christians, that we might go to meet Him at His coming with joy. " While the Father has delivered up the judgment to the Son in order to honour Him (Jn. 5:22) He has also done so in order that He might tenderly spare the conscience of believers who would otherwise have to tremble before His judgment seat."² Christ metes out judgment according to the attitude of men towards Him and His grace, as the gospel bears witness. Whether we can await with joyful confidence the last day depends on how far we have surrendered ourselves to the mercy of God revealed in Christ. Only through faith in His mercy can we entertain the hope of eternal life. " For He will be our Judge, but only in the sense that He will judge us according to the measure of our acceptance of the gift of grace which He has purchased for us."³ By our attitude towards the message of Jesus Christ the Saviour it is decided whether in the judgment we shall receive eternal blessedness or eternal damnation. " For if Jesus Christ must come in order to punish all those who have refused to believe in His gospel and have withstood it, then we can and must infer that the world will be judged only according to its attitude towards the gospel. . . . All those therefore who believe in the gospel may without any doubt take comfort in the fact that Jesus Christ will come again as their Saviour."⁴

The judgment of Christ means the exposure of our true being which is determined by our relationship to Christ and His word. On that day the secrets of our hearts will be disclosed. " Then the books which are now shut will be opened."⁵

---

¹ *Loc. cit.*, p. 506.
² *Loc. cit.*
³ On Jude 21; *C.R.* 83, 499.
⁴ " Car si Jesus Christ doit venir pour faire vengence sur tous ceux, qui n'ont point creu en l'Evangile, mais y ont resisté, nous pouvons et devons conclure que le monde ne sera iugé que selon l'Evangile. . . . Tous ceux donc qui croyent en l'Evangile se peuvent glorifier sans aucune doute, que Jesus Christ viendra pour leur Redempteur." Sermon on 2 Thess 1; *C.R.* 80, 231.
⁵ On 2 Cor. 5: 10; *C.R.* 78, 65.

There will be punishment and reward. But not according to the standards of human retribution. While evil works will receive their merited punishment, good works will be rewarded not because of any intrinsic merit but will be accepted and recognized out of sheer mercy and grace. "As evil works are punished by God, the good also receive their recompense and reward. But there is this difference: while evil works are punished as they deserve, the recompense of good works is never based on merit and deserving. For no human work is perfect..."[1] By evil works Calvin means here the works of the godless; by good works the works of believers. The latter are not good in themselves but they become so through justification by grace flowing from faith in Christ, and this has its eternal ground in the election of God. Justification and the recompense of works do not therefore in the last resort contradict each other. "Man becomes righteous by grace and the benefits of Christ and yet he will receive the reward of his works from God. For as soon as God has accepted us in grace our works become well pleasing to Him, so that He considers them worthy of reward even though strictly undeserved."[2] It is in fact a pure reward of grace which He gives us in the judgment of Christ. Our works become good works through their acceptance by God's free mercy in Christ, and as such He rewards them by the same Christ through whom He has revealed to us His love. God gives the promised reward, not because we can approach Him with a certain complacency, "but because He crowns His earlier gifts by showering upon us new ones with the same generosity which He has manifested hitherto."[3] Thus God crowns in His children the work which He began in them. In the judgment of Christ God finally justifies His elect, although they too are sinners and their works evil and inadequate from the point of view of their vocation, so that they do not deserve justification and the heavenly kingdom of God. "They take possession of the kingdom, not because they have merited it by the righteousness of their

---

[1] *Loc. cit.*
[2] On 2 Tim. 4:8; *C.R.* 80, 390.
[3] *Loc. cit.*

works, but because God justifies those whom He had previously elected." [1]

Hence the concern to accomplish good works in accordance with the law of God is not superfluous, for justification in Christ challenges also to sanctification in Him in virtue of the power of the Holy Ghost. And not until we learn to love God and our neighbour as the fulfilling of the law do we show forth the fruit of justification by faith, and its divine ground, which is our election to eternal life whereby God first manifested His love towards us. " God always prevents us by His love, but in a man's love towards God is shown first of all the evidence of His election." [2] The crown of life is promised to such love. This can hardly be described as initiating the *syllogismus practicus* in Calvin;[3] it is rather the necessary allusion to the connexion between faith and works which is of particular importance in regard to the coming judgment. But for Calvin it is absorbed in the testimony to the grace of our Lord Jesus Christ, which alone saves us from eternal damnation in the hour of judgment. Thus our sole refuge is the grace with which the Lord accepts us and frees us from accusation of sin. Once that happens, then in God's free mercy our works too are acceptable and there can be no talk of reward.[4]

Believers as such who are saved and finally redeemed in judgment have a share in the ultimate triumph of Christ over His and their enemies. As His assessors they will judge the world which has rejected and persecuted Christ and His church. That is a great comfort to the church in the face of the attacks and the oppressions to which it is exposed. As certainly as the cross and the suffering of the church is also a judgment of the Lord upon His own house, yet the earthly suffering of Christians may not be in general interpreted as a manifestation of God's anger and temporal prosperity as a revelation of His favour; for we now live by faith, not by sight. " Since faith is a seeing of things invisible (Heb. 11) it

---

[1] On Matt. 25:35; *C.R.* 73, 688.
[2] On Jas. 1:12; *C.R.* 83, 389.
[3] Cf. for the problem of the *syllogismus practicus* in Calvin, W. Niesel, *Die Theologie Calvins*, pp. 162 ff.
[4] Cf. on 2 Tim. 4, *loc. cit.*

THE GENERAL RESURRECTION 151

is just as wrong to measure the wrath of God by the degree of our suffering in the world as it is to estimate His favour by the quantity of material goods which we have acquired." [1] When we consider that, the present prosperity of the ungodly need not worry us. " So when we are prostrate in misery while the ungodly are wallowing in secure prosperity let us learn to fear the retribution of God, which escapes earthly judgment, and let us find comfort and peace in the hidden consolations of spiritual life." [2]

In this connexion Calvin speaks about a compensatory justice of God. In the judgment of Christ the relative positions of the church and the world will be reversed. " It is absolutely certain that God as the righteous Judge can do no other but one day give rest to the weary who are now oppressed unjustly, and mete out to the oppressors of the pious their merited punishment." [3] Theodicy is for Calvin no mere postulate but a confession of faith based on Scripture and its revelation. Of course it is a question whether the justice of God may be understood in the human sense as a principle of compensatory justice and as the foundation of a moral world-order. It is in any event not a principle from which can be inferred independent consequences that might affect the transcendent freedom of God in the exercise of His grace. Here emerges the problem of Calvin's doctrine of God, which is also the problem of his doctrine of predestination; but to consider it in detail falls outside the scope of this work.[4]

In answering the question about retribution in judgment Calvin is in danger of prescribing a certain " must " to God. " If God is a just judge of the world, He must balance what is now so topsy-turvy, for nothing so contradicts all divine order than that the ungodly should with impunity oppress the righteous and give unbridled expression to their hate while the pious without any fault are cruelly tormented." [5] Calvin

[1] On 1 Thess. 1 : 10; *C.R.* 80, 145. [2] *Loc. cit.*
[3] On 2 Thess. 1 : 5; *C.R.* 80, 189.
[4] Cf. with regard to this H. Otten, *op. cit.* Cf. also pp. 131 ff.
[5] " Nam si iustus est mundi iudex Deus, restitui oportet, quae nunc sunt confusa; atque nihil magis inordinatum quam impios impune molestos esse bonis, et effraeni violentia grassari; bonos autem nulla sua noxa crudeliter vexari." On 2 Thess. 1, *loc. cit.*

might have been content to bear witness to the word of Scripture about the ultimate glory of believers and the damnation of unbelievers. To sit in judgment with Christ is promised above all to His immediate disciples, but in a broader sense can be extended to the whole church. " He promises His disciples that they shall be companions with Him in His ultimate triumph. In promising to them seats in the kingdom from which they shall judge the twelve tribes of Israel He compares them with ambassadors or ministers who in the council of the king take the first places." [1] " Nay, they will themselves be allowed to reign with Him as kings . . . Jesus here makes His disciples not merely the possessors of an inheritance, but kings, because He shares with them the rule which He has obtained from His Father. With Paul we may extend that, although with a certain difference, to all the saints of God who at the last are consecrated to His service by Christ the Judge." " So Paul reminds us of the high honour of which God has deemed His saints to be worthy: He has appointed them as judges over the whole world." Like the disciples, they are assessors of Christ their Head in His judgment.

Calvin here thinks especially of judgment on the demons. " We shall pronounce judgment on the fallen angels. But if we are to judge beings who are not only of most noble origin but also retained immortality after their fall and superiority to the transient world, should then earthly things be withdrawn from our judgment?" [2] The church is already proclaiming judgment upon the world by the preaching of the word, and in the process of that preaching judgment is now manifest. " The preaching of the gospel is already a disclosure of the kingdom of Christ." [3] Through it His rule both in the positive and negative sense is being established and expanded in the world, concealed but yet effectual. In proportion as we share in this service of the whole church we shall be sharers in the revelation and consummation of His kingdom at the last. " In the last judgment the servants of Christ will participate in

---

[1] On Matt. 19:28; C.R. 73, 544.
[2] On 1 Cor. 6:3, C.R. 77, 389.
[3] On Matt. 19:28; C.R. 73, 545.

His glory and triumph according as they have helped to extend His kingdom on earth." [1]

(b) *The judgment of wrath*

As we have seen, judgment upon the reprobate is closely bound up with the gracious judgment of the elect; indeed the former is judgment in the true sense of the word. Hence Calvin can describe the dual significance of the second coming of Christ as His coming to bring about the resurrection of believers and to judge the ungodly. " Christ is preached as the resurrection for the former and the judge for the latter, and both functions are centred in the day of judgment." [2] The last judgment is identical with the future disclosure of the wrath of God. Calvin understands the wrath of God chiefly in an eschatological sense. " Wrath without further qualification is the meaning of divine judgment." [3] It is the wrath that is to come of which Paul speaks, and which on the return of Christ will be fully manifest and operative, while even now it threatens all that is hostile to God; and this means in effect the whole of mankind in its fallen state. " The wrath of God and eternal destruction menaces the whole human race because all have sinned and come short of the glory which they should have in the presence of God." [4] Whosoever does not escape this wrath through the grace of Christ must look forward to a terrible judgment.

Of course it is precisely unbelievers who cradle themselves in security and are as they that sleep. For all such the sudden coming of Christ to judgment will mean a dreadful awakening. " The ungodly who surrender themselves recklessly to their lusts will be caught unawares by the second coming of Christ, for wrapped in darkness they notice nothing, and where God is not known thick darkness prevails." [5] This darkness and blindness is at one and the same time destiny and guilt.

---

[1] " Christi ministros, prout quisque regnum eius propagaverit, gloriae et triumphi in extremo die fore participes." On 1 Thess. 2:19; C.R. 80, 153.
[2] On Rom. 2:16; C.R. 77, 20.
[3] On 1 Thess. 2:16; C.R. 80, 153.
[4] On 1 Thess. 2:9 f.; C.R. 80, 145.
[5] On 1 Thess. 5:4; C.R. 80, 169.

While God illumines the elect He blinds the reprobate. "As God enlightens our hearts by His spirit so that He may dwell with us and His word display its power in us, in the reverse sense He abandons those whom He has appointed to damnation, so that as though bewitched and with blinded eyes they hand themselves over to Satan and his servants in order to be deceived by him." [1] But by their own free will they become guilty before God. They suffer a punishment which fits their impiety. Those who are lost have no reason to attempt to bargain with God, for they have obtained what they sought.[2] " God's rejection of them despite its eternal appointment is also a retribution for their turning away from the truth of God. Hence God allows false teaching to operate as a kind of touchstone to prove the hearts of men, so that they decide for or against His word. We must hold fast to what is written in Deuteronomy 13:2, viz. that God uses false teachers in order to try the hearts of men; for such teachers obtain no influence over those who love God with an upright heart. But whoever finds pleasure in unrighteousness also harvests its fruit . . ." [3]

Thus the judgment on unbelievers begins here and now in the decision that men make in the face of God's word and those who represent it. Hence Calvin can characterize Antichrist at once as the executioner of just punishment on those who despise the gospel.[4] The measure of the punishment depends on how far we have knowingly despised the word and the truth of God; but also unwitting sin must be paid for. " So much is certain, that our ignorance goes hand in hand with punishable negligence. Hence there is no comfort in saying that he who has failed unwittingly is free from guilt; rather the heavenly Judge declares that even people who sin unwittingly will receive their punishment, though in slighter measure." But a still more terrible punishment on the Day of Christ threatens those who consciously despise the message of the wrath to come and the defiant and dissolute manner of life which is the consequence. " Thus the more instructed a

---

[1] On 2 Thess. 2:11; C.R. 80, 204.
[2] *Loc. cit.*
[3] *Loc. cit.*
[4] See above, pp. 120 f.

person is so much the more occasion is there for punishment when he persists in disobedience." [1]

Not only rejection of the word of God but also persecution of His church which flows from it means that the future judgment on the world is already beginning. Such persecution is, so to speak, the outward sign of the same thing. Although the ungodly scorn the message of the coming Lord, they secretly tremble and so they wish to get rid of the tiresome prophet—the church of Jesus Christ—which by its preaching constantly reminds them of their awful doom. "For the ungodly the return of Christ spells terror; the reminder of it drives their thoughts away from heaven rather than exalting them towards it; for they take every possible means to escape from the Judge whom they must expect from heaven. . . . It is a sign of unbelief when any one, as often as that theme is in question, becomes afraid." [2] The fear of divine judgment is naturally linked with hatred of the church of God. But the world, by fighting against the church, draws upon itself all the more the judgment of Christ. "When the godless fight against God it is a foreshadowing of their future destruction, and the more they rage against the pious the more they hasten towards their sure doom. . . . These persecutions to which the children of God are subject are the mark of their status as Christians, provided that they bear them bravely and calmly. But for the ungodly they are a testimony of damnation because they are stumbling against the stone which will crush them." [3]

Here again Calvin draws inferences *e contrario*, following his thought of the compensatory justice of God. "If then we hold firmly to this principle, that God is a righteous Judge of the world and that He will reward every man after his own works, the conclusion is unquestionably that the contrary nature of our present circumstances is a proof of His still-hidden judgment." [4] It is precisely in the apparent or temporary judgment on the church, which its persecution by the world suggests, that God gives a clear adumbration of His

[1] On Luke 12:47; C.R. 73, 681.
[2] On Phil. 3:20; C.R. 80, 56.
[3] On Phil. 1:28; C.R. 80, 21.
[4] On 2 Thess. 1:5; C.R. 80, 189.

imminent judgment on the ungodly—a judgment that is now concealed but that in the future advent of Christ will be manifest to all. Though God at present spares them and even allows them to prosper, for the most part, more than His own, yet their future punishment is certain. This implies both a comfort and a warning to believers. " We must learn to place our hopes in the judgment to come, because God now spares evil-doers although they have merited punishment for their misdeeds. At the same time believers must recognize that they have no reason to envy the godless on account of their present prosperity, since this will soon have a frightful end." [1] To the question as to why the godless prosper so well, Calvin, who like Luther is fond of calling the enemies of God and His church (2 Pet. 2:12) by the names of certain animals, gives the short answer: " Because the Lord is feeding them like pigs for the day of slaughter ".[2] He means by this that the ungodly, just because of the earthly blessings which God confers upon them, become ripe for judgment upon their guilt.[3] God can afford to wait, but they can never escape His avenging hand. " He bears with the wicked for a time but does not let them go unpunished. God is not in such a great hurry as men." He has as it were already seized unbelievers and taken them into His secret custody. " The idea that God is keeping them expresses more than might be at first sight supposed: they have not escaped His hand but with secret cords are held and bound until the day when they will be dragged before the seat of judgment." [4]

The last day as the day of the judgment of Christ upon His enemies is depicted by Calvin in the darkest colours as the *dies irae*, especially in his sermons. It is the day before which even the devils tremble, because they are then brought into subjection along with the ungodly. In this connexion Calvin alludes to the prophetic message of the day of the Lord, con-

---

[1] On 2 Thess. 1:6; *C.R.* 80, 190.
[2] " Interea lautior est ut plurimum impiorum fortuna: quia Dominus eos instar porcorum saginat in diem occisionis." On 1 Cor. 15:19; *C.R.* 77, 544.
[3] Cf. *Inst.* III, 25, 9; *see above*, p. 144.
[4] On 1 Pet. 2:9; *C.R.* 83, 464.

trasted as it is with the false and frivolous hopes entertained by the people of Israel. The day of the Lord will be darkness and not light. Calvin applies this to nominal Christians in the church. " Just so to-day we see some of the most notorious evil-doers who open their mouths wide and cry : ' What is all this? Do you suppose that we do not fear God and do not aim to be as good Christians as anyone else? ' But look, in fact they are loose-living people full of ungodliness who have about as much religion in them as dogs and pigs. When you examine their lives you discover that they are full of dishonesty and have neither faith nor morals, no more than foxes. . . .[1] For all such the day of Christ will be a terrible and fearful day, a day of dread and mourning." At this point Calvin exhorts the church to sanctification, for he does not wish to draw merely an apocalyptic picture of horror nor confine himself to uttering threats to outsiders; his purpose is always to challenge the Christian church to adopt a right attitude of vigilant expectation towards the coming of its Lord. " We must therefore note from this chapter of Saint Paul that it is essential for us—if we desire the coming of our Lord Jesus Christ to be to our good and to find in Him on that day our Saviour—to consecrate ourselves to a life of holiness and to keep ourselves unspotted from the world." With this he connects the summons to faith which is the " source of all holiness ".[2]

Calvin's teaching about the judgment of Christ makes to a large extent the impression of being simply an outcome of his consistent doctrine of predestination (in its later form), so that only the coming Saviour is preached to believers who can now by experience be plainly distinguished from unbelievers, while to the godless it is simply a question of proclaiming their coming Judge. In that case it would be impossible to associate with the thought of judgment the note of warning to the church nor an invitation to the world to accept Christ as Saviour. But just when Calvin employs his doctrine for the purposes of preaching, hence notably in his sermons, he shows himself to be a witness to the gospel which never announces

[1] Sermon on 2 Thess. 1 : 6 ff.; *C.R.* 80 235 f.
[2] *Loc. cit.*

judgment apart from grace nor grace apart from judgment. Calvin well realizes that the final unambiguous and decisive word can be uttered only by Christ Himself, and it is He who will utter it at the day of judgment.

(c) *The question of the millennium*

The judgment of Christ as the last judgment is for Calvin the final establishment of the rule of Christ or its culmination in the kingdom of God. " Now the Lord reigns in the world only through the gospel and we give honour to His majesty only where faith recognizes it in the word . . . thus we see that at present prophecy is only beginning to be fulfilled. It will be completely fulfilled only on the day of the general resurrection when all the enemies of Christ will be under the sole of His feet. That this might come to pass, the Lord must first execute His judgment." [1] This kingdom of Christ will be an eternal kingdom because it is the kingdom of God. Calvin emphasizes this with vigour. Hence he decidedly rejects the chiliasm of the fanatics which would make of the kingdom of Christ a purely temporal and transient one. Calvin sees in chiliasm a deceptive fantasy by means of which Satan began to corrupt the Christian hope soon after apostolic times. " I dismiss the notion that Satan began already in the time of Paul to ruin this hope (cf. the passage about the resurrection). But shortly afterwards the Chiliasts arose who fixed and narrowed the conception of Christ's kingdom as being of a thousand years' duration." [2]

Calvin considers this a childish fantasy which hardly deserves the credit of refuting. Yet, for him, what is at stake here is the eternal character of the kingdom and therewith the whole expectation of the future cherished in the life of faith. Scripture testifies that both the blessedness of believers and

---

[1] " Non aliter nunc regnat in mundo Deus quam per Evangelium; nec aliter rite honoratur eius maiestas quam ubi ex verbo agnita suspicitur . . . Hinc apparet inchoari quidem in praesenti vita vaticinium istud: sed a sua perfectione abesse, donec dies ille ultimae resurrectionis illuxerit, quo prosternentur omnes Christi hostes, ut fiant scabellum pedum eius. Porro id quoque fieri non poterit, nisi in iudicium sederit Dominus." On Rom. 14:11; C.R. 77, 263.

[2] *Inst.* III, 25, 5; *O.S.* 4, 439.

the damnation of the ungodly will be endless. The hope of the elect would be undermined by a temporal limitation of the expected kingdom and the redemption it consummates. " Any one who prescribes for the children of God only a thousand years' enjoyment of their inheritance in the future does not see what a disgraceful implication this is for Christ and His kingdom.[1] Since the communion of Christ and His church is that of an indissoluble connexion between the Head and the members, such a limitation of the kingdom would jeopardize not only the heavenly transfiguration of the pious but also that of their exalted Head." " For if believers are not clothed with immortality, then also Christ Himself, into the likeness of whose glory they are to be changed, has not been received into eternal glory; if the blessedness of believers is to have an end, then also the kingdom of Christ on the everlastingness of which that blessedness is based becomes a temporal one."[2] Calvin can only regard the idea of the millennium as due to the failure of faith and insight or as a diabolical seduction. " These people (the exponents of chiliasm) are either entirely inexperienced in all heavenly things or with secret malice are trying to shake the grace of God and the power of Christ."[3] Like the opponents of the resurrection with whom Paul argues in 1 Corinthians 15, they make the Christian hope into a hope that is merely relative to this world and thereby dissolve the true hope which is directed to the eternal future of the Lord and His coming kingdom. The saving work of God in Christ finds its secure and abiding fulfilment only if on the day of the Lord " sin is effaced, death is swallowed up in victory, and the kingdom of eternity is fully and wholly established."[4]

Thus Calvin is concerned about the exclusive orientation and concentration of hope on the ultimate appearance and revelation of the Lord for the general resurrection and the last judgment on all. He sees in chiliasm an impoverishment, not to say a destruction, of the Christian hope. In this he agrees with the

[1] *Inst., loc. cit.*, p. 440.
[2] *Loc. cit.*
[3] *Loc. cit.*
[4] *Loc. cit.*

Lutherans who in the Augsburg Confession—no doubt in view of the increase of sectarian fanaticism—stated: " Here we reject the teaching of those Judaizers who visualize that before the resurrection of the dead the proud saints and pious will enjoy a worldly hegemony in which all the godless will be wiped out " (C.A. 17).[1] The confession of the reformers also adopted this judgment on ecstatic chiliasm.[2]

As certainly as the repudiation of a false temporalization of the Christian hope, such as the reformers met with in the Anabaptists, is justified and necessary, yet it is to be questioned whether they do justice to that concern of Scripture which the latter misrepresented. We find here in Calvin something parallel to his polemic in regard to the question of the state after death. In both cases he sees in the Anabaptists the danger of a materialization of the gospel and in his zeal to oppose it he is apt to overlook that aspect of Biblical truth which it suggests, though in a perverted form. His exegesis of the chief proof text of chiliasm (Rev. 20 : 1-6) which the fanatics used to give colour to their error, is by no means convincing. He rightly points out that the thousand years does not mean the eternal blessedness of the church, but it is equally contrary to the text to suggest as he does that it is merely a question of various revolutions which the church militant on earth must expect.[3] Here he follows the teaching of Augustine—so decisive for the eschatology of the Western church—who, following the example of Ticonius in his commentary on the Revelation of John, made the millennium instead of an eschatological factor merely a period in church history (H. Reuter),[4] since he understood by it the whole time of the church from the epiphany to the parousia.

Calvin does not indeed adopt this notion as such, which forms the presupposition to Augustine's teaching about the city

---

[1] *Bekenntnis Schriften der ev.-luth. Kirche,* 1930, p. 70.
[2] " Damnamus praeterea Judaica somnia, quod ante iudicii diem aureum in terris sit futurum seculum, et pii regna mundi occupaturi, oppressis suis hostibus impiis." *Conf. Helv. post.* 11; *Bekenntnis Schriften der ref. Kirche,* 1903, p. 185.
[3] *Inst., loc cit.*
[4] *Augustinische Studien,* 1887, p. 114; quoted after H. Eger, *op cit.* p. 48.

of God, but he does interpret the testimony of the Revelation more in terms of church history than of eschatology, just as he does the Biblical doctrine of Antichrist and his kingdom which is the antithesis to the millennium.[1] The dual resurrection of Rev. 20:5 ff. is, according to Calvin's exegesis which again is plainly a spiritualizing one, on the one hand the spiritual resurrection of the soul in regeneration, on the other the resurrection of the flesh at the second coming. "Hence John affirms a dual resurrection corresponding to the dual death. Without doubt the first is that of the soul in judgment, the second that which takes place when the body is raised up and with the soul is exalted to glory; blessed, he says, are those who have a part in the first resurrection; over them the second death has no power." [2]

The kingdom of a thousand years is then the spiritual rule of Christ over indivdual souls in their earthly life until the completion of their course in death and the general resurrection. This means that the millennium, which according to Scripture is a visible kingdom and a communion of believers with their head, Christ, is not only spiritualized but also individualized. Scripture, however, states that the millennium is neither a purely spiritual nor a purely earthly kingdom, but an intermediate one which no longer belongs to this aeon—but neither does it wholly belong to the new world-aeon of God. It is an eschatological event, but is not in itself the end nor yet the eternal kingdom of God. According to the witness of Paul (1 Cor. 15:20 ff.) the outbreak of the new aeon takes place in a series of God's appointment: the resurrection of Christ, His return, His victory over His enemies, and His surrender of all rule to the Father. We cannot simply describe this as the apocalyptic dress of a pure eschatological truth, but it is an unmistakable allusion to the coming of the kingdom of God "in earth as in heaven"; of that kingdom which indeed spells the end of history, although when it dawns it sets up within history a final prefiguring of the consummation because this world must be changed into the new world of

---

[1] See above, p. 116 ff.
[2] *Psy.* 57; 198.

God. "There is therefore a chiliasm which has Biblical foundations and is justified, and remains unaffected by the condemnatory verdict of the Augsburg Confession" (O. Michel),¹ and we would add: and by that of Calvin. We must indeed just here be on our guard against all visualization of the future which is not warranted by Scripture, and take to heart Calvin's warning : "In regard to all those matters which lie hidden from us and far surpass the reach of human understanding we must either try to attain certainty through the clearly revealed word of God or entirely resign all such certainty ".²

4. THE ETERNAL CONSUMMATION IN CHRIST

If we may discriminate between the various acts of the end which is brought about by the central event of the parousia of Christ and which Calvin summarily describes as the general resurrection, then the final act, the final deed of Christ as Mediator, is the deliverance of His rule to the Father after the eternal separation in the judgment scene has been completed. This consummation also implies the dual aspect of the eternal reign of God—an aspect sealed by this ultimate judgment of Christ : eternal blessedness and eternal damnation, both of which must serve the glory of Christ.

(a) *The deliverance of the Kingdom*

The consummation of the reign of Christ spells the end of all other rule and authority; not merely of that which is inimical to God. It means the triumph of Christ over the devil and his dominion, but also the end of those social arrangements intended for the maintenance of temporal life, e.g. marriage and the state, and even in a certain sense the end of the church. "At present the devil is engaged in a conflict with God, and the godless in manifold ways rebel against the ordinances of God, throw all things into confusion, and confront us with monstrous vexations; in such a situation it is not

---

¹ *Op cit.*, p. 28.
² *Inst.* III, 25, 5; *loc. cit.*

at all clear that God is all in all. But when Christ shall have performed the function of judge with which God has invested Him and has crushed beneath His feet Satan and his hosts, then the honour of God will be perfectly manifest in this work of destruction." [1] Of course the submission of the enemy and his power will not be voluntary, but these hostile armies too must bow their knee before Christ. " Naturally I grant that the devils will never surrender with voluntary obedience, but neither does Paul suggest that such obedience is coerced." [2] This does not mean that in the end—although reluctantly—they will be saved; they are certainly subjected to the reign of Christ but they have no share in His salvation.

Those ordinances of God which are appointed as resources for our earthly pilgrimage are also in conflict with the consummation of His reign. This applies also to the natural ordinance of marriage, the dissolution of which will concern us when we come to speak of the perfecting of the individual man.[3] But Calvin means here especially the state and all earthly hierarchies. Worldly rule is indeed based on divine authority in so far as it fulfils the mission with which God has entrusted it; it can in fact plainly " represent the power of God whose rule it vicariously exercises ".[4] But this is only a temporary arrangement made for the passing world and earthly time. " Civil government has the task, as long as men live in community, of promoting and protecting the outward veneration of God, of defending the sound doctrines of piety and the well-being of the church, and of shaping our life for the general good . . . of maintaining the common peace and public security." [5] True humanity among men depends in this intervening time

---

[1] " . . . nunc quod diabolus reluctatur Deo, quod impii ordinem ab eo institutum confundunt et permiscent, quod infinita scandala oculis nostris observantur, non liquido apparet Deum in omnibus esse omnia: sed ubi Christus iudicium exsequutus sibi a patre mandatum, Satanam et impios omnes straverit, in ipsorum exitio gloria Dei erit conspicua." On 1 Cor. 15:28; *C.R.* 77, 54.
[2] On Phil. 2:10; *C.R.* 80, 29 f.
[3] See below, pp. 175 ff.
[4] " . . . ea enim significatur, mandatum a Deo habere, divina authoritate praeditos esse, ac omnino Dei personam sustinere, cuius vices quoddammodo agunt." *Inst.* IV, 20, 4; *O.S.* 5, 474.
[5] *Inst.* IV, 20, 2; *O.S.* 5, 473.

upon the maintenance of civil justice by duly constituted authority until such time as God will bring to pass the new heaven and the new earth, in which the perfect justice of His kingdom will prevail. "If it is God's will that while we are striving to reach our true home we should wander upon earth, and if our pilgrimage here requires such resources, then it means that whoever attempts to remove them is robbing man of his true humanity (*humanitas*)." [1] But when the still hidden life and kingdom of Christ, which begins already here in the soul or the inner man,[2] shall be fully disclosed, then these ordinances are superseded.

It is typical that Calvin in this connexion also sees the dawn of the provisional ending of the kingdom in the death of the individual or the release of the soul: "all these things become superfluous when the kingdom of God, already within us, extinguishes our present life".[3] But for the world as a whole this supersession of earthly authority takes place on the day of Christ when He hands over the kingdom, i.e. His consummated rule, to the Father. In regard to this subjection of all authority it is not merely a question of the powers that are inimical to Him. "We have no reason to think only of dominions and powers which do battle against Christ. The apostle speaks in general terms of powers under which he includes the rightfully constituted civil authorities.[4] The kingdom of Christ which now exists only in embryo will be completed on the Last Day, and that means the end of all other kingdoms. "Then all that is exalted must be put down so that the honour of God alone may shine forth." [5] The end of this life and this world means the end of all its authorities. "For all earthly rank and rule contributes only to the good order of this life in time. As certainly as the world will have an end, so certainly will states and their governments, laws and hierarchies, dignities and ranks fall to the ground. Then there will be no more distinction between slaves and masters, kings and peoples, authority

---

[1] *Loc. cit.*
[2] *Inst.* IV, 20, 1; *O.S.* 5, 471.
[3] *Inst., loc. cit.*, p. 473.
[4] On 1 Cor. 15:24; *C.R.* 77, 546.
[5] *Loc. cit.*

THE GENERAL RESURRECTION 165

and subjects."[1] All these bearers of power must, through Him to whom all power is given in heaven and on earth, yield up their borrowed authority to the real *auctor* of all rule and all power. This applies also to sacred and righteous rulers. For they stand in the way of the complete manifestation of the ineffable glory of God. "At present they as it were hinder God from disclosing Himself to us immediately. But once God quite personally takes into His hands the reins of rule over heaven and earth (*absque medio*) He will be all in all for all things, persons, and creatures."[2]

The completion of the reign of Christ in the realized dominion of God implies the fulfilment of the church, but also its end as an earthly ordinance wherein Christ exercises His rule only through the mediation of men in the ministry of the word and sacraments. The church stands indeed in a peculiar relation to the kingdom of God, but may not be identified with the latter, or only in so far as it bears the embryonic spiritual kingdom of Christ. The rule of Christ begins in this world through the word which the church preaches and which is believed in it;[3] the church is the proper sphere of His present reign. "For His rule is not first to be found in the assembly of the elect in heaven but already in His church on earth."[4] Yet its ministry in the word and sacraments is limited. The functions of the church end with the consummation of the reign of Christ and His church, just as do the ministries of the word and the sacraments; then the Lord will rule His kingdom and His own directly. Even the mediatorial services of the angels will be superseded. "The authority of the angels in heaven and the functions of the church on earth will come to an end. For then God will no more exercise His rule through men or angels but will reign directly in His own Person."[5] The glory of the angels and

---

[1] " Deinde scimus omnes principatus et honores terrenos pertinere ad conservationem vitae praesentis. . . . Ergo sicuti finem accipiet mundus: ita et politia, et magistratus, et leges, et distinctiones ordinum, et gradus dignitatum, et quidquid tale est: non differet amplius servus a domino, non rex a plebeio, neque a privato magistratus." *Loc. cit.*
[2] On 1 Cor. 15:28; C.R. 77, 550.
[3] See above, p. 158. [4] On Eph. 1:14; C.R. 79, 154.
[5] On 1 Cor. 15:24; C.R. 77, 547.

the church is not thereby diminished but rather consummated. "But the authority which at present the angels exercise in His name and at His behest will then be terminated, and the leaders and teachers of the church will resign their functions."[1] We have already referred in the appropriate places to the end of the ministry, of the means of grace—the word and the sacraments—which is the basis of church office.[2]

But not only the word of the preacher, the word of Scripture, but also the Word of God Himself which became incarnate will—Calvin thinks—be no longer in the centre of the picture when His task is fulfilled and the kingdom of God realized. Christ in bringing His reign to its culmination also terminates it; by the very fact that He hands it over to the Father. Of course Calvin, following Scripture, can describe the kingdom of Christ as an eternal kingdom, but only in so far as He is the Son of God through whom we enter the eternal kingdom of the Father. "The writer of 2 Peter refers to the kingdom of Jesus Christ because only under His leadership and guidance can we aspire to heaven."[3] When He has completed His work of mediation and has submitted all things to Himself, then He will surrender His special Lordship and power to the Father from whom He received it. "On the day of the Lord will Christ be exalted in order to deliver up the kingdom to the Father so that God may be all in all."[4] Calvin here quotes 1 Corinthians 15:24–28. This is the chief proof text for Calvin's special doctrine of the end of the kingdom of Christ and His mediation, even in a certain sense of the humanity of Christ, as he points out in the exegesis of this text.

We here meet a special Christological concern of Calvin.[5] On the one hand he sees the completion of the work of Christ in the culmination of His kingly rule through the submission of all other powers and dominions, but on the other in the termination of this rule, in so far as it is that of a Mediator,

[1] Loc. cit.
[2] See above, pp. 51 and 86.
[3] On 2 Pet. 1:11; C.R. 83, 451.
[4] On 2 Pet. 3:12; C.R. 83, 477.
[5] See also p. 126.

through its surrender to the Father. "The apostle here establishes two points: (1) everything must be brought into obedience to Christ before He surrenders His world dominion into the hands of the Father; (2) The Father in entrusting sovereignty to the Son reserved to Himself the ultimate rule."[1] The mediation of Christ has only the sense of being a means of bringing us to the Father. When that is done it recedes into the background. "The present mediatorial work of Christ must serve to guide us ultimately to the Father Himself. But Paul adds immediately (v. 28) that the Son too, after subjecting all things to God, will Himself become subject to the Father. It is as if He wanted to exhort us: wait patiently until the day when Christ as the Victor over all His enemies will restore us to the secure government of God and fully establish God's kingdom within us."

Calvin himself tries to meet the obvious objection to such a limitation of the mediation of Christ and His kingdom: it is that the Bible consistently attests the eternity of the kingdom of Christ. "But here the testimony of the whole of Scripture seems to contradict us. How can we reconcile the two facts: His kingdom is an everlasting kingdom, and yet He subjects Himself at the last?"

In his reply Calvin first points out that the assumption of power by the Son of God was relative strictly to His incarnation. As He who was made man He is God revealed in the flesh. That is Calvin's constantly recurring formula for the unity and distinction of divinity and humanity in the Person of Jesus Christ, which he likes to use in his comment on 1 Timothy 3:16 agreeably with the Chalcedonian definition (*Deus manifestus in carne*). First we must establish that Christ received His power only as the Incarnate Son of God. "Of course in His human nature He was not only humbled but also exalted. As the Lord and King over the world he is, however, only God's vicegerent, governing in union with the Father but without this implying ultimate dominion. Christ holds the reins of government as the vicar of God, but not as though He were active and God were passive—for how would that be

[1] On 1 Cor. 15:27; C.R. 77, 549.

conceivable, since Christ is the Father's wisdom and counsel and is of one substance with Him—indeed is God Himself?" But we come to know God only in the incarnate Lord. The reign of Christ is therefore the reign of God in terms which are apprehensible to us. " Thus we have faith in God as the supreme Lord, but we see Him only in the face of the man Jesus."[1] It is of God's great mercy that He condescends to seek us in such human terms, because otherwise we could not know Him and His saving dominion. " When it is said that Jesus Christ has a name that is above every other name (*un nom souverain*) and is the image of God His Father, this is because of our obtuseness and weakness; likewise when He is called the vicegerent of God " (*Lieutenant de Dieu* : the same title which Calvin uses for civil authority) " Christ is only the means by which God Himself reigns ".[2]

But Calvin thinks that one day the Mediator will have finished His work of mediation. This happens when as Son He hands over the kingdom to the Father. Then we shall see God face to face and no longer in the face of the incarnate Son. " On that day Christ will surrender the kingdom to the Father so that we may be united perfectly and immediately with God." The humanity of Christ which now mediates to us the knowledge of and communion with God is yet a limitation which hinders perfect union with God. In the final consummation it will no longer stand between us and God. For the humanity of Christ is a veil (*velum*) in which God clothes Himself in order to draw near to us. But in eternity this will no longer be necessary. Then the veil will be withdrawn and we shall see without further mediation the glory of the God who rules His kingdom; " the humanity of Christ will no longer be the medium which prevented us from enjoying the ultimate vision of God."[3] Thus the kingdom of Christ is consummated in such wise that the government passes from His

---

[1] *Loc. cit.*
[2] Sermon on Eph. 1 : 19-23; *C.R.* 79, 339.
[3] " Tunc autem restituet Christus quod accepit regnum, ut perfecte adhaereamus Deo . . . Sic ergo subiicitur patri: quia tum remoto velo palam cernemus Deum in sua maiestate regnantem: neque amplius media erit Christi humanitas, quae nos ab ulteriore Dei conspectu cohibeat." On 1 Cor. 15 : 27; *C.R.* 77, 549.

humanity to the absolute Godhead. It is no longer the kingdom of the Incarnate but still, and in fact all the more, the eternal kingdom of Christ. " Thus His kingdom will have no end, but in a certain sense (*quodammodo*) Christ will transfer it from His humanity to the glory of the Godhead. Then that access will be open to us which at present our weakness still blocks."[1] As the humanity of Christ in which He performed His special work as Mediator and Governor recedes, He will Himself become ultimately subject to the Father after subjecting all things to Him. That does not mean that His reign ceases but rather that in truth it is consummated in the communion which He has with His own.

Calvin strongly emphasizes this in the already quoted Ephesians sermon, in which he discusses the apparent contradiction between Ephesians 1:21 and 1 Corinthians 15:24 or 28. When it is a question of the immediate relation in which our glorified nature stands to God, it does not imply that Christ vanishes from the picture, for He will rather then be in the state of final consummation. And Calvin infers this from what Scripture says about our consummation in Him. At this point he again alludes to Colossians 3:4. " When Jesus Christ appears, then we shall attain the glorious blessedness which has been won for us . . . and He will gather all unto Himself so that we shall be sharers of His glory, each according to his measure and degree."[2] Now it is precisely in His humanity that Christ has been glorified, and Calvin asserts that specifically in this context, but he obviously understands this in the sense that the glorification of Christ is so spiritualized that there can no longer be any question of His humanity as incarnate, and certainly not when we ourselves have put off the weakness of the flesh and are able to know His Godhead directly. " Christ has been so glorified in His human nature that He is truly God of one substance with the Father. This will then be fully known, whereas now we have only a dim

---

[1] " Neque hoc modo regnum a se abdicabit, sed ab humanitate sua ad gloriosam divinitatem quodammodo traducet: quia tunc patebit accessus, quo nunc infirmitas nostra nos arcet." *Loc. cit.*
[2] Sermon on Eph. 1; *C.R.* 79, 339.

perception of it." [1] Hence in Calvin's opinion we see Christ in eternity only in so far as He is God in His unity with the Father, and His kingdom will be an eternal kingdom inasmuch as He can be described, in the words of the prophecy of Isaiah 9, as Himself the everlasting Father. Through His Godhead Christ reigns eternally and perfectly with the Father. "Nothing is so exalted or so glorious that it is not subject to the majesty of Christ. This applies not merely to this world but also to the one that is to come. Hence Isaiah (9:5) calls the Messiah whose position as ruler is not confined to this world but extends to the eternal kingdom of God, 'the everlasting Father'. All in all: the apostle smites to the ground all the glory of men and angels that the majesty of Christ may stand forth supreme." [2]

It remains a question whether Calvin thinks that the humanity of Christ is completely cancelled in the eternal consummation; that it is dissolved in His Godhead. He himself leaves it somewhat in the balance by his significant *quodammodo*. But in any case His function as Mediator is terminated. The Son of God was made man only in order to effect the atonement, and when that redeeming work is completed the flesh which He has assumed for the sake of humanity loses its significance. With the return of Christ for the consummation of His work, the soteriological significance of His God-manhood is ended. "Here the mission of Christ (as God-man), which the fall had rendered necessary, is completed" (E. Emmen).[3]

It is noteworthy that in this matter Calvin tends to forget the fact of the communion of Christ with believers, which elsewhere he takes so seriously. From the point of view of the communion of Christ, however, his teaching about the end of the humanity of Christ, or at any rate of its mediatorial office, becomes somewhat problematical, for it calls in question

[1] "Et aussi nous sentirons que quand Jesus Christ nous est apparu homme mortel, que tellement il a este glorifié en sa nature humaine, que vrayement il est Dieu, d'une mesme essence avec son Pere. Cela (di-ie) sera pleinement cognu, là ou auiourd'huy nous n'en avons qu'un petit ombrage." *Loc. cit., C.R.* 79, 340.
[2] Commentary on Eph. 1:21; *C.R.* 79, 159.
[3] *De christologie van Calvijn*, 1937, p. 109.

the eternal union of Christ and His own. While in regard to the resurrection of the dead Calvin emphasizes the conformity between Christ and believers who are corporeally raised up by Him, here that conformity finally disappears. For if at the last Christ lays aside our flesh, what comfort can it be to us that in our flesh He rose again and ascended into heaven? Has the resurrection of the flesh any eternal significance? If he were to be true to his conception of abiding communion with Christ, should not Calvin have taught a final dissolution of our humanity or our corporeality? What he says about the pure spirituality of the vision of God in eternity might be viewed as pointing in this direction, for spiritual always implies for Calvin non-corporeal. But perhaps we should not thus reduce Calvin *ad absurdum*. There remains in him a contradiction: that between his tendency to spiritualism—which here brings him into the region of docetic Christology—and on the other hand his Biblical realism.

(b) *Eternal blessedness*

The consummated reign of God, which is brought about by the Son's surrender of the kingdom to the Father, consists really in the final salvation of the children of God and also in the perfecting of the new creation to the honour of its triune Lord.

(i) *The perfecting of believers*

For Calvin, the consummation consists primarily in the ultimate blessedness of believers who are justified and sanctified by Christ, and also attain through Him the heavenly glory and felicity which is the crown of His saving work. The eternal blessedness of the elect springs from the culmination of their communion with Christ, their Head, which implies perfect fellowship with God, as a result of which they see Him face to face and are partakers of His nature. " Once we are reconciled with the Lord we have before us the prospect of eternal communion with Him." [1] We shall be forever with the Lord; that is the hope of eternal life. The Christ who is to come imparts to us in that perfected fellowship the fullness of

[1] On 1 Thess. 4: 17; *C.R.* 80, 167.

His divine glory, so that we become entirely transformed into His likeness in body and soul. " We shall be conformed to the heavenly life of our Lord Jesus Christ . . . He comes to enable us to participate in His glory so that everything in Him to which must be ascribed all dignity honour and praise . . . may be communicated to us. In brief, Paul declares that our Lord Jesus in no sense reserves His glory to Himself but possesses it only in order to radiate it to all the members of His body." [1]

Of course there remains a certain distinction between Him and us : the perfection of communion with Christ is no mystic union but the complete transformation into His image, which spells not identity but resemblance. "The apostle does not say: we shall be equal to Him. There must be a distinction between Head and members. But we shall be like Him, because He will make our vile body like unto His glorious body." [2] Thus Calvin thinks that the eternal image of Christ in man consists precisely in the transfiguration of the body that it may be like unto the glorified body of Christ. This transfiguration is completed through the vision of the glory of the Lord. "The vision of Christ makes us to resemble Him." [3]

In his exegesis of 1 John 3:2 Calvin equates the vision of Christ—and that in His corporeal humanity—with the vision of God: in the consummation we see God in Jesus Christ and are thus transformed into the image of God. It is one and the same vision which spells terror and ruin to the godless, blessedness and life to believers. For "our seeing is an experience of the spirit which the godless could not endure without being afraid." Such seeing is vouchsafed to us when we are born again and made new creatures through Christ. "In so far as the image of God is brought to life in us we are rendered capable of seeing God." This process begins now already but will not be completed until we have quite laid aside our sinful

---

[1] ". . . il viendra pour nous faire participians de sa gloire: que tout ce qui est en luy qui merite d'estre honoré et reveré, tout cela, di-ie, nous sera alors communiqué. Brief, S. Paul declare que nostre Seigneur Jesus ne viendra point retenir sa gloire à luy seul, mais afin qu'elle soit espandue sur tous les membres de son corps." Sermon on 2 Thess. 1:6 ff.; *C.R.* 80, 234.
[2] On 1 John 3:2 f.; *C.R.* 83, 331.
[3] *Loc. cit.*

and transient nature, which like a veil (*velum*) hides from us the full vision of God (the same metaphor which Calvin uses to express the idea of the manhood of Christ as limiting the perfect vision of God. See above, p. 168).

"Hence the majesty of God which is now hidden will not be seen as it is in itself until the veil of this mortal and corrupt nature is withdrawn." We see then that the beginning of our regeneration in this aeon by Christ and His spirit is the presupposition for our ultimate and glorious transfiguration through the perfect vision of God. "Our nature could never come so near to God if it were not through and through spiritual and destined for heavenly and blessed immortality." But even the perfected vision of God remains a vision at a distance in the abiding gulf which yawns between God and man, Creator and creature, as that finds visible expression in the distinction between the glorified body of Christ and our own glorified bodies. "Our glory will not be so perfect as to be able to comprehend the Lord in His absolute Godhead. Even at the last there will remain an impassable distance between Himself and us."[1] Even in the eternal kingdom we are not dissolved in the Godhead, but just in the full communion of the ultimate vision remain a living response to God's own being. Then we shall no more merely see His reflection, but Himself, and shall stand in confrontation with Him as it were face to face.[2] "While now He shows Himself to us only in signs and symbols, we shall then see His being itself in unhindered clarity: a new and utterly ineffable mode of vision."[3]

The eternal vision of God implies also fullness of communion with Him. In fellowship with the eternal love of God we shall enjoy Him utterly and forever. "When the Lord communicates His glory, power and righteousness to the elect, when they taste the perfect joy of His presence, and—what is still more glorious—in some sense increase in communion with Him—then we should bear in mind that in such benefits every kind of felicity is included."[4] Thus Calvin combines

[1] *Loc. cit.*
[2] On 1 Cor. 13:12; *C.R.* 77, 514.
[3] On 1 John 3, *loc. cit.*
[4] *Inst.* III, 25, 10; *O.S.* 4, 453.

with the *visio* the *fruitio Dei* (like Augustine) which he represents almost as a *unio mystica*. The highest blessedness consists in the full possession of God Himself. " If God bears in Himself like an inexhaustible spring the plenitude of all good, then those spirits which aspire to attain the highest good and perfect blessedness can want for nothing beyond Him." [1] Calvin praises this highest bliss, which is spiritual, in the most exalted terms, realizing well that it far exceeds our present capacities of understanding. " Even if we had said all that could be said in human language about this transcendent glory, we should hardly have skirted the fringe of its smallest part. For although we truly understand that the kingdom of God will be full of splendour and joy, full of blessedness and glory, yet all that these words express remains far removed from our consciousness and as though shrouded in mystery—until that day comes when God Himself exposes to us His glory and allows us to see it face to face." [2] In such naked vision we shall enjoy God through the power of the spirit. Thus Calvin attests with Scripture : " I shall be satisfied with the vision of Thy countenance " (Ps. 17 : 15).[3] At the same time he insists on the abiding gulf and distinction between God and ourselves.

In general, Calvin uses in describing the eternal consummation of the redeemed the two conceptions of blessedness and glory *promiscue*, yet in a certain sense he makes a distinction between them. Blessedness spells complete salvation in Christ, perfect release from sin and death and all the sorrow and pain of earthly life, which is imparted to all believers equally. Glory is the heavenly reward which indeed all receive but in different measure. " Our blessedness consists in the fact that we live unto God. In our regeneration the process begins, but it reaches its term only when we are fully redeemed, when God removes us from the cares of earthly life and gathers us into His kingdom. To this blessedness proper is added our participation in the glory of heaven." [4]

The idea of blessedness as a conquest of and freedom from

---

[1] *Loc. cit.*
[2] *Inst., loc. cit.*, pp. 452 ff.
[3] *Loc. cit.*
[4] On 2 Tim. 2 : 10; *C.R.* 80, 364.

all earthly distresses and needs was characterized in various ways. We shall here confine ourselves to pointing out just one aspect of the life of the blessed which marks it in particular as heavenly angelic life: that is, the dissolution of the sexual impulse and therewith of marriage, which, however, does not mean the removal of all sexual differentiation. Calvin sees the reason for this with Lk. 20:36 in the fact that in the life of eternity the mortality of human life is ended; therefore there is no longer any need for the continuance of the human race as such. In the kingdom of God we are not transformed into angels, but in this respect we shall be like the angels. " Christ does not mean that the children of God after the resurrection will be like the angels in every respect, but only in so far as they will be freed from all the frailties of their present life; they will no longer be subject to the needs of this ever-decaying and transient life. Luke explains still more precisely in what way they will resemble the angels, viz. that they will die no more and that therefore there can be no further question of a continuance of the race by procreation as on earth." [1] Thus marriage is merely a temporal, not an eternal, fellowship; for the favourable or the unfavourable decision of God which will be manifest in the last judgment of Christ may separate in the spiritual world husband from wife. It is characteristic that Calvin uses this eschatological possibility (cf. Lk. 17) for the purposes of moral exhortation: " Some day husband and wife will be separated. This thought should warn the faithful not to permit themselves to be hindered by the bonds which here below bind human beings together. For it is a matter of common experience that one has such concern about another that he neglects his own spiritual progress thereby. In order that each man for himself, free from all fetters, may hasten to run the race, Christ attests that of two who are closely linked the one may be taken and the other left." [2] But for Calvin this does not exclude the possibility of religious communion in marriage. " This does not mean that human ties must always thus be dissolved; rather the effect of the holy bond of faith

---

[1] On Matt. 22:30; C.R. 73, 606.
[2] On Matt. 24:40; C.R. 73, 675 f.

will be that the pious wife clings to her pious husband all the more. By His word Christ wills only to remove obstacles and encourage each individual to hasten forward so that they who are already alert and prepared lose no time in dallying with their companions." [1] Such fellowship in the faith outlasts marriage, which like all earthly ties vanishes with the passing away of this world. The only eternal society, Calvin thinks with Scripture, is that founded by Christ, namely, the church, whose earthly form too will be done away, as we saw, after the completion of its temporal mission.

Whereas the eternal blessedness of all the members of the body of Christ is the same, the degree of their heavenly glory varies according to the diversity of the gifts of the Holy Ghost which they already receive in this aeon. "As God proceeds variously in the distribution of His gifts to the saints in this world and allows them in unequal measure to feel His radiance, so also in heaven, where God will crown His gifts, the measure of glory will be unequal." In this Christ manifests the rich variety of His gifts of grace. Thus it is not a question of any special recognition of outstanding accomplishments by specific believers, but of the reward of grace by which the Lord marks the effect of His own gifts and work in His children. Together with blessedness each one, according to the gift of grace and the spiritual inspiration with which God has endowed him in this life, receives a corresponding eternal glory. "If anyone pays close heed to Scripture he will discover that it promises to the faithful not only eternal life but to each individual his special reward." [2] Thus for example the apostolic service of teaching and preaching receives a special promise from the Lord. "Paul realized . . . that for him according to the measure of his efforts a special crown was laid up." In a broader sense this applies to the preaching office as a whole. "Thus we find too in Daniel: 'Teachers will shine as the

---

[1] *Loc. cit.*
[2] "Nempe sicuti varie Deus sua dona Sanctis in hoc mundo distribuens eos inaequaliter irradiat, ita non fore aequalem gloriae modum in caelis, ubi dona sua coronabit Deus. . . . Ac siquis attente Scripturas consideret: non modo vitam aeternam promittunt fidelibus, sed specialem cuique mercedem." *Inst.* III, 25, 10; *O.S.* 4, 454

light of the firmament and they that lead many to righteousness as the stars everlastingly '. Thus the eternal consummation in Christ, while ending our functions, crowns them with their glorious reward like that of the church as a whole." As Christ allows His glorious body to begin its course in the world with a diversity of gifts and step by step increases them —here Calvin's idea of progress comes out—so too in heaven He will perfect them and glorify them.[1]

(ii) *The perfecting of the church*

The perfecting of the church consists not only in the ultimate redemption of believers as individuals but also in their consummation as a totality. This will be manifest above all in the assembling of its scattered and separated members by their Head. The unity of the church as a visible communion of all the elect is for Calvin an eschatological reality. The return of the Lord is so important for the church because it brings about the perfect unity of the body of Christ, which is still only an object of faith.[2] " This hope forms the great consolation of Christianity in face of its present confusions and weakness. It is of course in a certain sense the lot of the church in discipleship to its Lord that it should bear these mortifications as the suffering servant in this world. Thus the holy people, the church, is destined to wander on earth as pilgrims who are scattered and separated. Such has been the case up to the present."[3] The church lives under the sign of the cross, so that it dies daily, and is resurrected again and again only by the wondrous grace of God until the day of its ultimate and perfect resurrection. " God is the Saviour of His church until the end, but the manner in which He saves it must not be judged according to our natural feeling; for until the time of its final victory the church will ever resemble a dead corpse."[4]

But the divisions and weakness of Christendom are for Calvin an occasion of lamenting and penitence, for they are at

[1] *Loc. cit.*
[2] On 2 Thess. 2:1; *C.R.* 80, 194.
[3] On Dan. 12:17; *C.R.* 69, 297 f.
[4] " Deus ecclesiae suae servator quidem erit usque ad finem, sed modus ipse servandi ne aestimetur ex sensu carnis, quoniam ecclesia similis erit mortuo cadaveri usque dum resurgat." On Dan. 12:2; *C.R.* 69, 299.

the same time due to the guilt of Christians. " What a sad state of division in the church we have to bewail to-day . . . where do we see anything of the unity of the church as one body? And where has that unity been seen in the history of Christendom? Everywhere we see only torn and scattered parts."[1] But the note of praise to God in Calvin sounds more strongly than this lament. The maintenance of the church in its earthly distress is for him more marvellous than its final salvation at the last day. " In the meantime let us note what is here said; viz. that this abjectly mutilated state of the church must be until Christ restores it wholly at His second coming; and if we could consider the matter in its true light we should think it a still greater miracle of God that He rules His church in such a human and peaceable manner. . . . Is it not a miracle that Jesus Christ gathers together His church out of members which are as it were scattered and torn limbs? Behold, we see no form in the church, and yet God effects a secret unity of His own . . ."[2]

But the return of Christ will bring about the transfiguration of the church as well as the revelation of that unity which at present is visible only in its Head. The Lord will unify His church not only in full manifestation but in such a way as to lead it to that perfection which He has promised us.[3] " In this ultimate unification and consummation of the Body of Christ the angels will play a special part, for the glorification implies its union with the hosts of heaven to the eternal praise and service of God." " The angels of God will befriend the state of the church as we cannot do."[4] The teaching about the final unification of the church is a comfort and an exhortation to the Christian society which is still militant here in earth. " If at present the wiles of Satan scatter the church, or if it is threatened by the anger of the godless or falls into confusion through false doctrine, then we must think of the consolation with which Christ restored the disciples and look forward to the promised unification of believers . . . For however heavily

[1] On Dan. 12:7; *loc. cit.*
[2] Sermon on Dan. 12:5–7; *C.R.* 70, 159.
[3] *Loc. cit.*
[4] *Loc. cit.;* cf. also above, p. 124.

the pressure of human sin burdens the church, disrupts and threatens it, and leaves it no refuge in the world, yet we must be in good heart and hope because the Lord will hold it together not by human means but by His all-controlling divine power." [1] But the promise of this all-embracing hope makes the unity of the church a challenge to us also. The unity of Christians must be as close as is the unity of a living body which is animated by a soul. " It should not show itself spasmodically but penetrate the whole." The illuminating reason for this is, according to Ephesians 4:4, that we are called to cherish this great hope.

" If we wish to be united in our aspirations towards this goal then we must live in unity in this world." The unity of the coming kingdom makes all disunity of the church on earth an inner impossibility. "Would that it were ineffaceably impressed upon our minds that the law of the church of God makes it as impossible for the children of God to strive with each other as for the kingdom of heaven to be divided." [2] Whoever disrupts the true unity of the church in faith and love robs himself of the hope of membership in the glorified body of Christ. "Let us learn from Paul that those have no share in the common inheritance who are not one body and one soul." [3]

The glorification of the church produces finally the culmination of its lordship over the world. Even in the first creation man stands at the centre of the picture. "The children of God are the heirs of all things . . . It is well known that the world was created for the sake of humanity . . ." [4] Man is appointed by His creator to make the earth subject to himself. After the loss of this inheritance through the fall, this design finds its fulfilment in a higher sense in the second creation: dominion over the new creation is granted to the saints of God under the leadership of their Head and Lord Jesus

[1] On Matt. 24:31; *C.R.* 73, 668.
[2] On Eph. 4:4; *C.R.* 79, 190 f.
[3] *Loc. cit.*
[4] " Scimus filios Dei esse mundi haeredes . . . Et nota est satis doctrina illa, creatum esse mundum humani generis gratia." On Dan. 7:18; *C.R.* 69, 66 f.

Christ. And indeed this dominion begins already with the establishment of the kingdom of Christ and the preaching of the gospel (in this world). "God conferred the Kingdom upon His chosen people when to the ends of the earth He became known as the Saviour of the world . . . In any event the conferring of the kingdom on the elect took its beginning when by the power of the Holy Ghost the teaching of the gospel found acceptance on all sides." [1] The rule of the church is not an independent fact but coheres only in and with the rule of Jesus Christ. "Thus the saints began to reign 'under heaven' when Christ by the spread of the gospel inaugurated His kingdom." [2] Hence neither Jews nor papists may appeal to Scripture concerning the dominion of the church or the people of God, because they do not admit Christ alone as Lord. Only in so far as it is the body obedient to the Head has the church a share in His dominion. "It is not as though the church had the ground of its authority in itself; its authority arises from the fact that Christ as its sole Head reigns above it and exercises His sovereignty . . . for the common good of all His members." [3] But this rule promised to the church still awaits its ultimate fulfilment. Only in the consummation effected by Christ in His eternal kingdom will His members inherit the kingdom of the earth. "For it is not without reason that the Last Day is called in truth the day of redemption and is said to give to the children of God new courage and to make them new creatures. So let us then be patient until that day when we shall take possession of the inheritance that our Lord here promises us, and shall see the earth given into our charge." [4]

What Calvin says about the church as the corpus of a new humanity and its lordship over the world does not go beyond occasional indications. For he is less interested in the fulfilment of the church as a society than in the salvation of its individual members. (But the communion of the perfected body of Christ because it is centred in Christ is also communion among

[1] On Dan. 7:27; C.R. 69, 82 f.
[2] Loc. cit., p. 84.
[3] Loc. cit.
[4] Sermon on Matt. 5:5-7; C.R. 74, 788.

His members.) For this reason in speaking of the consummation in general he refers not to the church but mostly to the elect believers, children of God, etc. At the same time he always implies thereby the church as a totality. But these terms are characteristic of the individualizing tendency in the eschatology of Calvin which necessarily coheres with the spiritualizing tendency. For the church as a fulfilled community has no greater significance for Calvin, simply because he is able to say much about the heavenly glory which is promised to Christians but only little about the new earth over which they are to reign with their Lord.

(iii) *The perfecting of the world*

Over and above the redemption of man and the consummation of the church Calvin teaches a perfecting of the world or cosmos as a whole; that is, of the whole created order. That too is in need of renewal, and such renewal comes about only by a dying; by an entire transformation. For Calvin the lot of the creatures is bound up with that of man, as Scripture attests. As a result of the fall man has dragged the creatures along with himself into the pit of corruption, so that by the ordinance of God they are also the victims of mortality.

" Since Adam by his fall destroyed the integrity and order of nature, the servitude to which the creatures are subjected through human sin is oppressive and painful; not because they are endowed with any kind of sensitivity but because their natural impulse drives them to seek the integrality from which they have fallen." [1] The creature sighs and groans, as Paul in Romans 8 poetically expresses it (says Calvin), as we do, to overcome the transiency of this life. " No part of the universe is untouched by the longing with which everything in this world aspires to attain the miracle of resurrection." [2] The enormity of our lostness and guilt, and also the unfathomability of the mercy promised us in Christ, is mirrored for us in the creation. " In this respect we may note how frightful

[1] *Inst.* III, 25, 2; *O.S.* 4. 434.
[2] " Nullum esse elementum nullamve mundi partem, quae non veluti praesentis miserae agnitione tacta in spem resurrectionis intenta sit." On Rom. 8: 19; *C.R.* 77, 152.

must be the damnation which we deserve when all the innocent creatures between earth and heaven have to bear with us the punishment of our sins. For it is our fault that they suffer from the common corruption." [1] " On the other hand the future glory of the children of God stands out clearly : for in order to enhance its radiance the whole of creation must be transformed into a new status." [2] As the creation was punished because of the old man, so it will be glorified to correspond with the new man. Hence the creatures long for the manifestation of our future glory. " It is a new proof of the immeasurable greatness of our eternal glory that it is able to evoke a burning aspiration in the whole universe." [3] Of course the glorification of creation is not the same as that of believers, but it will be manifest only with the latter. " The creature who is now subject to vanity will not be freed until the children of God attain the fullness of their redemption. In longing for its own release the creature is thus looking forward to the dawn of the kingdom of heaven." [4]

The future glory of creation consists essentially in the restoration of its original innocence and immortality. The apostle does not say " that it will share in the glory of the children of God, but that it will experience an elevation and redemption after its own manner : in completing the redemption of man God will restore order to the present confusions of earth." [5] Calvin does not dare to say more about the new status of creation. At this point it is not clear in what the amelioration of the second as against the first creation consists. Here too Calvin wants to guard himself against over-subtle and worthless speculations which go beyond the warrant of Scripture. " We are content with the simple doctrine that such measure and order will prevail in the world as will exclude all distortion and destruction." [6] For the sake of the eternal plan of salvation which God has for His fallen humanity, He preserves creation

[1] On Rom. 8:21; *C.R.* 77, 153.
[2] *Loc. cit.*
[3] On v.19, *loc. cit.*
[4] On v.20, *loc. cit.*
[5] On v.21, *loc. cit.*
[6] *Loc. cit.*

also for that its ultimate and corresponding redemption. " For the result of the sad disorder ensuing upon the fall of Adam would have been at any moment to break up the machinery of the world, to bring its wheels to a standstill, if a mighty power of another order in accordance with its secret purpose had not intervened to hold it together . . . Because God gives the hope of a brighter future the creature clings to that hope and ever longs for the manifestation of the promised immortality." [1]

But the consummation of the world comes about like that of man, only through the end of its present mode of being. The last judgment effects not only the end of history but also that of nature as it is known at present. The end of this aeon which will dawn with Christ and His return brings about the end of all things. The parousia of Christ spells not only the perfect renewal of man but also the total transformation of the world. For Scripture bears witness " that Christ will speedily come in order to bring all things to an end." [2] Nothing in creation is eternal, but the whole cosmos receives through Christ the promise of eternal life. " All that is created is subject to mortality but the kingdom of Christ is an eternal kingdom. Hence all creation must be fashioned anew and transfigured." [3] This is possible only through complete re-constitution and radical change. The present structure of the creation and of the whole cosmos must pass away and give place to another one. The creatures too must undergo a certain judgment of death.

" Whoever infers from the great age of the earth its continued existence is deliberately blinding himself to the clear judgment of God." [4] Already we can observe enough signs of this judgment in the perishable character of all things earthly. Calvin declares with 2 Peter that the world is only maintained by the divine grace and patience and does not possess the intrinsic power to preserve itself. Rather it bears in itself those elements by which the creator will one day bring about its end.

[1] On v.20; loc. cit.
[2] On 1 Pet. 4:7; C.R. 83, 274.
[3] On Heb. 12:27; C.R. 83, 185.
[4] On 2 Pet. 3:4; C.R. 83, 473 f.

"The power of nature in no sense suffices for the maintenance and preservation of the world. On the contrary, the material which is to produce its destruction lies hidden in it by God's good pleasure. We must not forget that the world can properly be maintained by no other power but that of the word of God." The powers of nature are in this only His instruments. "The whole order of nature serves exclusively the will of God."[1] But Calvin attributes to no one elemental power the agency by which God will destroy the cosmos. He is not concerned with the how but with the fact itself; namely, that the almighty word of God both creates and transmutes the world. "It is fundamentally of no consequence whether this comes about by fire or water."[2]

In regard to the idea of the transfiguration of the cosmos Calvin makes the same distinction between substance and quality which he makes in regard to the resurrection of the human body. While the character of the world wholly changes, its essence remains the same. "The fundamental materials of the world will pass away in order that, as it were, a new structure may arise; but their inner kernel remains."[3] Thus for Calvin, who here follows the ancient tradition of the church in contrast to Lutheran teaching,[4] the consummation is brought about not by destruction but by transmutation. The world must be changed in order to provide the right sphere for the kingdom of Christ and His glorified church. "Heaven and earth will be purified by fire so that they may be in harmony with the Lordship of Christ."[5] This promise is made to the whole cosmos by the coming of Christ into the world.

In Calvin cosmic eschatology is never divorced from the Christological and eschatological vision of the end. Hence his

[1] On v.5, *loc. cit.*
[2] On v.7, *loc. cit.*
[3] On 2 Pet. 3:10; *C.R.* 83, 476.
[4] Cf. Quenstedt: "Forma consummationis huius non in nuda qualitatum immutatione, alteratione, seu innovatione, sed in ipsius substantiae mundi totali absolutione et in nihilum reductione ... consistit." Quoted after H. Schmid, *op cit.* p. 544. Luther himself on the contrary taught the conception of transfiguration (as a complete renewal of the world); cf. Althaus, *Die letzten Dinge*, pp. 337 ff.
[5] "Sic enim ratiocinatur, coelum et terram incendio purgatum iri, ut regno Christi respondeant." On 2 Pet. 3:10; *loc. cit.*

statements about the end and the change of the world always develop into exhortations to man about his renewal. In this matter he warns us against cosmological speculations. " It is bad to take much trouble over intellectual subtleties. All that the apostle says about the cosmos forms only the point of departure for warnings against impiety." [1] For the reason for the ending of the world lies in us men. The creatures of God are in themselves unspoilt. But by our guilt we drag them down into the misery of mortality. " Heaven and earth because of us will pass away." They must be freed from the harm which has been caused by us. " The corruptions of heaven and earth will be purified by fire, and yet the creation of God is pure." But if the latter must be purified, how much more ourselves. " What must happen to us who are so deep in the mire ... Hence for man regeneration is a far greater necessity." [2]

Calvin does not discuss in greater detail the meaning of the new earth for the new humanity. But although he speaks mostly of heaven only as the sphere of the perfected church and sees blessedness to consist in the purely spiritual vision and enjoyment of God, he turns aside from any mystical spiritualism which considers the visible things of creation to be wholly worthless in the final state of glory. He considers such conceptions to arise from idle enquiry and investigation into the details of future glory and all such speculation he regards with repugnance. " Men who crave for vain knowledge and would like to understand what distinction there will be between prophets and apostles, or again between apostles and martyrs, how far virgins will take precedence of the married—leave in short no corner of heaven outside the scope of their vain enquiries. Then they also take it into their heads to ask what purpose will be served by the transformation of the world, when, however, the children of God out of their incomparable abundance will not need a single thing, but will be like angels who because of their eternal blessedness do not eat." [3] Calvin concedes that

[1] *Loc. cit.*
[2] *Loc. cit.*
[3] *Inst.* III, 25, 11; *O.S.* 4, 454 f.

in the new heaven and earth there will be no real need for these earthly things, but that we shall find our highest and purest enjoyment in the sheer vision and awareness of the creaturely. " There will be so much enjoyment in mere vision, so much delight in mere knowledge without sensuous taste, that such felicity will far surpass all our earthly resources." In this aeon the enjoyment of earthly good is often prevented by our weakness or depraved by our lack of restraint. " Let us suppose that we were placed in the richest part of the earth where no pleasure failed: who would not at times be hindered in the use of such benefits of God by his own frailties? And whose course is not often disturbed by his own lack of restraint? From this it follows that the highest felicity consists in pure enjoyment free from all earthly weakness, even when there is no normal use of this passing life." [1] Thus Calvin teaches that man's eternal relation to God is the foundation of his eternal relation to the world: the perfect enjoyment of the creatures corresponds to the perfect vision of God; we can enjoy the former only in God.

The final purpose of the eternal consummation of the cosmos together with that of the church is that there may be universal praise to God. Nothing is asserted here (Rev. 5:13) but that the various parts of the world from the heights of heaven to the centre of the earth should in their way proclaim the honour of the Creator.[2] " The end of the glorification of man and the world is the glory of God."

(c) *Eternal damnation*

Calvin teaches that not only the eternal salvation of the elect but also the punishment of the damned serves the greater glory of God. Their final ruin must serve the honour of the Lord who does not with impunity allow His offer of salvation to be despised by the godless. Hence there is a dual resurrection, a dual judgment, and a dual issue. Eternal damnation is related to eternal blessedness as the negative to the positive.

[1] *Loc. cit.*
[2] " Quo non aliud affirmatur quam singulas orbis partes, a summo caelorum vertice ad usque terrae centrum, suo modo creatoris gloriam enarrare." *Inst.* III, 5, 8; *O.S.* 4, 140.

Whilst eternal salvation is perfected communion with God, the eternal curse of damnation implies completed removal from the presence of God. " We must in this matter think of the pain caused by being cut off from fellowship with God." [1] But the eternal distress of unbelievers is not only absence of eternal life in and with God, but also a suffering under the eternal wrath of His offended majesty. The sight of God spells ruin to men when it is not through Christ changed into the vision of His holy love.

" It is the eternal lot of the godless to feel . . . the divine majesty standing against them so that its crushing weight is inescapable." [2] Unbelievers fear the sight of God, which they cannot endure. "Apart from the fact that they flee from and tremble before the sight of God, His glory so dazzles their eyes that they must be overwhelmed and smitten by it." [3] After Adam's fall from God this applies to all men in so far as the image of God is not restored in them by Christ. " We see how Adam on account of his guilt fears the presence of God. And God in general terms declares to men : ' No one can see me and live ' " (Ex. 33 : 20).[4] The awareness of the wrath of God and the sight of His glory is like a consuming fire to which the reprobate are eternally exposed. " His wrath is a raging fire which utterly consumes all that it touches." [5] The eternal fire in which according to Scripture the damned will find themselves is for Calvin only a symbol of the wrath of God. " The image of fire suggests how severe the punishment will be. The fact that it is not a question of a real fire is clear from Isaiah 30 : 33 where the spirit of the Lord is compared with the wind which fans the flame." [6]

Calvin refuses to go into a more detailed description of this fire, since we cannot comprehend it with our human thoughts. " I leave it to the foolish curiosity of others to brood over the exact nature of this fire. It suffices me to maintain what Paul

---

[1] *Inst.* III, 25, 12; *O.S.* 4, 456.
[2] *Loc. cit.*
[3] On 1 John 3 : 2; *C.R.* 83, 331.
[4] *Loc. cit.*
[5] *Inst., loc. cit.*
[6] On Matt. 25 : 41; *C.R.* 73, 690.

also in this connexion insists on, viz. that Christ will be a severe recompenser of the godless." [1] Calvin is content to emphasize that the fire will be eternal, since damnation is as endless as blessedness. " It is important only to notice that, like the glory promised to believers, the fire will last eternally." [2] The fire of the eternal wrath of God is death-bringing. Thus Calvin represents damnation as an eternal dying. " St. Paul adds further what is the manner of the said punishment, namely, an endless ruin, a death which does not die." [3] And this death is rendered eternal by the eternal glory of God in Christ, before whom unbelievers must die eternally for the sake of His honour. " It is to be inferred from that that this death is determined by the glory of Christ which is eternal and without end. Hence the sting of this death will never cease. We can measure the terribleness of the punishment by the fact that it will correspond to the greatness of the glory and majesty of Christ." [4]

Calvin insists that all the statements of Scripture about eternal damnation are only to be understood as metaphors. This metaphorical mode of expression is due to our weakness and obtuseness. " Because no description can do justice to the severity of the divine vengeance on the damned, their sufferings and torments are pictured to us by means of physical things such as darkness, howling, and gnashing of teeth (Mt. 8:22) undying fire (Mt. 3; Mk. 9) or under the image of the worm which gnaws endlessly (Is. 66). For it is certain that the Holy Spirit by such modes of speech has aimed at overwhelming all our senses with fear." [5] In this matter Biblical prophecy uses foreshadowings of this eternal calamity in the extraordinary and terrible happenings of nature and history. " As often as the prophets instil fear into our minds

---

[1] On 2 Thess. 1:7; C.R. 80, 191.
[2] On Matt, 25, loc. cit.
[3] On 2 Thess. 1:9. loc. cit.
[4] " Mortis perpetuitas ex eo probatur, quod Christi gloriam habet sibi adversam. Atqui ea aeterna est, nec finem habet. Itaque vis eius nunquam cessabit. Inde et terribilis poenae atrocitas colligi potest: quia tanta futura est quanta est Christi gloria et maiestas." Loc. cit.
[5] Inst., loc. cit. p. 455.

by their metaphors, they express nothing that we in our frailty cannot understand, but they mingle with their words such symbols of the future judgment as are manifest in sun and moon and the whole structure of the world." [1] The eternal torment itself is for Calvin essentially spiritual. The vision of the majesty of God and His wrath forever deprives the godless of all peace of conscience and tortures them endlessly. " Thus these unhappy consciences find no peace but are painfully caught up in terrible whirlwinds, they feel how the angry God tortures them, they are pierced and mangled by death-dealing arrows, cower in terror before the thunderbolt of God and are crushed by the pressure of His hand so that it would be easier to be swallowed up by some abyss or gulf rather than endure for a moment such terrors." [2] But even here Calvin does not remain consistently spiritual. For just as the visible creation contributes to the eternal felicity of the blessed, Calvin also thinks that it has a part to play in the eternal damnation of the godless. For this reason the punishment must be bodily also. " Then all creatures serve the end of the Lord's judgment so that the ungodly must experience how heaven and earth and the sea, as all animals and everything that is created, are inflamed against them with violent wrath and armed to destroy them: for in this way the Lord makes His anger plain to them." [3] Thus in the eternal consummation creation is both the instrument of the saving mercy of God and of His vengeful righteousness. In this two-fold sense it becomes in its renewal the scene for the manifestation and vindication of the eternal honour of God.

Hell as the abode of the devil and the demons, who are damned with the godless whom they rule, is not, Calvin thinks, a sphere independent of the sovereign sway of God but only another way of suggesting the fire of eternal punishment. Satan will possess a certain kingdom—the antithesis of the kingdom of Christ—only until the consummation of the Lordship of God. Then with his followers he will receive the ulti-

[1] *Loc. cit.*, p. 456.
[2] *Loc. cit.*
[3] *Loc. cit.*

mate punishment for which they have been eternally destined. " As the head of all the reprobate the devil is the adversary of Christ. For although all the devils are fallen angels, in many parts of Scripture one of them is represented as the head, who gathers together under his power all the impious into one mass of corruption just as believers are assembled under the Lordship of Christ ... The statement of Christ that eternal fire is prepared for the devil, Gehenna, deprives the godless of all hope of escape since they are to receive the same punishment as the devil who obviously is damned in Gehenna without any hope of redemption." [1] Yet Calvin makes a certain distinction between the devils and the godless. Unbelievers also are called by the word of God, but their eternal rejection becomes manifest in their refusal of grace, as a result of which they deliberately surrender themselves to the ruin to which Satan and his angels have already fallen a prey. " Of course the godless, like the devil, are the victims of eternal ruin, but because the former who are called to the hope of salvation through the gospel prefer to perish with Satan, despise the Saviour and give themselves up to eternal sorrow, the reason for their punishment, viz. their sin, is more plainly visible. Thus although the lost are already before their birth fore-ordained to eternal death by God's secret judgment, yet so long as they live they are not regarded as heirs of death or partners of Satan; but in their unbelief the curse becomes manifest which in secret weighs upon them." [2] The two-fold issue is thus the final result of the double predestination. The sin of unbelief is only the apparent reason, but their rejection by God from eternity is the real reason for their eternal damnation.

Calvin's doctrine of election, together with his teaching about the judgment of Christ, excludes the hypothesis of a ἀποκατάστασις πάντων. For him neither before nor after the final judgment is there any possibility of universal salvation. " For it is only just that Christ at His appearing should crush the rebels who despised His kingdom as long as they could not see Him ... it is therefore foolish to hope for universal redemp-

[1] On Matt. 25:41; C.R. 73, 690.
[2] Loc. cit.

tion, for they will notice too late Him whom they have pierced."[1] The grace of God is certainly offered to all men, but it would be exceedingly foolish to suppose that all men without exception will be saved. "The consummation of the kingdom of God through Christ does not mean that Satan and his followers will be finally saved." We cannot infer from the "God shall be all in all" (1 Cor. 15:28) that even the devil and all the godless will finally be saved.[2] It is certainly true that all creatures must return to God as the starting point and the goal of their being and be always bound to Him. But in regard to the enemies of Christ that happens against their will; for their nexus with God implies that they are destined to eternal punishment. It is precisely in that punishment that they are to praise the glory of God and Christ. "Then in their destruction the honour of God will be perfectly vindicated."[3]

This defeat, however, does not mean annihilation but eternal death. The eternal glorification of God is the whole meaning and purpose of eternal damnation. Calvin's descriptions of the ultimate fate of the godless are only brief in comparison with his account of the eternal salvation of the elect. This again confirms that in harmony with Scripture the centre of gravity of his eschatology and theology rests not upon the law but upon the gospel.

---

[1] On Matt. 24:30; C.R. 73, 667.
[2] On Rom. 11:32; C.R. 77, 229.
[3] On 1 Cor. 15:28; C.R. 77, 549 f.

CONCLUSION

The Significance of the Eschatology of Calvin

SINCE already in the course of our essay we have given an appreciation at various important points of the eschatology of Calvin, it now remains for us in conclusion only to sum up the outstanding results of our enquiry.

The authentic Christian stamp of the eschatology of Calvin is to be seen in the fact that it does not speak of the ultimate in general terms but that in obedience to the word of God it bears witness to the future coming of Christ. In this part of his teaching, as in the whole of his theology and preaching, Calvin is concerned with the " Last " who is also the " First " (Rev. 1 : 17); hence the centring of the hope in the communion of Christ, the emphasis on the second coming as the decisive eschatological event, the stress on the saving significance of judgment as the final salvation of the elect; hence the interpretation of the interval after death as pointing to the general resurrection and the consummation of the divine society in Christ. Thus Calvin's eschatology is essentially Christology.

With this is connected its conscious foundation in Holy Scripture. Calvin endeavoured in his eschatology, as in his whole teaching and preaching, to bring out the witness of the Bible—the witness to Christ as the central truth of the word of God. He emphasizes this specifically again and again, especially when he finds himself in controversy with opponents who as decisively as himself refer to Scripture, i.e. in his defence of the immortality of the soul against the Anabaptists. But just at this point our criticism had to begin, for it is here that Calvin's eschatology is least scriptural.

Here and in other places there is discovered in his teaching a certain tension between his loyalty to the Biblical message of the return of Christ and of the kingdom of God as a visible all-embracing reality, and on the other hand his humanistic tendency to confine and spiritualize the hope in the direction of the salvation of the individual.[1] The Biblical contrast of the present and the future aeon is to this extent even in Calvin identified with the metaphysical antithesis between the temporal and the eternal, the earthly and the heavenly, the bodily and the spiritual. Hence he thinks of the future life preeminently as a heavenly and spiritual life which definitely begins at death with the liberation of the immortal soul, and which is completed in the immediate vision of God without the mediation of the humanity of Christ. For this reason the new creation, in so far as it is a new earth and the new Jerusalem, the fulfilled communion of the saints in the new world, is only occasionally referred to by Calvin. But we saw that this spiritualizing tendency in the eschatology of Calvin was constantly interrupted and rectified by the influence on his teaching of Holy Scripture with its concrete hopes, especially in regard to the resurrection of the flesh as the resurrection of this body. The orientation of Calvin's eschatology (and of his theology) as a whole towards the general resurrection preserves its Biblical character, even though that character is seriously threatened by the other aspect of his thought.

But this danger, which is only a threat in Calvin, became acute and ruinous in later Protestantism, not only in Reformed but also in Lutheran. It is especially typical for the development of Protestant eschatology that the great architect of Lutheran orthodoxy, Johann Gerhard, in his doctrine of the state after death represents not the standpoint of Luther but that of Calvin.[2] Real and universal eschatology continually declines both among the Lutherans and the Reformed. This is particularly clear in hymnology. Evangelical hymn books con-

[1] This spiritualizing tendency of Calvin derives from the point of view of the history of dogma, not only from humanism but also in part from the profound influence of Augustine to whom we have made allusion in various places. Augustine, as the father of Western mediaeval theology, is also the real founder of the eschatology of the mediaeval church, in which that of Calvin is in many respects rooted. In this connexion Calvin often and with pleasure refers to the teaching of the great church father. The characteristic feature of the eschatology of Augustine is its combination of Greek spirituality and Biblical realism; in this Calvin to a certain extent follows it.
[2] *Loci theologici*, loc. 26.

tain no doubt a great number of poems on the theme of eternity, but with a few exceptions they are mostly filled with the idea of a definite individual and spiritual expectation of eternal life. Correspondingly the hope of the church was weakened to a pale longing for heaven. Eschatology in general became a foster child of Protestantism (Nietzsche). But the reformers themselves are not so much responsible for this as the growing influence of mysticism and the modernism which succeeded it. As far as the reformers are concerned they brought eschatology into its own (and this applies particularly to Calvin) in connexion with their central evangelical message. Yet the very example of Calvin has shown us also that the reformed doctrine of the last things (that of Calvin more than that of Luther) did not do full justice to essential Biblical concerns. As a result there arose cracks in the structure of evangelical theology which later produced its distortion and collapse.[1] Of course in the nineteenth century attempts were made to re-establish an evangelical theology on the basis of the Biblical message, but up to now the reformed churches suffer from the consequences of that corruption of the Biblical expectation of the future.

But theological work in the last twenty or thirty years, following in the footsteps of the reformers, has brought about a thoroughgoing re-orientation of evangelical teaching as a whole in the direction of eschatology.

Connected with this is a new effort to reach a correct understanding of the last things themselves. Here attention must be concentrated on those aspects of eschatology which were neglected by the reformers, and its true Biblical content clarified i.e. within the limits which Holy Scripture itself prescribes for the insights of faith. To-day even more than in the time of the reformation it is necessary to bear witness to the Christian hope in all its grandeur and splendour and also to define it as against falsely seductive versions of it. Only so will evangelical theology and preaching at the present time perform rightly

---

[1] A. Vilmar says with regard to the ambiguity of the evangelical doctrine of the state after death " that it has largely promoted the modern Mohammedan doctrine of immortality " (*Dogmatik*, 1874, II, 302).

the service which its Lord, the Lord of the world and of the church, requires of it. In the confusions and distresses of the present, the church of Jesus Christ needs clear teaching and persuasive preaching about the coming of its King and His Kingdom which is alone eternal, so that it may give out its message as a herald to a slumbering or mad world whether it be for salvation or for judgment. The church which lives by this confession may in the woes of our time joyfully look upward to its coming Saviour, and amid ever-increasing oppression pray to Him with growing longing, as did Calvin, and indeed still more fervently than did he:

"*Quousque Domine?*"[1]

---

[1] Thematic phrase on the title page of the later editions of the *Institutio*, and the prayer of Calvin on his death-bed (cf. W. Dahm, *op. cit.*, p. 51.)

INDEX

Abraham, 82, 85, 86, 87, 91, 92, 94, 100
Adam, 63, 66ff., 143, 187
Althaus, P., 100, 105, 184
Anabaptists, 52, 55, 82, 91, 112, 160, 192
Angels, 69, 70, 71, 93, 100, 124f., 152, 165f., 175, 190
Animal, 63, 64f., 67, 181f., 189
Antichrist, 117ff., 154, 161
Apocalyptic, 1ff., 109, 113, 115, 123, 158ff.
Aristotle, 73
Assaults (by trial and temptation), 29, 34f., 57, 114, 155, 195
Augustine, 62, 80, 83, 94f., 106, 160, 174, 193

Baptism, 59, 98, 107, 135
Barth, P., 72
Bauke, H., 53
Believers (see also Church), 25, 34, 47, 77, 111, 125, 129, 147f., 161, 177, 180f.
Blanke, F., 101
Blessedness, 19, 37, 80f., 86, 92f., 94, 106, 161, 176
Body, 32, 46, 58f., 81f., 84f., 89, 97f., 135f., 175, 193
Brunner, P., 19, 72
Burial, 136f.
Butzer, M., 52

Childhood, 23, 35
Chiliasm, see Millennium
Christ:
  Cross, 34f., 48, 76, 103, 134
  Resurrection, 19, 35, 78, 126f.
  Descent into hell, 76f., 80
  Ascension into heaven, 20, 41, 44, 48, 80, 109f.
  Victory, 122, 152, 167
  Return, 12, 16, 18, 26f., 192
  Divinity, 173
  Humanity, 168f.
  Form of a servant, 123
  Glory, 22, 123, 138, 182, 188
  Reign, 20, 90, 109, 123, 158f., 162f., 166, 186
  Mediation, 168f., 199
Christ as Saviour, 12, 148, 198
  as Judge, 145f., 188
  fellowship of, 20f., 34f., 73f., 81, 87, 90, 134f., 162f., 170f.
Christology, 22, 47, 109, 126, 171, 192
Chrysostom, 91
Church, 12, 90, 114, 117f., 128, 155, 159f., 177f., 194f.
Church Fathers, 91, 103
Civil power, 163f.
Conscience, 71, 75, 93, 105
Consummation, 32f., 41f., 56f., 81
Cosmos, see World
Creation, 12, 62f., 64, 67, 69, 73, 124, 137, 189, 193
Creationism, 62
Cross, of Christ, see Christ
  of Christian, 34f., 114, 155, 177

Dahm, W., 112, 195
Damnation, 12, 92f., 106, 148, 155f., 159, 186f.
Death (eternal), see Damnation
Devil, 29, 93f., 120, 154, 156, 158, 162f., 189f.
Dinkler, E., 95

Doumergue, E., 52, 60

Earth (new), 13, 161, 164, 185f., 193
Eger, H., 94, 106, 160
Ellwein, E., 40
Emmen, E., 170
Erasmus, 51f.
Ethics, 15, 31, 53, 54
Expectation (of imminent end), 111

Faber, C., 55
Faith, 11, 13, 16f., 31, 44, 49f., 84f., 95, 148, 150, 158
Flesh and Spirit, 32f., 39, 57f., 74f., 98f., 139f.
Fröhlich, K., 33
Fruitio Dei, 174

Gerhard, J., 193
Gloede, G., 72
God:
  Almighty power, 133, 142
  Honour, 82, 120, 133, 147, 152, 163, 172, 186
  Justice, 142, 151, 153f., 189
  Glory, 126, 188
  Love, 154, 173, 187
  Wrath, 156f., 187, 189
  Communion with, 127, 173, 187, 191
Göhler, A., 38, 49, 53
Gospel, *see* Word of God
Grace, 13, 146f., 158, 191

Hauck, W. A., 20
Heathen, 71f., 105f., 116, 136
Heaven, *see* Kingdom of God
Hell (*see also* Damnation), 76, 93f., 186f.
Heppe, H., 108
Heretical teachers, 31, 118, 160, 178
Hoffman, G., 88
Hope, 11, 15ff., 194

Humanism, 11, 51f., 65, 72f., 192f.
Humanity (new), 23, 179f., 185
Hymns, 193f.

Image of God, 38, 64, 67f., 141, 172
Immortality (of the soul), 55f., 68f., 96, 192
  (of God), 69f.
Inheritance (eternal), 19, 22f., 159, 179
Israel, 116, 136, 157, 180
Issue, two-fold, 12, 53, 162, 171f.

Jerusalem (heavenly), 86, 92, 193
Judgment, Last, 12, 47, 93f., 104f., 134, 145f., 156f., 183
Justification, 1, 13, 18, 149f.

Kattenbusch, F., 52
Kingdom of God, 12, 90, 105, 114, 117, 123, 125, 149, 158f., 162f., 192, 195
Kolfhaus, W., 20, 39
Koopmans, J., 91

Lang, A., 52, 112
Lapse, 94, 113, 119f.
Last Supper, 50f., 62, 98, 135
Life, earthly, 133f.
  new, 18, 26, 30, 33f., 46f., 83
  future, 17, 39, 41f., 171f., 193
  contempt of, 43, 45f.
Love, 25, 30, 149, 179
Luther, 11f., 15, 52, 54, 56, 58f., 77, 91, 97ff., 107, 112, 122, 156, 160, 184, 193

Marriage, 162, 175f.
Martyrdom, martyrs, 37, 94, 107, 185
Meditatio vitae futurae, 40ff., 51ff., 66, 80
Melanchthon, 52
Michel, O., 96, 162

INDEX

Militia Christi, 29f.
Millennium, 158ff.
Ministry, 103, 165f., 176, 194f.
Mission, 114f.
Mohammed, 119

Niesel, W., 51, 53, 54, 55, 150
Nietzsche, 194

Old Testament, 21, 60, 95, 104, 131, 135f.
Otten, H., 146, 151

Papacy (and Roman Church), 11, 103, 118f., 180
Peace, eternal, 92
Penitence, see Regeneration
Persecution, 34f., 114, 150, 155
Pessimism, 41, 43, 52f., 60
Philosophy, 42, 45, 47, 71, 72f., 100, 108, 128
Pilgrimage, 24, 27f, 48, 50, 57, 163
Pinet, A. du, 55
Plato, 72f.
Praise of God, 178, 186
Prayer, for the departed, 102, 105f.
Predestination, 24, 145f., 151, 157, 190, 191
Preutz, H., 122
Proclamation, see Ministry and Word of God
Progress (of regeneration and the Kingdom of God), 31f., 39, 61, 79, 83f., 114, 179f.
Promise, 16f. (see also Word of God)
Purgatory, 12, 102f.

Quenstedt, 184
Quintin, 50

Redemption (to come), 12, 18, 36, 146f., 177f.

Regeneration, 31, 38, 65f., 173
Religion, 66, 71, 120, 157
Rest, blessed, 82ff.
Return, see Christ
Reuter, H., 160
Reward, heavenly, 30, 88, 91, 149, 174, 176
Ritschl, A., 52

Sanctification (see also Regeneration), 31, 38, 90, 157
Schmidt, H., 108, 184
Schniewind, J., 96, 113, 137
Schott, E., 98
Schultz, M., 51ff.
Schwarz, R., 55, 112
Scripture, Holy (see also Word of God), 13, 16, 53, 72f., 86, 87f., 95, 98f., 101, 102f., 108, 130f., 161f., 166, 192, 194
Self-denial, 38, 40, 52
Servetus, 69
Signs (of the end), 113, 124
Sin, 43, 69, 74f., 154, 178, 181f.
Soul, 44, 55ff., 107, 128
Speculation 11, 101, 125, 166, 182, 185
Spirit, Holy, 24, 33, 50, 65, 69, 74, 90, 103f., 127, 135, 150, 188
Spiritual, spiritualization, 1, 52, 62, 65, 94, 98, 116, 123, 137, 161, 171, 185, 189, 193
Stange, C., 100
State, 163f.
Steadfastness, 17, 25f., 34
Syllogismus practicus, 150

Tertullian, 91
Theology (natural), 71f., 135f.
Thurneysen, E., 96
Ticonius, 160
Traducianism, 62
Transformation (of man), 140f. (of the world), 181f., 184f.
Troeltsch, E., 52

Ungodly, 45, 76, 92f., 110, 122, 125, 145, 153f., 162, 178, 186f.

Vigilance, 27, 110f., 117, 125
Vilmar, A., 62, 194
Vision (of God), 85, 95, 168, 186

Wernle, P., 53

Word (of God, Gospel), 9, 16, 20, 82, 84, 96, 98, 102f., 106, 114f., 121f., 129f., 154, 158, 166, 183, 191, 193f.
World, new, 164, 180f., 184

Zimmerli, W., 55f., 80

www.ingramcontent.com/pod-product-compliance
Lightning Source LLC
Chambersburg PA
CBHW062040220426
43662CB00010B/1587